DIGITAL COMPUTER PRIMER

McGraw-Hill Series in Information Processing and Computers

J. P. Nash, Consulting Editor
Richard W. Hamming, Associate Consulting Editor

DIGITAL COMPUTER PRIMER

EDWARD MACK McCORMICK

National Science Foundation
Washington, D.C.
and
Lecturer in Government and Public Administration
American University
Washington, D.C.

McGRAW-HILL BOOK COMPANY, INC.

New York   Toronto   London

1959

QA 76.5
M118

DIGITAL COMPUTER PRIMER

Library of Congress Catalog Card Number: 58–13011

8 9 10 11 12 13 14 15 – MP – 1 0 9 8 7

44867

To Cleta, Susan, and Patti

Preface

This book has been written to substantiate its author's belief that automatic digital computers are devices which can be understood by the well-informed layman. Unfortunately, much publicity concerning this very significant tool of our modern civilization is misleading and inaccurate. Although the first use of automatic digital computers was for the solution of highly specialized mathematical problems, the present generation of computers is being used for a wide variety of activities in many fields—including business, industry, social sciences, religion, languages, and library science, as well as the physical sciences. Computers are being used by many people who are not *super*human, despite the assumptions of science fiction.

The intent here is to present automatic digital computers as devices which are really not so new or mysterious as may sometimes be suggested. Many of the essential concepts in their design and use are merely logical extensions of concepts an informed layman takes for granted. The equipment used is frequently that which is encountered daily in business and communications. The resultant computer—although a significant, useful tool—can be understood by mere mortals. This book is intended for everyone who (1) has a reasonable curiosity and background and (2) is sincerely interested in learning about digital computers. Much of the material given on each topic is intended for the general reader. The student who wishes to delve further should use the specific references at the end of each chapter or the general bibliography at the end of the book. Some topics not of interest to the general reader are marked as such and may be skipped. Problems are given at the end of some of the chapters; other problems and exercises are suggested in the main body of the material.

This book contains some material presented in various classes of "Automatic Digital Computers," a course taught for UCLA, in the Mathematics Extension of the Orange Belt Graduate Program. Much credit goes to those students who sat many long hours in the evening listening to the author's lectures. Although their reaction was often indirect (as measured by the ability of the instructor to keep them awake), it has molded and will continue to mold the course and will eventually result in changes in the material and in the manner of presentation.

Acknowledgment is given to the various computer manufacturers who furnished information for this book. Their many and well-done instruction and operation manuals are the backbone of instruction in this dynamic field. The principal sources were Burroughs Corporation, International Business Machines, and Remington-Rand. Specific acknowledgment is made to the International Business Machines Corporation for permission to reprint material from their following copyrighted manuals: *IBM Electronic Data-Processing Machines—Type 705 Preliminary Manual of Instruction*, Copyright 1955; *IBM 305 RAMAC Manual of Operation*, Copyright 1955; and *IBM Type 650 Technical Information Manual*, Copyright 1955. Regrettably, it has not been possible to list all other sources of information individually.

The comments and criticism of Loren P. Meissner are also gratefully acknowledged. He made many worthwhile suggestions which have been included in the book.

Finally, the author would appreciate comments from readers with respect to his mistakes, oversights, and omissions.

E. M. M.

Contents

Everyone should firmly persuade himself that none of the sciences, however abstruse, is to be deduced from lofty and obscure matters, but that they all proceed only from what is easy and more readily understood.—DESCARTES

CHAPTER 1

Introduction

Man's technical progress is reflected in the tools he has invented. From early times he has been ceaselessly creating and improving devices to assist his brains and muscles in completing tasks that would otherwise be difficult or impossible. From simple tools such as the wheel he has developed the complex machines in use today. In his search for ways to ease his mental labor, the invention of writing is perhaps man's greatest single achievement, for it has enabled him to keep records to supplement his memory and to transmit to his descendants information about his other advances.

Throughout the centuries man has developed and refined this ability to record, process, and communicate information. The invention of the printing press and the typewriter, for example, are major milestones in the development of mental effectiveness. In the past century and a half man has learned to use physical phenomena—especially electricity—more fully than ever before. These years saw the development of the telegraph, the telephone, radio, and television—all of which improved the speed with which ever-increasing quantities of information could be handled.

The human brain does not only record and interchange information; it can also modify, process, and respond to it. The training and experience of our lifetime are stored in the brain and used by it in responding to the new information it is continually receiving. This process whereby the brain stores and uses information is little understood even today, but mathematical operations are fundamental to our method of understanding and representing many of its functions, and devices to aid in arithmetic and other mathematical processes are old. The abacus, slide rule, and calculating machines are some of the devices man has built to help him solve his mathematical problems.

These devices rely on the person using them, however, for much of the requisite brain power. Hence their use is restricted by the limitations of the human part of the system. Now, with the advent of automatic digital computers, man has created devices that can solve complete prob-

1

lems without the need for human intervention during the course of solution. Freed from his own limitations, man has been able to take advantage of the tremendous speed of operation that advances in electronics permit computers to attain.

Although operations that computers generally perform are the very unsophisticated ones of addition, subtraction, multiplication, and division, great speed of operation is more than compensation. So much so, in fact, that computers have been able to solve many problems that, although not inherently difficult, were considered insoluble because of their sheer computational magnitude. This doesn't mean computers think. They don't. (They can, in a sense, learn, however, as we shall subsequently see.) What they can do is perform onerous computational tasks at lightning speed, thereby liberating human brain power for more creative efforts, for example, programming new uses for computers. In fact, success in using computers to solve abstruse problems depends greatly on man's ability to *program* the problem in terms the computer can handle. In sum, in a kind of self-regenerating process, the computer's ability to do routine work rapidly has spurred the development of better computers and better techniques for using them.

The principal use of computers has been in the area of applied mathematics. Many devices that go beyond the limitations of slide rules, adding machines, and mathematical tables have been developed in the last 75 years. For example, a series of *electric accounting machines* (EAM) has been developed. Included are sorters, collators, and tabulators, as well as arithmetic devices, which together constitute a system of machines that complement each other. This "system" concept has also been extended to much more powerful, comprehensive, and rapid devices called *electronic data-processing machines* (EDPM).

The application of computers to more strictly scientific problems has come later than the original business application of EAM equipment, and many of the techniques and much of the equipment now used in scientific work was developed earlier for business applications. Although mathematicians first defined the need for the immediate predecessors of present-day computers, computers are no longer reserved exclusively for them. The trend instead has been toward broadening the use of computers, to linguistic applications, for example, rather than limiting them to numerical data. Thus a computer was used as an aid in preparing the index of this book and in performing certain editing functions, which are but small indications of possible nonnumerical usefulness.

Computers have been of increasing importance as basic tools for analysis. To use a computer for solving a problem, it is necessary to define the problem in great detail, breaking it down into elemental units.

This operation requires highly refined and flexible techniques. It is noteworthy that techniques developed for use with digital computers have been applied to many other information-processing devices, such as analog computers, process controllers, and data-reduction equipment.

The general-purpose automatic digital computer, then, is the subject of this book. It is really a very simple device, incapable of performing anything much more sophisticated than elementary arithmetic operations. The subject matter of first-year algebra is beyond its scope directly. But its lightning speed of operation coupled with the ingenuity of a human programmer make it the most versatile device yet developed by man. It is capable of solving very complicated problems, provided the human brain spells out these problems completely, specifically, and in minute detail. Yet this also means that the usefulness of a digital computer is generally limited only by the imagination of the human directing it.

SCOPE

Apart from the more complex applications and the engineering details of computer design and construction, the basic principles can be understood by anyone who can add. It is the purpose of this book to present these basic principles. Many of them will not be new, since they are fundamental concepts of arithmetic and logic known to most of us even though we may not be familiar with their application to computers. Computers encompass the fields of mathematics, engineering, electronics, accounting, and many others; and it is necessary to discuss certain aspects of each of these fields. This book is not for the specialist in any of these areas; it is intended, rather, to provide general background material for anyone who is interested in computers, as an operator, applications specialist, designer, or in any other capacity. It is intended to emphasize neither the scientific nor business application of computers, since both areas are well covered by other texts, but rather to present basic material common to both. We shall consider only general-purpose stored-program automatic digital computers of the general EDPM type (or its scientific equivalent) and ignore many limited-purpose computers, even those used for a large number of special-purpose applications. Electric accounting machines (EAM) used extensively in business record keeping will not be considered as such here. However, much that is said in this book will also apply to the EAM. In fact, the field of automatic digital computers owes much to the EAM field; the widely used Card-Programmed Calculator which preceded most automatic computers, for example, comprises a combination of conventional EAM equipment.

One purpose of this text is to present the words, terminology, and nomenclature of the computer field. There is considerable variation in the terms used by different groups. As far as possible, the terms and definitions of the Association for Computing Machinery and of the Institute of Radio Engineers have been used as standards. In addition, terms encountered in the manuals and other literature pertaining to computers have been included in an attempt to indicate similar or equivalent nomenclature. Although not all variants could be listed, a reasonable number is included.

The critical reader may notice some misstatements; many times a generalization is made without qualifications, given or implied, although there are known exceptions. The reasons for this are (1) the general statement covers most instances, and (2) the inclusion of all necessary qualifications would not only water down the generalization but might frequently make it difficult to follow the main theme and thus needlessly confuse the issue. Stating the necessary qualifications and exceptions does not necessarily result in a more rigorous presentation, but may at best reflect the present state of the art as known to the author. Both the state of the art and the author's knowledge may reasonably be subject to change. Hence a rigorous statement would be both too temporal and in conflict with the basic tenet to present fundamentals only. Delving deeper into any specific phase of the subject will make one aware both of what has been glossed over and why. Exceptions pertain to the special-purpose one-of-a-type computers, which frequently represent the state of the art at the time of their construction or which were experimental models to test new ideas of their ingenious designers, builders, and users. Generally, the state of the art has progressed so rapidly that these machines will not be duplicated, even though each of them may continue in use for a considerable period of time.

Generalizations made here are intended to apply to most automatic digital computers of the predictable future; the possibility of encountering exceptions will probably grow smaller as standardization evolves.

COMPUTER OR CALCULATOR?

Before studying computer systems it is necessary to differentiate between computers and calculators. The terms computer and calculator have, by connotation, two distinctly different meanings. The term calculator will refer to a machine (1) which can be used to perform arithmetic operations, that is, to add, subtract, multiply, divide or, sometimes, calculate the square root, (2) which is mechanical, (3) which has a keyboard input, and (4) which has manually operated controls. Adding machines and most desk calculators belong to this category.

The term computer will refer here to *automatic* digital computers. These (1) can be used to solve complete problems, not merely the arithmetic operations, (2) are generally electronic, except for input-output equipment, (3) have various rapid and versatile input-output devices, and (4) have internally stored control programs. Speed and general usefulness make a computer equivalent to thousands of calculators and their operators. An automatic digital computer, thus, is considered a computing device or system which, after its initial set-up, is capable of solving complete *significant* problems without further human intervention. The term digital implies that quantities are represented in the computer by discrete levels. The advantages of limited discrete levels will be elaborated in subsequent chapters. The word significant implies a problem which involves many operations to obtain the answer. This means that a device, such as an adding machine, which will solve a problem by adding two numbers without further human intervention is excluded, because a single simple addition is hardly significant. Many more powerful calculating devices widely used for accounting and other business applications are also excluded. In these data-processing machines, the complete task is broken into various phases, and a human operator is required to complement the machine functions.

BIBLIOGRAPHY

Although automatic digital computers have been developed mainly since 1945 and the development has been quite rapid, there is interesting background before 1945. The history of computers is given in the following references. (The contribution of Charles Babbage and Countess Ada Augusta Lovelace is thoroughly treated in Bowden.)

Bowden, B. V., ed.: "Faster than Thought," pp. 3–31 and 341–409, Pitman Publishing Corporation, New York, 1953.

Grabbe, E. M.: Data-processing Systems: How They Are Used, *Control Eng.*, vol. 2, no. 12, pp. 40–45, December, 1955.

Ivall, T. E., ed.: "Electronic Computers," pp. 1–12, Philosophical Library, Inc., New York, 1956.

Richards, R. K.: "Digital Computer Components and Circuits," pp. 1–35, D. Van Nostrand Company, Inc., Princeton, N.J., 1957.

Stibitz, G. R., and J. A. Larrivee: "Mathematics and Computers," pp. 45–63, McGraw-Hill Book Company, Inc., New York, 1956.

The difference between a calculator and a computer is important. For those unfamiliar with calculators the following is recommended.

Engineering Research Associates: "High-speed Computing Devices," pp. 135–145, McGraw-Hill Book Company, Inc., New York, 1950.

The question as to whether computers can "think" is debatable. This matter is considered in the following work.

Bowden, B. V., ed.; "Faster than Thought," pp. 311–337, Pitman Publishing Corporation, New York, 1953.

CHAPTER 2

Organization of Computers

A digital computer usually consists of large blocks of equipment (called "hardware") containing many tubes, transistors, or other basic components. Most computers are organized, however, into four major units: arithmetic, storage (or memory), control, and input-output units. These units have their analogies in any computational process. In a simple mental calculation, for example, the human brain performs the arithmetic, storage, and control functions; that is, it calculates, remembers partial answers, and decides what to do next. The input is, say, the family grocery bill, and the output is how much you are over your budget. For a more complicated problem, pencil and paper may be used as aids. The brain still performs the arithmetic and control functions, but the paper serves as the storage. When a standard desk calculator is employed, the brain is needed only to exercise the control function. An automatic digital computer, given properly prepared input data, performs all functions.

In this chapter we shall study briefly the requirements for each of a computer's four major units, note some special computer characteristics, and define certain basic terms, in other words, give a summary of a complete computer system. Later, we shall take up each unit in detail.

COMPUTER UNITS

Arithmetic Unit. The need for this unit is self-evident, since a means of doing arithmetic operations is essential to the solution of a mathematical problem (see Fig. 2.1).

Storage Unit. As indicated by the other blocks in Fig. 2.1, however, other operations are involved in solving a problem besides those performed by the arithmetic unit. The solution of any complex problem requires that the steps in the solution be written down or somehow "memorized." Thus the storage of a computer memorizes *instructions* (or commands) to be fed into the arithmetic unit. These instructions generally consist

6

of a sequence of computations that the arithmetic unit must perform to solve the problem.

Control Unit. Generally the instructions are not in a form that will operate the arithmetic unit directly. A *control* function to interpret them is necessary. The human operator of a desk calculator exercises a control function, as, for example, when he decides what keys must be depressed to solve a given problem. In high-speed automatic digital computers, the control task is performed electronically.

Input-Output. Yet it is not enough to know how to solve a problem and to have an arithmetic unit capable of doing the actual calculations.

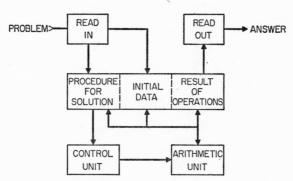

Fig. 2.1. General organization of an automatic computer system.

It is also necessary to have the *initial data* which are a part of the problem and are needed to initiate the solution. As soon as the process of solving a problem starts, it is necessary to store the results of all completed operations, just as we jot down numbers that will be used later when we solve a problem by the use of pencil and paper. Subsequent steps will consist of using the original data and/or the results of previous operations, performing further basic arithmetic operations, and again storing the results.

When the problem is completely solved and the final answer obtained, the calculation is stopped, and the output, or answer, is *read out*. The information thus obtained may be recorded on a sheet of paper, so that the read-out is simply a matter of reading the recorded numbers. However, in an essentially electronic computing system the answer ordinarily exists in the computer in a form impossible for the operator to interpret directly. The read-out device usually consists of physical equipment that records the computer output either as a curve or as a set of printed numbers.

Similarly, there is need for specialized *read-in* equipment. The operation of putting a problem and relevant data on paper is normally taken for granted. However, when the storage for information comprises relays and vacuum tubes, or exists in the form of invisible small regions of magnetization, special read-in equipment is required so that the information will be in a form the computer can use.

The above outline of the basic organization of a computer is analogous to the pad-of-paper manual-calculator approach to a problem, and most computers are organized in this way. Computers used for business applications require that the emphasis be on input-output equipment and on large storage facilities for record keeping. Such computers thus are sometimes block-diagrammed with the arithmetic, control, and storage units shown in Fig. 2.1 combined into a *processing unit*, as shown in Fig. 2.2. Sometimes the arithmetic unit is even secondary to storage and input-output equipment.

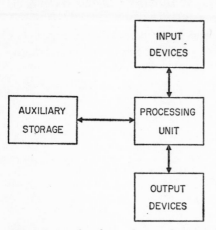

FIG. 2.2. Another form of general computer organization.

As stated, computers are used to solve "significant" problems. This implies that the storage in the computer is large enough and the speed of arithmetic operations fast enough to permit useful (i.e., nontrivial) problems to be solved, and for the solution to be accomplished in a reasonable period of time.

ESSENTIAL CHARACTERISTICS OF AUTOMATIC COMPUTERS

Although the four major parts of an automatic digital computer are analogous to calculating aids familiar to everyone, there are some essential characteristics that are not necessarily recognized as such. General-purpose computers with their great versatility and flexibility are possible only because of the following three general features which collectively have earned for computers the nickname "giant brains."

Information-handling Ability. Modern automatic digital computers characteristically have storage capacities large enough for thousands or millions of numbers. They must also be able to transfer data from one part of the system to another in a period of time measured in thousandths or millionths of a second (milliseconds or microseconds). Storage size and speed of information interchange make it practical to solve problems which would otherwise be virtually insoluble. The *common storage* of both instructions and data, and the possible interchange between them, will be considered here. The input-output equipment, which essentially communicates information between the computer and the outside world, is an important part of this information-handling ability.

Modification Ability. Automatic digital computers are designed to modify the information they handle. The modification processes generally considered are the arithmetic operations (addition, subtraction, multiplication, and division). However, computers are not limited to arithmetic operations. Some of the more potentially useful jobs involving nonarithmetic operations for which computers may be used will be discussed in later chapters. The stored-program feature and the modification ability mean that data may not only be handled arithmetically, but that the instructions used to solve a problem can be modified and changed. Potentially, this makes it possible for a computer to learn, in other words, to change its response to a situation as a result of information fed back from its environment. The speed of these operations again determines the usefulness of a computer. In fact, the average time for multiplication or addition (for nine additions and one multiplication, for example, as an *average calculating time*) is frequently quoted for comparison.

Decision-making Ability. The third essential common characteristic of computers is the ability "to make decisions." The usefulness of a computer is seriously limited if only a fixed sequence of operation can be performed. Decision-making ability means that the computer can, on the basis of criteria specified in advance, choose alternative sequences or courses of action. This occurs at a rate of speed far exceeding that at which the human mind makes and implements decisions. Thus the computer can decide the precise sequence of operations necessary to solve a problem on the basis of conditions arising during the process of solution.

TERMINOLOGY

The terminology used by various computer groups varies considerably. The terms "store" or "storage" and "memory" are often used synonymously. We shall use the term *storage*. The items of information which cause a computer to perform specific operations are synonymously called "instructions," "commands," or "orders." We shall use the term *instruction* for this purpose; the terms "command" and "order" will be restricted to their accepted connotations. The electrical signals which cause an electronic computer to perform various operations are commands; order will be used to indicate sequence.

The storage of a computer is of great importance. It is divided into many individual units called *locations* (or cells), each of which is capable of storing either a number (which may be original information or the result of an operation already performed) or an instruction. Each location is specified by a number called the *address*. Instructions generally are expressed numerically, and the computer will consider the contents of a given storage address in the same manner whether these contents consist of a data number or an instruction in numerical form. It is not necessarily possible by examining any given storage address to determine whether its contents are an instruction or data. The term generally used to indicate the contents of a storage location is "word." Hence, the capacity of the storage of a computer is given as a definite number of words; thus a computer is said to have a storage capacity of, say, 2,000 words, 4,096 words, or 20,000 words. Word size is expressed by the number of decimal digits or binary bits (terms that will shortly be taken up); it may, for example, be 10 decimal digits or 40 binary bits.

Program. It is impractical to build a computer capable of interpreting the wide variety of instructions a human being could understand, so that computing procedures are broken down in terms of relatively few different types of instructions. Hence, the general plan of action (commonly called a *program*) written out (or encoded) as a specific set of operational instructions may be long, even for an apparently simple problem. Because of its stylized form, such a set is generally called a *routine*. Substituting numbers or symbols for the specific operations to be performed by the computer (translating into machine language) is called *coding*. To facilitate coding and to make it more efficient, computers have instructions that permit the modification of other instructions where the same or similar operations are to be performed on the data. This, too, is an important characteristic; it permits a computer to follow a general set of instructions in a manner more analogous to the way in which a human being would conceive and execute the same.

The characteristics that make automatic digital computers so extremely flexible and versatile also make it necessary for all actions to be defined in great and precise detail. Hence, a major part in solving a problem on a computer is preparing the program. Frequently, many man-days of preparation are required to prepare for a few minutes of actual computer operation. If one does not pursue the analogy too far, this may be compared with the years of training, education, and experience a human being requires to enable him to perform tasks that in themselves last, at most, hours at any one time. The use of computers to do a great deal of the routine work involved in preparing programs for their own operation will be among the topics considered later.

SEQUENCE OF OPERATIONS

Briefly, assume that a computer starts with the control unit taking the contents of the first storage location (whose address is 00) and interpreting this as an instruction. The digits in that instruction determine (1) the operation to be performed and (2) the storage address associated with this operation. The instruction could, for example, be "bring the number of storage location 20 into the arithmetic unit." The word in this location is called the *operand*. The computer control unit next takes the contents of storage location 01 (next to 00 in numerical sequence) and again performs the operation indicated by the instruction with respect to the address given. This operation might be, for example, "multiply the number in the arithmetic unit by the number in storage location 21, and leave the product in the arithmetic unit." The computer control unit next takes the contents of storage location 02, and is instructed by the operation and address digits therein. To continue our example, this next step might be, "put the contents in the arithmetic unit (the product formed in the previous step) into storage location 22." Then the control unit takes the contents of storage location 03 as its next instruction, and so forth.

The sequence of instructions does not specify the value of operands, merely their location. Hence, a computer can perform the same sequence of operations on different sets of data without any alteration of the program. Only the contents of the data storage locations are changed. The contents of the addresses containing the instructions are unaltered.

Although the usual sequence of operation is the numerical order of the storage locations for each succeeding instruction, it is necessary that deviations from this sequence be possible. If the computer continued in sequence in the example quoted, it would take the contents of storage location 20 as its twenty-first instruction, whereas—in this case—storage location 20 contains a number rather than an instruction. For that reason, all computers are designed with the so-called *unconditional transfer* instruction, which simply causes the control unit to go, for its next instruction, to a specified storage location other than the next sequential address.

All general-purpose stored-program digital computers are designed to make decisions; this means that the control unit can obtain its next instruction either (1) from the next storage location in sequence or (2) from the storage location specified in the instruction. The choice depends on a condition which the computer itself examines. This is called a *conditional transfer of control;* it makes it possible, for example, to have the subsequent sequence of instructions to be obeyed by the computer determined by the positive or negative value of a number in the arithmetic unit.

PROBLEMS

1. Consider the way you prepare an income tax return (long form) in terms of the organization of a computer as given above. For example, what corresponds to arithmetic unit, control unit, storage? Where is the input, the output? Where are there unconditional transfers in the procedures? Where are there conditional transfers?

2. Similarly, consider making a pie from a recipe as a form of process control. How may it be considered analogous to the organization of computers?

3. Sometimes an automatic digital computer is considered to be a "speeded-up" desk calculator. Review how such a computer differs significantly from a calculator.

BIBLIOGRAPHY

The organization of computers is considered in most of the books given in the bibliography. Some of these are:

Booth, A. D., and K. H. V. Booth: "Automatic Digital Calculators," pp. 22–26, Academic Press, Inc., New York, 1953.

Chapin, N.: "An Introduction to Automatic Digital Computers," pp. 4–28, D. Van Nostrand Company, Inc., Princeton, N.J., 1957.

Eckert, W. J., and R. Jones: "Faster, Faster," pp. 1–18, McGraw-Hill Book Company, Inc., New York, 1956.

Engineering Research Associates: "High-speed Computing Devices," pp. 6–11, McGraw-Hill Book Company, Inc., New York, 1950.

Noe, J. D.: Data-processing Systems: How They Function, *Control Eng.*, vol. 2, no. 10, pp. 70–77, October, 1955.

CHAPTER 3

Elementary Coding

In order to understand fully the fundamental principles of computer operation, it is necessary to know how a digital computer solves problems. Although it is not the purpose of this book to teach the reader digital-computer coding or to discuss in detail the many applications of digital computers, some simple problems involving almost trivial mathematics will be considered as basic examples. We shall describe in detail how these sample problems are solved, digit by digit, word by word, and instruction by instruction.

The fundamentals considered here apply, of course, to the practical problems solved on automatic digital computers. Among the basic distinguishing characteristics of computers to be described and illustrated here by specific examples are instruction and number interchangeability, instruction modification, cycling, iterations, loops, and conditional and unconditional transfers. To begin, we will consider certain aspects of how a simple computer could be used for solving easy problems.

CHARACTERISTICS OF AN ACADEMIC COMPUTER

As one elementary example, take a computer with 1000 storage locations (or cells) numbered from 000 to 999 inclusive. Assume that in solving a problem this computer will first execute the instruction in storage location 000 and proceed to the instruction in storage location 001. It will then execute the instruction in storage location 001, and so on, unless it is instructed otherwise. We shall not consider input-output, but assume that instructions and numbers are already placed in storage and that the answers need not be read out but may be left in storage. Assume further that there is the usual *accumulator register* in the arithmetic unit. The accumulator is that part of the arithmetic unit into which numbers are brought from storage, in which the results of operations remain, and from which numbers may be taken for storage. This

13

arrangement is similar to the operation of registers on hand-operated calculators.

Finally, assume that the computer is capable of executing any one of the seven following instructions.

A (m). Add the number at storage location m to the number already in the accumulator. A (231) means "add the number in storage location 231 to the contents of the accumulator." Parentheses $(\ )$ are generally used to indicate "contents of." Note also that this does not indicate the magnitude of the numbers to be added together, but that it merely gives their locations. Taking a number from storage does not alter the contents of that storage location. If the accumulator contained zero before this instruction was executed, it will afterward contain the same number as the number in storage.

S (m). Subtract the number in storage location m from the number in the accumulator.

M (m). Multiply the number in storage location m by the number in the accumulator, and leave the result in the accumulator.

D (m). Divide the contents of the accumulator by the contents of storage location m. Leave the quotient in the accumulator.

C (m). Copy the number in the accumulator into storage location m, leaving zero in the accumulator. This will also erase the previous contents of that storage location, so that it will contain only the number that was in the accumulator.

T (m). Instead of continuing in sequence, transfer control to storage location m, perform the instruction found there, and proceed in sequence. This will not affect the contents of the accumulator.

R (m). If the number in the accumulator is zero or positive, continue to the next instruction in sequence. If the number in the accumulator is negative, clear the accumulator, shift the control to storage location m, and perform the instruction found there and in succeeding storage locations.

The above instructions have been given alphabetic abbreviations. ADD is represented by an A, SUBTRACT by an S, etc. This general technique of alphabetic abbreviations is in common use as a mnemonic device; however, many digital computers do not recognize instructions given as alphabetic symbols but can accept instructions only in numerical form. Hence, although alphabetic abbreviations are used in coding, they must be translated into numerical form. In the examples we shall consider 1 means ADD, 2 SUBTRACT, 3 MULTIPLY, 4 DIVIDE, 5 COPY, 6 TRANSFER, and 7 CONDITIONAL TRANSFER. These numbers, rather than the alphabetic abbreviations, will be used to represent computer operations. Although there are computers capable of handling *alphanumeric* symbols directly, they will not concern us now, but will be discussed in a later chapter. Even in this application, however, a translation is required if a mnemonic system for operations is used, because such a system is generally not identical with the operation symbols used directly in the computer.

We shall further assume a "word" to be composed of 10 decimal digits plus sign. As a number, for example, 8950 could be represented as 895 000 0000. (We will divide the 10 digits 3-3-4 for convenience.) A negative quantity such as −144 could be represented as 144 000 0000−. Note that the minus sign may sometimes be at the right of the number, and that some groups consistently use it in this position because of certain output characteristics.

If the word is an instruction, the five digits farthest left are 0s, the sixth digit is the *operation* part of the instruction, the seventh digit is 0, and the three least significant digits are the address of the operand in the instruction. Thus the instruction word 000 001 0897 means "add to the accumulator the contents of storage location 897." Similarly, the instruction word 000 004 0793 means "divide the contents of the accumulator by the contents of storage location 793." And lastly, the instruction word 000 006 0037 means "instead of taking the next instruction from the next storage location in sequence, go to storage location 037 for the next instruction." A minus sign with an instruction word will be interpreted as having no special significance at this time.

COMPOUND-INTEREST EXAMPLES

The use of this basic set of instructions to solve a problem is illustrated by the program illustrated in Table 3.1,* which computes the value of a sum of money when the interest earned is allowed to accumulate and accrue to the principal.

The program assumes the computer goes first to storage location 000 and interprets the word contained there as an instruction. Since the operation indicated is an ADD (numerically, 1), the computer will take the contents of the operand specified (storage location 020) and add it to the contents of the accumulator. The accumulator is assumed to have been initially clear, so that after execution of the first instruction the accumulator contains a copy of the set of numbers, namely, the word in storage location 020. This number represents the value of the principal. We shall not indicate a specific value for this principal, nor for the interest rate, as the program is effective for a wide range of values.

---

* For verisimilitude, Tables 3.1 through 3.6 are reproduced directly from a computer's printing device. The columns headed "Instr Cell" in these tables refer to what we call "storage locations" in this book.

After executing the instruction in storage location 000, the computer will automatically go to 001 and execute the word there as its next instruction. Here the 3 0021 (nonsignificant zeros to the left are disregarded) is an instruction to multiply the contents of the accumulator by the contents of storage location 021. Since storage location 021 contains the interest rate, the accumulator will, at the end of this step in the program, contain the amount of interest accrued for the specific values of principal and interest rate for the time period.

Again having no specific instructions to the contrary, the computer

Table 3.1. Basic Compound-interest Problem

INSTR CELL	INSTRUCTION OR NUMBER	REMARKS
000	000 001 0020	TAKE PRINCIPAL
001	000 003 0021	MULTIPLY BY INTEREST RATE
002	000 001 0020	ADD PRINCIPAL
003	000 005 0020	STORE NEW PRINCIPAL
004	000 006 0000	REPEAT
•		
•		
•		
•		
•		
•		
020		PRINCIPAL
021		INTEREST RATE

will go to the next storage location, namely, 002, for its next instruction. As a result, the contents of storage location 020 (the value of principal) will be added to the contents of the accumulator which contains the accrued interest. The accumulator will then contain the new value of the principal. Next, in executing the instruction in storage location 003 this new, rather than the initial, value of principal is stored in location 020. The initial value is thereby erased.

As the fifth step of the program, according to the instruction in storage location 004, the computer is instructed to go no longer to the storage location next in numerical sequence but rather to return unconditionally to storage location 000 for its next instruction, whereby the computer will repeat the operations detailed above. Repeating a sequence of steps in this manner is called *looping*.

This loop of five steps will continue to repeat. The value of the increasing principal could be noted in each cycle of the loop by reading the contents of storage location 020. Thus, if the value of the principal after 20 loops of computation is desired, the computer will execute five instructions for each loop and at the end of 99 steps will have stored the twentieth new value of principal; it would thereafter be about to return to storage location 000 to repeat this loop for the twenty-first interest calculation.

Decision Making. This program obviously has some limitations. Basically, it will continue indefinitely, and there is no way of stopping it.

Table 3.2. Compound-interest Problem Illustrating a System for Causing a Computer to Branch to Another Program after a Predetermined Number of Iterations (Cycles)

INSTR CELL	INSTRUCTION OR NUMBER	REMARKS
000	000 001 ´0020	TAKE PRINCIPAL
001	000 003 0021	MULTIPLY BY INTEREST RATE
002	000 001 0020	ADD PRINCIPAL.
003	000 005 0020	STORE NEW PRINCIPAL
004	000 001 0022	TAKE TALLY
005	000 001 0023	ADD ONE
006	000 005 0022	STORE AS NEW TALLY
007	000 001 0022	TAKE NEW TALLY
008	000 002 0024	SUBTRACT 20
009	000 007 0000	TEST FOR RECYCLE
•		
•		
•		
•		
•		
•		
020		PRINCIPAL
021		INTEREST RATE
022		TALLY
023	000 000 0001	
024	000 000 0020	

In general, however, it is desired to have the computer indicate the result of its computation at some specific place in the program. Furthermore, having finished a specific set of computations, the computer should either go on to another program or at least stop.

A method that permits the computer to make such a decision is shown in Table 3.2. The first four instructions (000 through 003) are the same as encountered in Table 3.1. In storage locations 004, 005, and 006, however, the computer takes the contents of location 022 (which is blank when the problem starts), adds 1 to it from location 023, and stores this as a tally in location 022. Thus, after the interest, and hence the new principal, has been computed for the first period, location 022 will contain a 1, which during the second cycle becomes a 2, during the third cycle a 3, and so forth. The contents of location 022 at any time is thus the number of time periods for which the computation has been made. At the end of 20 periods, after the count-up operation of 004–006 is completed, storage location 022 contains a 20.

This preparatory counting enables the computer to decide whether a predetermined number of interest periods have been computed. The instructions in storage locations 007, 008, and 009 result in the actual decision. In location 007 the computer puts this count back into its accumulator; in location 008 the count contained in storage location 024 is subtracted from the accumulator. To have the program stop after computing for 20 periods, the contents of location 024 must be 000 000 0020. Thus, as the number of interest periods computed is 1, 2, 3, . . ., 18, 19, the result in the accumulator will be negative after the subtract instruction in storage location 008 has been executed. Thus the conditional transfer in storage location 009 will result in a change of control back to storage location 000, and the entire process is repeated.

However, when the twentieth new value of principal has been computed in storage locations 000–003 and the count in storage location 022 has been increased from 19 to 20 according to the instructions in locations 004–006, the situation is different. The execution of the instructions in locations 007 and 008 will now result in a zero value in the accumulator. By definition, the CONDITIONAL TRANSFER instruction will cause the computer to go to storage location 010 for its next instruction instead of returning to location 000. Thus the compound interest for 20 periods will be computed, and after the twentieth period the computer will "decide" to branch out. The beginning of some other program or a STOP instruction, if desired, could be stored in location 010. In all, the computer will execute 200 steps before it gets to location 010.

Instruction Modification. Another important characteristic of an automatic-digital-computing system is its ability to modify its own instructions, as illustrated in Table 3.3. In this variation of the compound-interest problem, the amount of interest earned in the first period is stored in location 030, the amount for the second period in location 031, the third in 032, fourth in 033, etc. Since it is not particularly pertinent for this example, no means for stopping the computation will be considered.

The first two instructions (000 and 001) are the same as in the other programs. However, in 002 the value of interest is stored in location 030, as the new condition requires. In 003 this value is brought back into the accumulator, 004 the value of the principal is added, and in 005 the new principal is stored in location 020.

Before the value of the principal at the end of the second period can be computed, it will be necessary to modify the address portions of the instructions in storage locations 002 and 003, by replacing each of them with 031 instead of 030. This is done in storage locations 006–008 for the instruction stored in 002. In storage location 006 the instruction itself, namely, 000 005 0030, from storage location 002 is brought into the accumulator, and, in storage location 007, the contents of storage location

Table 3.3. Compound-interest Problem Illustrating Instruction Modification

INSTR CELL	INSTRUCTION OR NUMBER	REMARKS
000	000 001 0020	TAKE PRINCIPAL
001	000 003 0021	MULTIPLY BY INTEREST RATE
002	[000 005 0030]	STORE INTEREST
003	[000 001 0030]	TAKE INTEREST
004	000 001 0020	ADD PRINCIPAL
005	000 005 0020	STORE AS NEW PRINCIPAL
006	000 001 0002	TAKE 002 INSTRUCTION
007	000 001 0023	MODIFY OPERAND
008	000 005 0002	STORE NEW 002 INSTRUCTION
009	000 001 0002	TAKE NEW 002 INSTRUCTION
010	000 002 0025	MODIFY OPERATION
011	000 005 0003	STORE AS NEW 003 INSTRUCTION
012	000 006 0000	RETURN TO 000
•		
•		
•		
•		
•		
•		
020		PRINCIPAL
021		INTEREST RATE
022		
023	000 000 0001	OPERAND MODIFIER
024		
025	000 004 0000	OPERATION MODIFIER

023 (a 1 in the least significant digit) is added to it. This arithmetic operation results in the modified word 000 005 0031 in the accumulator. In storage location 008 this instruction is stored back into 002 in place of the previous instruction. Subsequent execution of this modified instruction in storage location 002 would result in the contents of the accumulator being placed into storage location 031 instead of 030. Note the use of brackets [ ] in Table 3.3 to indicate an instruction which will be modified.

Only the address portion of the instruction in the above example needs modification. In locations 009–011 the address of the instruction in location 003 could have been similarly modified and stored for subsequent execution in modified form.

However, an alternative method has been used. Note that the instruction in storage location 003 differs from that in 002 only in the operation portion of the instruction. The addresses of the storage locations of the operand involved are the same. Thus, to obtain the new instruction for storage location 003 we need only modify the operation portion of the instruction in storage location 002, which is done in storage locations 009–011. In storage location 009 the new instruction of storage location 002 is brought into the accumulator. Subtracting 4 0000 from the 5 0031 in the accumulator results in 1 0031, which is the desired instruction for storage location 003. In storage location 011 this instruction is caused to be stored in storage location 003 for subsequent execution.

In this case, this operation results in modifying only the operation portion of the instruction. The 0000 portion of 4 0000 assured that the address portion was not altered.

This ability to modify all parts of an instruction by arithmetic operations entirely under the computer's own control is very important. Skillfully applied, it results in the ultimate utilization of computer potentialities and makes computers a very powerful and useful tool.

ITERATION

Speed of operation and associated coding problems often make it practical for computers to solve problems in a manner not always practical for other methods of computation. Frequently, a straightforward (explicit) method for solving a problem is either not known or impractical to code; then an iterative (implicit) procedure is used instead. In the iterative method an estimated (approximate) value of the unknown is assumed, and the computer determines how well this assumed value fits the equation. Next the error due to this first approximation is used to calculate a second approximation, and the process repeats (iterates). If the process is convergent, as it must be to use the iterative technique, the second computed value will be better than the first. That is, the error this time will be less; then it in turn is used to compute a third approximation to the value of the variable. This process will be repeated until the calculated value of the variable is as close to the actual value as desired. For many computations this general technique is the best way of solving the problem. Sometimes it is the only way.

Square Root. An example of the iterative technique involves taking the square root of a number. Although there are straightforward (noniterative) procedures for taking the square root,* † an iterative procedure is generally used with digital computers.

Although the initially assumed value may be far from correct, the iterative procedure causes the answer to be obtained for most numbers with relatively few iterations. The basis of the computation is that, by definition, the square root of a given number, when divided into the number, will equal the square root. For example, we know the square root of .010 000 0000 is .100 000 0000. However, let us assume that the computer will always start with .999 999 9999 as the initial approximation. Dividing this into .010 000 0000 results in .010 000 0000. If we average the initial trial divisor, .999 999 9999, with the result of the division, .010 000 0000, we have .505 000 000, which is a better approximation than the initial .999 999 9999. Then, dividing .505 000 0000 into .010 000 000 and again averaging the quotient with the trial divisor results in .262 400 9900 as the third approximation. Repeating the process a fourth time results in .150 255 3012; a fifth time in .108 404 3468; a sixth in .100 325 7842. The seventh approximation is .100 000 5290; and finally, the eighth is .100 000 0000, the correct answer.

Thus, although it started with a grossly wrong approximation, the iterative procedure resulted in rapid convergence on the correct answer. Had the initial approximation been closer to the answer, the number of iterations would have been less; if further from the answer, then more would have been required. It is neither practical nor necessary to determine in advance the number of iterations required for a given problem.

The detailed coding for this procedure is shown in Table 3.4. The instructions in storage locations 000–002 obtain a quotient by dividing the trial divisor (initial approximation) into the number whose square root we wish to determine. Locations 003–005 contain a check to see if this quotient is equal to the trial divisor; if it is not, the computer prepares to iterate. Locations 007–013 are used to average this trial divisor and the quotient to obtain a better trial divisor. In location 014 the computer goes back to cell 000 to repeat the process. When the square-root value has been determined to the accuracy desired, the test in 005 causes

---

* One method is based on the binomial expansion; another involves subtracting successive odd numbers. Some automatic hand calculators use the latter method. It is possible, of course, to program a computer to determine the square root of a number by either of these methods. There are also some computers [9] in which square root is built in and programming for it is not required.

† Superscript numbers throughout the text refer to the specific list of computers or major components of a computer system given on page 201. These computers or components have the characteristic cited. Although several computers may have a common characteristic, only one will generally be cited, since it is impractical to list all computers having the same given characteristic.

the computer to go to location 006; it will then stop if not instructed otherwise.

The detailed steps in solving for the square root of .160 000 0000 by this method are shown in Table 3.5. The first column (Step) has nothing to do with the computer or its solution to the problem. It merely serves as a guide in understanding the action. The Instruction Cell column

Table 3.4. Routine for Taking the Square Root of a Number by Newton's Method of Successive Approximations

INSTR CELL	INSTRUCTION OR NUMBER	REMARKS
000	000 001 0015	TAKE X
001	000 004 0016	DIVIDE BY TRIAL DIVISOR
002	000 005 0017	STORE QUOTIENT AS APPROX ANS
003	000 001 0017	TAKE THIS APPROX ANS AND
004	000 002 0016	SUBTRACT TRIAL DIVISOR
005	000 007 0007	TEST DIFFERENCE
006	000 000 0000	STOP IF ZERO OR POSITIVE
007	000 001 0016	IF NOT, TAKE TRIAL DIVISOR
008	000 003 0018	AND HALVE IT
009	000 005 0019	STORE IT TEMPORARILY
010	000 001 0017	TAKE THIS APPROXIMATION AND
011	000 003 0018	HALVE IT ALSO
012	000 001 0019	ADD HALF THE TRIAL DIVISOR
013	000 005 0016	STORE AS NEW TRIAL DIVISOR
014	000 006 0000	RETURN FOR NEXT ITERATION
015		X
016	999 999 9999	INITIAL TRIAL DIVISOR
017		SUCCESSIVE APPROX ANSWERS
018	500 000 0000	ONE HALF
019		TEMPORARY STORAGE

gives the storage location from which the computer takes each instruction in sequence or as otherwise directed. Notice that it starts with 000, proceeds in order through 014 (omitting 006), and repeats this five times. The column Instruction lists the instruction located at the address given in the previous column. The operation part of the instruction is separated from the address part merely to facilitate observation.

The next column, Accumulator Contents, shows the contents of the accumulator in this computer after the operation indicated has been performed. Again the 10 digits are grouped 3-3-4 to make the numbers easier to read. The last column, Operand, shows the contents of the address specified in the instruction.

Thus the first step in computing the square root of .160 000 0000 involves executing the instruction in address 000. The instruction there is 1 0015, which means "add the contents of address 015 to the accumulator." The contents of 015 (the operand), as shown in column 5, is 160 000 0000. Since the accumulator was assumed initially clear, its contents after the operation has been performed, as indicated in column 4, is 160 000 0000. In a similar manner all 77 steps in the solution can be observed in detail. Note that the intermediate approximations of .579 999 9999, .427 931 0344, .400 911 5285, and .400 001 0361 are obtained in steps 12, 26, 40, and 54 of the solution. The final answer .400 000 0001 (correct to one count in the least significant place) is obtained in step 72 of the process.

If one were to code a straightforward method for computing the square root (for example, the subtracting of odd numbers), the number of storage locations required to store the program would be considerably more than those needed with this iterative method. Further, the straightforward method will likely require more time for the computer to obtain an answer. These are two good reasons why the iterative procedure is generally used for square-root problems.

FLOW DIAGRAMS AND CHARTS

With a well-defined simple problem and a thorough knowledge of machine language it is possible to write the routine directly, as was done in the previous example. The program to be coded need not be very complicated, however, before it becomes impractical to go directly from the problem to the detailed machine-language code. In fact, except for relatively simple problems, it is impossible to incorporate all the pertinent data into the routine when thinking directly in machine language. This is especially true when the solution involves a number of decisions and alternate paths. Hence an intermediate representation of the problem is necessary, and this is generally what is called a *flow diagram* or *flow chart*.

A flow diagram is a means for visualizing the over-all problem. Usually it consists of a series of rectangular blocks connected by lines and arrows indicating the sequence of operations involved in the solution. A sample flow diagram of the simple square-root routine just considered is given in Fig. 3.1. (Notice that it is independent of machine language and might be implemented in a number of ways.) In the initial flow diagram of a problem, each box usually represents a major part of the problem. For complicated problems, each block might represent functions requiring hundreds or even thousands of detailed computer instruc-

Table 3.5. Step-by-step Results in Computing a Square Root

STEP	INSTR CELL	INSTRUCTION	ACCUMULATOR CONTENTS	OPERAND
1	000	000 001 0015	160 000 0000	160 000 0000
2	001	000 004 0016	160 000 0000	999 999 9999
3	002	000 005 0017	000 000 0000	000 000 0000
4	003	000 001 0017	160 000 0000	160 000 0000
5	004	000 002 0016	839 999 9999−	999 999 9999
6	005	000 007 0007	000 000 0000	000 000 0000
7	007	000 001 0016	999 999 9999	999 999 9999
8	008	000 003 0018	499 999 9999	500 000 0000
9	009	000 005 0019	000 000 0000	000 000 0000
10	010	000 001 0017	160 000 0000	160 000 0000
11	011	000 003 0018	080 000 0000	500 000 0000
12	012	000 001 0019	579 999 9999	499 999 9999
13	013	000 005 0016	000 000 0000	999 999 9999
14	014	000 006 0000	000 000 0000	000 000 0000
15	000	000 001 0015	160 000 0000	160 000 0000
16	001	000 004 0016	275 862 0690	579 999 9999
17	002	000 005 0017	000 000 0000	160 000 0000
18	003	000 001 0017	275 862 0690	275 862 0690
19	004	000 002 0016	304 137 9309−	579 999 9999
20	005	000 007 0007	000 000 0000	000 000 0000
21	007	000 001 0016	579 999 9999	579 999 9999
22	008	000 003 0018	289 999 9999	500 000 0000
23	009	000 005 0019	000 000 0000	499 999 9999
24	010	000 001 0017	275 862 0690	275 862 0690
25	011	000 003 0018	137 931 0345	500 000 0000
26	012	000 001 0019	427 931 0344	289 999 9999
27	013	000 005 0016	000 000 0000	579 999 9999
28	014	000 006 0000	000 000 0000	000 000 0000
29	000	000 001 0015	160 000 0000	160 000 0000
30	001	000 004 0016	373 892 0226	427 931 0344
31	002	000 005 0017	000 000 0000	275 862 0690
32	003	000 001 0017	373 892 0226	373 892 0226
33	004	000 002 0016	054 039 0118−	427 931 0344
34	005	000 007 0007	000 000 0000	000 000 0000
35	007	000 001 0016	427 931 0344	427 931 0344
36	008	000 003 0018	213 965 5172	500 000 0000
37	009	000 005 0019	000 000 0000	289 999 9999
38	010	000 001 0017	373 892 0226	373 892 0226
39	011	000 003 0018	186 946 0113	500 000 0000

tions. The flow diagram itself, however, is simply an orderly representation of the problem, and no special knowledge is necessary to make one. Anyone who knows the problem should be able to diagram it.

Symbols. There are many forms of flow diagrams. Perhaps the simplest and most popular type uses rectangular boxes and simple lines

Table 3.5. Step-by-step Results in Computing a Square Root (*Continued*)

STEP	INSTR CELL	INSTRUCTION	ACCUMULATOR CONTENTS	OPERAND
40	012	000 001 0019	400 911 5285	213 965 5172
41	013	000 005 0016	000 000 0000	427 931 0344
42	014	000 006 0000	000 000 0000	000 000 0000
43	000	000 001 0015	160 000 0000	160 000 0000
44	001	000 004 0016	399 090 5439	400 911 5285
45	002	000 005 0017	000 000 0000	373 892 0226
46	003	000 001 0017	399 090 5439	399 090 5439
47	004	000 002 0016	001 820 9846-	400 911 5285
48	005	000 007 0007	000 000 0000	000 000 0000
49	007	000 001 0016	400 911 5285	400 911 5285
50	008	000 003 0018	200 455 7642	500 000 0000
51	009	000 005 0019	000 000 0000	213 965 5172
52	010	000 001 0017	399 090 5439	399 090 5439
53	011	000 003 0018	199 545 2719	500 000 0000
54	012	000 001 0019	400 001 0361	200 455 7642
55	013	000 005 0016	000 000 0000	400 911 5285
56	014	000 006 0000	000 000 0000	000 000 0000
57	000	000 001 0015	160 000 0000	160 000 0000
58	001	000 004 0016	399 998 9639	400 001 0361
59	002	000 005 0017	000 000 0000	399 090 5439
60	003	000 001 0017	399 998 9639	399 998 9639
61	004	000 002 0016	000 002 0722-	400 001 0361
62	005	000 007 0007	000 000 0000	000 000 0000
63	007	000 001 0016	400 001 0361	400 001 0361
64	008	000 003 0018	200 000 5180	500 000 0000
65	009	000 005 0019	000 000 0000	200 455 7642
66	010	000 001 0017	399 998 9639	399 998 9639
67	011	000 003 0018	199 999 4819	500 000 0000
68	012	000 001 0019	399 999 9999	200 000 5180
69	013	000 005 0016	000 000 0000	400 001 0361
70	014	000 006 0000	000 000 0000	000 000 0000
71	000	000 001 0015	160 000 0000	160 000 0000
72	001	000 004 0016	400 000 0001	399 999 9999
73	002	000 005 0017	000 000 0000	399 998 9639
74	003	000 001 0017	400 000 0001	400 000 0001
75	004	000 002 0016	000 000 0002	399 999 9999
76	005	000 007 0007	000 000 0002	000 000 0000
77	006	000 000 0000	000 000 0002	000 000 0000

and arrows. This is often adequate, but special symbols and boxes of other shapes to indicate certain operations are frequently used. Thus a decision-operation box would be rounded in some manner to make it easy to recognize the decision or branching portions of the program. As another example, operations involving punched cards are represented by an outline of such a card.

Still another example occurs in Fig. 3.1, where circles are used to in, dicate *start* and *stop*. In general, such circles identify entries to or exits from the program. Thus, when it is impractical to show a complete program on one diagram, these circles indicate interconnections between the portions on various pages. When a program is considered by itself (as was the square-root routine), circles could represent start and stop.

The use of special symbols to represent other operations is widespread, but there are no generally accepted standards in flow diagramming.

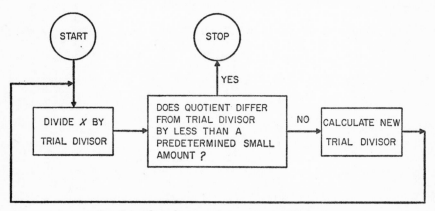

Fig. 3.1. Flow diagram for a square-root routine.

Programming. The defining of the problem that results in a flow diagram is called *programming*. Programming obviously can exist at more than one level. Thus, although the major outline of a problem could be shown on one diagram, others may be required to show portions of the problem in detail. Highly detailed flow diagrams are sometimes called *flow charts*. There is a limit to detailing. Some of the usefulness of a flow diagram disappears when each block represents only one or a very few basic machine-language instructions. Certainly when the nature of the operation in a single block is dependent on the specific instruction set of a computer, then this is no longer programming; rather it is coding. *Coding* is the process of translating the blocks of a programmer's flow chart into sets of specific machine-language instructions. Groups using computers are frequently divided organizationally into programmers and coders. The former emphasize the statement of the problem itself, while the latter are concerned with the detailed computer solution.

SORTING

Another detailed computer program that illustrates further ramifications of coding is one for sorting a set of numbers. Sorting is a standard operation, generally considered to be nonmathematical.

Let us assume that the numbers to be sorted are stored in consecutive storage locations. The sorting method will be to take adjacent pairs of numbers and compare the second number in the pair with the first. If it is less than the first, the storage locations of the two numbers are interchanged; if not, they are left as they were. Then the third number is compared with the second in a similar manner, the fourth with the third, etc. When all numbers in the set have been so ordered, the process is recycled, starting at the beginning. There

ORIGINAL DATA	DATA AFTER EACH CYCLE OF SORT							
	1	2	3	4	5	6	7	8
4	4	~~4~~3	3	3	~~3~~1	1	1	~~1~~0
5	~~5~~3	4	4	~~4~~1	~~3~~2	2	~~2~~0	1
3	5	5	~~5~~1	~~4~~2	3	~~3~~0	2	2
7	7	~~7~~1	~~5~~2	4	~~4~~0	3	3	3
9	~~9~~1	~~7~~2	5	~~5~~0	4	4	4	4
1	~~9~~2	7	~~7~~0	5	5	5	5	5
2	~~9~~8	~~8~~0	~~7~~6	6	6	6	6	6
8	~~9~~0	~~8~~6	7	7	7	7	7	7
0	~~9~~6	8	8	8	8	8	8	8
6	9	9	9	9	9	9	9	9

Fig. 3.2. Example of a sorting method where pairs of adjacent numbers are compared and interchanged if out of order.

may have to be many such cycles before all numbers are in order. This is not a very efficient sorting method but one that is relatively easy to code.

Example. An illustration of this in sorting 10 digits is given in Fig. 3.2. The digits struck out, such as 7, represent an interchange. For example, on the first cycle the 5 is compared with the 4 and the two will be left as is. However, when the 3 is compared with the 5, an interchange is effected; the 5 and the 3 change places. There are five other interchanges in the first cycle, which result in partial ordering of the numbers. The second cycle also results in five interchanges and a more nearly orderly set of numbers. It takes eight cycles to give a complete sort.

Routine. The program itself, shown in Table 3.6, occupies 45 storage locations (000–044); auxiliary data occupies seven storage locations (050–056). The data to be sorted is located in storage locations from 060 on. The program is not limited theoretically as to the number n of numbers to be sorted. However, n must be known in advance. In this case it is taken to be 10. The program will handle negative numbers, zero-value numbers, and duplicate numbers.

Flow Diagram. The flow diagram is given in Fig. 3.3. The numbers above each box refer to the storage locations where particular items of

Table 3.6. Program for Sorting

INSTR CELL	INSTRUCTION OR NUMBER	REMARKS
000	[000 001 0060]	TAKE FIRST NUMBER
001	[000 002 0061]	SUBTRACT NEXT NUMBER
002	000 007 0013	TEST IF INTERCHANGE NEEDED
003	000 005 0050	DUMP ACCUMULATOR CONTENTS
004	[000 001 0061]	TAKE NEXT NUMBER
005	000 005 0050	STORE IT
006	[000 001 0060]	TAKE FIRST NUMBER
007	[000 005 0061]	STORE IT IN NEXT POSITION
008	000 001 0050	TAKE NEXT NUMBER
009	[000 005 0060]	PUT IT IN FIRST POSITION
010	000 001 0051	TAKE INTERCHANGE TALLY
011	000 002 0052	SUBTRACT ONE FROM IT
012	000 005 0051	STORE NEW INTERCHANGE TALLY
013	000 001 0000	TAKE 000 INSTRUCTION
014	000 002 0053	SUBTRACT 000 001 0068 FROM IT
015	000 007 0020	TEST IF RECYCLE NECESSARY
016	000 005 0050	IF SO, DUMP ACCUMULATOR
017	000 001 0051	TAKE INTERCHANGE TALLY
018	000 007 0023	TEST IF TIME TO STOP
019	000 000 0000	IF SO, STOP
020	000 001 0052	TAKE ONE
021	000 005 0055	MODIFY INSTRUCTION
022	000 006 0027	SKIP TO 027
023	000 001 0054	TAKE A ZERO
024	000 005 0051	CLEAR INTERCHANGE TALLY
025	000 002 0056	PUT −8 IN ACCUMULATOR
026	000 005 0055	STORE IT FOR INSTR MOD
027	000 001 0000	TAKE 000 INSTRUCTION
028	000 001 0055	ADD INSTR MOD COUNT
029	000 005 0000	STORE NEW 000 INSTR
030	000 001 0001	REPEAT FOR 001 INSTR
031	000 001 0055	
032	000 005 0001	
033	000 001 0004	MODIFY 004 INSTR
034	000 001 0055	

the program are contained. The procedure is to compare the second number with the first in each pair of adjacent numbers, starting at the beginning of the set (storage locations 000–002). If an interchange is necessary, it is accomplished in 003–012. This constitutes one loop in the solution of the problem. After it has been determined that the first pair of numbers does not need to be interchanged (or, if it does, that this has been accomplished), then the computer in executing the instructions in 013–015 determines whether all nine combinations have been considered. If not, in 020–022 the computer modifies previous instructions

Table 3.6. Program for Sorting (*Continued*)

INSTR CELL	INSTRUCTION OR NUMBER	REMARKS
035	000 005 0004	
036	000 001 0007	MODIFY 007 INSTR
037	000 001 0055	
038	000 005 0007	
039	000 001 0000	TAKE MODIFIED 000 INSTR
040	000 005 0006	STORE IT AS NEW 006 INSTR
041	000 001 0009	MODIFY 009 INSTR
042	000 001 0055	
043	000 005 0009	
044	000 006 0000	RETURN TO 000 TO RECYCLE
045		
046		
047		
048		
049		
050		TEMPORARY STORAGE
051		INTERCHANGE TALLY
052	000 000 0001	ONE
053	000 001 0068	
054	000 000 0000	ZERO
055		STORAGE FOR INSTR MOD COUNT
056	000 000 0008	
057		
058		
059		
060	000 000 0004	START OF NUMBERS
061	000 000 0005	
062	000 000 0003	
063	000 000 0007	
064	000 000 0009	
065	000 000 0001	
066	000 000 0002	
067	000 000 0008	
068	000 000 0000	
069	000 000 0006	LAST NUMBER

so that the third in the set is compared with the second rather than the second with the first. Similarly, when the eighth has been compared with the seventh, the computer compares the ninth with the eighth. In storage locations 027–044 the actual instructions are modified by adding a 1 to the address portion. The bracketed instructions in storage locations 000, 001, 004, 006, 007, and 009 are those whose addresses refer to the locations where the numbers to be sorted are located. When these modifications are accomplished, the computer goes back to 000, the next pair of numbers is compared, and the process is repeated.

Generally, however, we must go back through the set after the nine pairs of numbers therein have been compared; that is, we must recycle. Thus, if in executing 013–015 the result is that all pairs have been examined, the computer diverts to 016 and (in 023–026) prepares to recycle (to subtract 8 from all addresses referring to storage locations of the data to be sorted). A cycle is started by comparing the number in 061 with that in 060; it is finished when 069 has been compared with 068. To repeat the cycle, 8 is subtracted from each address instead of 1 being added, as in 020–022.

It is also important to know when to stop this recycling process. Notice that, in 010–012, 1 was subtracted from an interchange tally stored in location 051. Even though the number in 051 starts at zero at the beginning of each cycle, one or more interchanges will result in a negative number being stored in 051 at the end of the cycle. If in 016–018 this number is examined and found to be negative, we know that at least one interchange occurred in the previous cycle and, hence, that the sorting operation is not necessarily completed and recycling is required. If recycling is necessary, in 023–024 zero is put in 051 as the initial interchange tally for the new cycle, the instruction modification for recycling is accomplished in 025–044, and the process repeats.

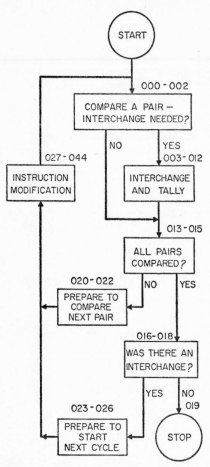

FIG. 3.3. Flow diagram for a sorting routine.

When the set of numbers has been completely sorted, the final cycle will involve no interchanges; at the end of the cycle 051 will still be zero, and the test in 018 will cause the computer to go to location 019, where the process stops. The sorting has been accomplished.

RED TAPE

This sorting routine illustrates another basic characteristic of most computer programs: Even when the method is simple, the program itself is likely to be rather involved. Here there were three instructions for comparing the two numbers in each set and seven more to effect the interchange when required. However, 35 other instructions were required for the computer to perform the mechanics of selecting other sets, recycling, modifying instructions, counting cycles, deciding when to stop, etc. A large portion both of the instructions required and of computer operating time is devoted to these "bookkeeping" operations, frequently called *red tape*.

Of course, the limited number of permissible instructions and their definitions as used here has caused this program to involve more instructions (and hence more steps in execution) than might otherwise be necessary. It is quite possible to define other or different instructions which would make this or any other program shorter and probably easier to code. The ultimate, of course, would be a single-order sort, and indeed some computers perform this operation directly.[17]

SCALING *

A very practical problem in the use of computers involves keeping the numbers within the limited range of the registers in the arithmetic unit. This is called *scaling*. If the registers were large enough to accommodate the full range of number values encountered in a problem, the magnitude of the numbers could be indicated by the position of the digits in the register. However, this is not practical, nor is it necessary. Most computations can be contained in 10- or 12-decimal-digit registers. Thus it is necessary to know why and how to shift the numbers in the registers and how to locate the decimal point. Let us consider some of the bases for these manipulations.

It is important to keep the digits of a number as close to the left of the storage register as possible. This minimizes the possibility of losing significance. If they are too far to the left, though, *overflow* will occur; i.e., the digit farthest left will not be accommodated in the register. For example, assume four-decimal-digit registers handling the sum of 6591 and 4037, which is 10428. But the four-digit accumulator would indicate only 0428, and the most significant digit in the sum would be lost. In

---

* This section may be skipped without loss in continuity. It involves some details in coding which, although important, are not of broad general interest.

most computers *overflow* is sensed and indicated so that, if desired, corrective action can be taken.

Fractional and Integral Operation. Arithmetic units which operate with the decimal point at the extreme left are called *fractional*, because all numbers are taken as less than 1. Most computers are fractional. One advantage of fractional operation is that multiplication can never cause an overflow. However, some computers operate with the decimal point at the extreme right. For obvious reasons, this is called *integral* operation. (The kind of operation used is most important for multiplication when there is a single-word accumulator for the product.[2]) Multiplication of one 10-digit number by another results in a 20-digit product. A fractional computer would keep only the 10 most significant digits in its one-word accumulator. In integral operation, only the 10 least significant digits would be retained. Fractional operation is standard even when the accumulators permit storing all digits resulting from multiplication. Our "academic" computer is assumed to be fractional; the M (m) instruction results in a product with the 10 most significant digits in the single-word accumulator.

Shift Instructions. Although the computer handles the numbers on a fractional basis, that is, with the decimal point always at the extreme left of the word, whoever does the coding may assume the decimal place to be anywhere in the register or not. To operate in this manner it must be possible to shift numbers in the accumulator. For this purpose, two new instructions will be defined for the academic computer.

SR (n). Shift the contents of the accumulator n places to the right. After such an operation, 0s will occupy the n positions farthest left in the accumulator. The n farthest-right digits of the number in the accumulator before the operation will be lost. Note that this operation involves the contents of the accumulator only and refers to no storage location. This instruction will be represented numerically by an 8.

SL (n). Shift the contents of the accumulator n places to the left. Zeros will replace the n least significant positions, and the digits in the n most significant positions will be lost. No overflow occurs on this instruction. This instruction will be represented by a 9.

Having these various operations available, let us see how they are used in scaling for various arithmetic operations.

Addition. In addition, the numbers added obviously must have the same number of decimal places. Thus the digits 895 000 0000 in a register are considered to be .895 000 0000 by the machine. However, if the coder wishes this to represent 8,950.00, then the decimal point is four places to the right of the left end of the register. If this is to be added to 101 230 0000, which the coder takes as 101.23, then before the addition the latter must be shifted right one place, becoming 010 123 0000. The answer, 905 123 0000, is interpreted as 9,051.23. Obviously the answer contains as many decimal places as were in the numbers added.

Let us consider that X represents a digit which could be something other than zero but may also be zero, and that 0 is always zero. In addition, therefore, it is not permissible to add $XXX\ XXX\ XXXX$ and $XXX\ XXX\ XXXX$, as it is quite likely to result in an overflow. One must add $0XX\ XXX\ XXXX$ to $0XX\ XXX\ XXXX$ to prevent such a possibility. In the sum, of course, the most significant digit will be either a 0 or 1.

Multiplication. Assume that an accumulator contains 800 000 0000 and that this is multiplied by the contents of a storage location containing 700 000 0000. The machine will obtain 560 000 0000 for the answer, as it considers this to be .8 multiplied by .7. However, the coder may have assumed that he was multiplying 800 by 70 and hence interpreted the answer as 56,000. Note that *the number of decimal places in the answer* (5) *is equal to the sum of the decimal places in the multiplicand* (3) *and in the multiplier* (2). This is the basic rule for determining the number of decimal places in scaling for multiplication. Also, the number of decimal places is negative if the decimal point occurs left of the far left of the register. Further, the number of decimal places can exceed the capacity of the register. For example, if 500 000 0000 and 400 000 0000 represent $500 drawing interest at the rate of 4 per cent, then the number of decimal places are 3 and −1 respectively. Thus we know that in the answer, 200 000 0000, the decimal point is two places to the right, that is, that the answer is $20. If this is to be added to the $500, it will be necessary to shift the decimal one place to the right before being able to perform this addition.

Note that if an n-decimal-place number is multiplied by another n-decimal-place number, the answer must be shifted left n decimal places in order to retain the n places in the product. Specifically, when multiplying a four-place number, $XXXX.XXXXXX$ by another four-place number $XXXX.XXXXXX$ the product would be marked off as $XXXXXXXX.XX$. To obtain a four-place answer, a left shift of four is required, resulting in $XXXX.XX0000$ in the accumulator.*

Division. The general rule for scaling in division is that *the number*

---

* To prevent this from causing the loss of significant digits in the product, the product must actually have been of the form, $0000XXXX.XX$. This means that the multiplicand and multiplier must have been of the forms (1) $00XX.XXXXXX$, (2) $0XXX.XXXXXX$ and $000X.XXXXXX$, or (3) any other form where there were at least n zeros in the most significant positions of the multiplicand and multiplier. It is not pertinent at this time to consider to what extent the least significant digits of the multiplicand and multiplier affect the significance of the product.

of decimal places in the quotient is equal to the number of decimal places in the dividend minus the number of places in the divisor. If 144 000 0000 were divided by 800 000 0000, the answer would be 180 000 0000. If this were assumed to be 1440 (4 places) divided by 8 (1 place), the answer must be 180, as we know that the decimal point in the answer will be three places from the left. If it were .00144 (−2 places) divided by 80,000 (5 places), then the answer would be interpreted as .000 000 0180, since the answer must have −7 decimal places. It will be noted that, to keep the decimal point consistent after division, a right shift of the quotient is required. Thus an n-decimal-place number divided by an n-decimal-place divisor must be followed by an instruction to shift right n places if it is desired to retain n decimal places in the quotient.

Overflow is possible in division, too. In a fractional computer, if the divisor is less in absolute value than the dividend, the quotient will be greater than 1 and will exceed the capacity of the register. To prevent such an overflow, the dividend could be shifted right before division. Division by zero obviously is as undesirable in computer operation as in mathematics in general. _____

PROBLEMS

1. Make a flow diagram of the procedure for preparing an income tax return. Make it general so that your diagram will include boxes for decisions such as "over $5,000? joint return? head of household," etc. Follow closely the instructions on the form itself.

2. Write a program for computing a bowling score using the instructions defined in this chapter. Assume the pinfall for each ball rolled on one frame is stored in consecutive storage locations. (There can be from 12 to 21 pinfalls.) Let the computer determine whether each pinfall represented a strike, spare, or flat, and score accordingly. This is not as difficult as it may first appear to be.

3. Devise a routine for calculating the square root of a number by subtracting odd integers. Contrast the amount of storage for this program with that required by the method of Table 3.4. Count the number of steps to calculate the square root of .160 000 000 and compare this with the solution of Fig. 3.5. (This is a tedious problem.)

4. Devise a routine for calculating the mean and variance of a set of numbers. (Mean is the sum of the numbers divided by the number of numbers; variance is the sum of the squares of the differences between the respective numbers and the mean, divided by the number of numbers.) Assume that up to 100 numbers are stored in storage locations 100, 101, etc. Each number may range in value from 10 to 9,999. This is meant to be a problem in scaling.

5. Why in the example of Table 3.4 was the new trial divisor obtained by adding half the previous trial divisor and half the previous approximation rather than by adding the previous trial divisor and the previous approximation and then taking half of the sum?

BIBLIOGRAPHY

The device of assuming a machine code of relatively few instructions and of using it to solve simple problems is frequently used. The following are some examples.

Booth, A. D., and K. H. V. Booth: "Automatic Digital Calculators," pp. 136–144, Academic Press, Inc., New York, 1953.

Canning, R. G.: "Electronic Data Processing for Business and Industry," pp. 74–88, John Wiley & Sons, Inc., New York, 1957.

Chapin, N.: "An Introduction to Digital Computers," pp. 363–386, D. Van Nostrand Company, Inc., Princeton, N.J., 1957.

Eckert, W. J., and R. Jones: "Faster, Faster," pp. 65–89, McGraw-Hill Book Company, Inc., New York, 1956.

Livesley, R. K.: "Digital Computers," pp. 1–14, Cambridge University Press, New York, 1957.

Metzger, R. W.: "Elementary Mathematical Programming," John Wiley & Sons, Inc., New York, 1958.

Richards, R. K.: "Arithmetic Operations in Digital Computers," pp. 354–363, D. Van Nostrand Company, Inc., Princeton, N.J., 1957.

Rock, S. M., and W. W. Klammer: Programming the Computer, *Control Eng.*, vol. 4, no. 3, pp. 119–123, March, 1957.

The subject of flow charts and block diagrams is given in the following references. (The referenced material disagrees with some of the statements in this book.)

Chapin, N.: "An Introduction to Automatic Digital Computers," pp. 115–128, D. Van Nostrand Company, Inc., Princeton, N.J., 1957.

McCracken, D. D.: "Digital Computer Programming," pp. 87–97, John Wiley & Sons, Inc., New York, 1957.

The subject of scaling in digital computers is considered in the following works.

Gotlieb, C. C., and J. N. P. Hume: "High-speed Data Processing," pp. 111–116, McGraw-Hill Book Company, Inc., New York, 1958.

McCracken, D. D.: "Digital Computer Programming," pp. 52–65, John Wiley & Sons, Inc., New York, 1957.

CHAPTER 4

Number Systems

Fundamental concepts of our number system are learned by all of us at an early age. Arithmetic, including the handling of negative numbers, is a required part of our school training. However, in digital computers numbers often are handled differently from the way they were in school, as we shall see in this chapter.

Let us review some basic number concepts. In ordinary computation we use a *decimal* system of numbers, with 10 symbols (admissible marks) to represent 0, 1, 2, 3, 4, 5, 6, 7, 8, and 9. In this decimal system the 10 is called the *base* or *radix*. That we should have 10 symbols and that they should be referred to as *digits* in the same manner as our fingers is no coincidence. Man found it helpful to use his fingers when first learning to use numbers.

POSITIONAL NOTATION

The number system we use has an important basic characteristic, namely, the positional value of a number. For example, in the number 327 the positions of the numbers indicate magnitude, the number farthest left being the greatest, the farthest right the least. The number 3 thus represents 300, or 3×10^2; the 2 indicates 20 (2×10^1); the 7 is 7×10^0, that is, simply 7. We recognize this positional value when we say that 327 is three hundred twenty-seven. Similarly, digits to the right of the *radix* point (decimal point in this case) would represent by their position one-tenth (10^{-1}), one-hundredth (10^{-2}), etc. Each position in a decimal system is called a *decade*.

Our concept of number also includes zero and negative numbers. For example, we know when we are decreasing by, say, one digit each time that a normal sequence of numbers would be 5, 4, 3, 2, 1, 0, -1, -2, -3, -4, etc. That is, to handle negative numbers we had to learn the rules of signs for arithmetic operations. However, an automatic digital computer does not necessarily handle negative numbers in this manner.

COMPLEMENT CONCEPT

To understand how a number of computers do handle negative numbers, consider a hand-operated calculator of the type that makes no provision for negative signs. When doing addition or subtraction on such a machine, where the result can be negative there must be a means of interpreting negative answers, for a negative result would cause the counter to turn backward beyond zero. For example, if one subtracted 521 from 321 the result would be 999 999 9800, assuming a 10-digit register. (The number of 9s in the result depends on the capacity of the register as well as on the value of the negative number.) However, we can interpret this result as −200, for it shows that the counter turned backward 200 counts after reaching the zero position. The 999 999 9800 is called the *complement* representation of −200. The complement, then, is the result of subtracting the original negative number from the full capacity of the register, in this case 200 from 1 000 000 0000.

Let us consider this counting-backward-beyond-zero kind of operation for a four-decimal-digit counter. See Table 4.1, where a sequence of

Table 4.1. Representation of Digits +5 through −5 by a Four-decimal-digit Register Using the Tens-complement System

Number	Counter
+5	0005
+4	0004
+3	0003
+2	0002
+1	0001
0	0000
−1	9999
−2	9998
−3	9997
−4	9996
−5	9995

counter values corresponding to the numbers between 5 and −5 is shown. This sequence applies to a counter which counts forward and backward, which has a maximum count in the register of 9999 and a minimum count of 0000, and which has a difference of only one count between the maximum and minimum counts. The presence of a 9 in the most significant position in this example indicates a negative number (i.e., that the counter has gone backward through zero). Although the counter has a capacity of 10,000 numbers (0000 to and including 9999), it actually represents from +8999 down to and including −1000. Thus 9000 would represent −1000, while 8999 would be +8999. Further, if desired, all numbers with a 9, 8, 7, 6, or 5 in the most significant position could be defined to represent negative numbers. In the last instance the counter capacity would range from +4999 to −5000. This system for representing negative numbers has been called the *tens complement*. Actually it is a 10^n complement; $n = 4$ in this case.

Basic Use of Complements. The important advantage of using a system of complements is the ability to subtract positive numbers or add negative numbers simply by adding complements. Hence negative-number operations can be performed by a device which merely adds. Such an ability is highly advantageous in automatic digital computers.*

Examples of arithmetic addition and subtraction with positive and negative numbers using this complement system are given in Table 4.2.

Table 4.2. Examples of the Use of a Complement Representation for Doing Negative Addition or Subtraction by Adding

	Number	*Counter*
(A)	+3	0003
	−1	9999
	+2	1 | 0002
(B)	+2	0002
	−3	9997
	−1	9999
(C)	−2	9998
	−3	9997
	−5	1 | 9995

Note that in examples (A) and (C) the addition of the negative number will cause the counter to overflow, that is, to turn forward more positions than the capacity of the register allows. This is indicated by the 1 to the left of the vertical rules which indicate maximum counter capacity. Further, assume that this overflow has no significance and

---

* Many computers use complements, but some can both add and subtract and hence do not use them. Similarly, some computers which can only subtract do addition by using complements. However, since the principles are much the same, we will consider only the basic adder-type computer here. Differences will be pointed out when pertinent.

that the counter recognizes only the four numbers within *XXXX*. The examples illustrate the consistency of such a complement system. They also point out that, although complements are useful for the internal performance of such arithmetic operations, it is necessary to convert to and from the complement system when entering and leaving the computer to obtain normal negative-number representation. The comparative difficulty of doing this with the tens-complement system is one reason why it is generally not used.

This "complementing" and "decomplementing" is difficult under the tens system, for it involves *borrowing* from digits to the left of the digit being complemented. (In the four-decimal-digit case it involves subtracting from the five-digit figure 10,000.) This borrowing operation is not easily mechanized in a computer; it is avoided by the widely used *nines-complement* system.

Nines Complement. If in the four-digit case, instead of subtracting from 10,000 or doing the equivalent operation, we subtracted from 9999 we would be using the nines complement. The complement for each digit in the nines system is obtained without regard for the other digits, and there is no borrowing. Thus a computer can do complementing operations on each digit in a number individually. This is an important practical consideration.

Now refer to Table 4.3 for the counter representation of the numbers

Table 4.3. Representation of the Digits +5 through −5 by a Four-decimal-digit Register Using the Nines Complement

Number	Counter	Number	Counter
+5	0005	−1	9998
+4	0004	−2	9997
+3	0003	−3	9996
+2	0002	−4	9995
+1	0001	−5	9994
0	9999		

around 0 in such a complement system. An examination of this table will result in some questions, especially when one notes that 0 is represented by 9999 and that there is no 0000. To understand the need for this, remember that the counter is only capable of adding, that is, that the count must always increase in any operation. (This contrasts with the hand-operated machines mentioned above, in which the wheels can turn either forward or backward.) Hence, as the counter counts up from 0001 to 0002, etc., it will ultimately progress to 9997, 9998, and 9999. When it advances one count from 9999, we would expect it to go to 0000. However, to use a 9999 complement, it is necessary to reduce the capacity of the counter from 10,000 to 9999 counts; that is, one count must be lost. This is done by what is known as the *end-around-carry* technique. As one count is added to a register with 9999 in it, there is an overflow as the register tends to turn to 1 | 0000. The digit farthest left overflows the four-digit capacity of the register and is carried around and added to the least significant position of the counter. Hence the adding of one count to 9999 results in 0001. This end-around-carry operation makes it impossible to obtain 0000; hence the capacity of the register is reduced by 1 as desired.*

Negative Zero. Since 0 is represented by 9999 in the case of addition, then by definition we are using a *negative zero*. That we can use a negative zero, as well as the normally assumed positive zero, is illustrated by the examples in Table 4.4. Thus adding either a positive number as

Table 4.4 Examples of Operations Involving 0 in the Nines-complement System

	Number	Counter	
(A)	+2 −0	0002 9999	
	+2	1 0001 0002	Before end-around carry After end-around carry
(B)	−4 −0	9995 9999	
	−4	1 9994 9995	Before After
(C)	−0 −0	9999 9999	
	−0	1 9998 9999	Before After

in (A) or a negative number as in (B) to this zero results in the correct answer. Of course, adding zero to zero (C) results in zero. In many computers it is possible to obtain either positive or negative zero as the

---

* When the basic arithmetic operation is subtraction, that is, counting backward, then 0 is 0000, but −1 becomes 9998 and 9999 will not exist. In this case end-around borrow is used. It can be demonstrated that this, too, results in a useful set of complements.

result of an operation, and it is necessary to take this into account in coding. Other nines-complement examples not involving zero are given in Table 4.5.

Table 4.5. Examples of Non-0 Operations Using the Nines-complement System

	Number	Counter		
	+5	0005		
(A)	−2	9997		
	+3	1 0002	Before end-around carry
		0003	After end-around carry
	+1	0001		
(B)	−4	9995		
	−3	9996		
	−2	9997		
(C)	−3	9996		
	−5	1 9993	Before
		9994	After

BINARY NUMBERS

Although all of us are accustomed to thinking and working with an arithmetic of decimal numbers, that is, of 10 states, digital computers are not so arranged. If computers were simply high-speed electronic versions of desk calculators, they would be decimal, since such calculators use wheels which have 10 discrete positions. However, it has not been found feasible to develop direct analogs of these calculators even for arithmetic units of automatic digital computers.

Reliability Need for Binary. One important reason for this is concerned with reliability. An automatic digital computer because of its speed, among other things, is required to be a phenomenally reliable device. A calculator whose wheels may turn 10 times per second would be tolerated if it made a few errors in a year of continuous operation. (Actually, the duty factor of calculators is so small that few actually operate this much in their useful life.) Yet a relatively slow automatic digital computer which makes one error in an 8-hour shift is suspect. However, in this 8 hours it will have done as many operations as a calculator does in a year of continuous operation. This comparison is conservative, for it assumes only 10,000 operations per second. Thus we see that much, much more reliability is expected of computers than has been required of calculators.

Although many direct 10-state decimal devices exist, designers of computers have found few that are (1) fast enough and (2) reliable enough for computers. The devices which have proved most practical are the *binary*, that is, those with only two states, on or off, high or low, conducting or nonconducting, etc. There is no in-between condition, and the possibility of indecision or wrong decision (unreliability) is minimal. Even where decimal operation is achieved with a multiplicity of binary devices, the over-all reliability is better than any practical true decimal device. The detailed reasons for this are outside the scope of this presentation.

Binary Arithmetic. Automatic digital computers, then, normally consist of a number of two-state binary devices. The arithmetic they use is obviously a simplified one; there can be only two coefficients, 0 and 1, which respectively indicate the absence or presence of a *bit* of information at a given position. Further, as with decimal numbers the position of a digit represents its magnitude—the magnitude at any position being a power of 2 rather than of 10. Thus, from the binary point to the left, the 0s and 1s in a binary number indicate the absence or presence of 1, 2, 4, 8, 16, 32, etc., in the decimal equivalent. For example, binary 1101 indicates an 8, a 4, and a 1, or a 13 in decimal notation. To the right of the binary point the possible values are $\frac{1}{2}$, $\frac{1}{4}$, $\frac{1}{8}$, etc. For example, the numbers $3\frac{1}{4}$ and $7\frac{3}{8}$ are 11.010 and 111.011, respectively, in binary notation.

Binary arithmetic naturally has simple addition and multiplication tables. Addition is

$$0 + 0 = 0$$
$$1 + 0 = 1$$
$$1 + 1 = 10$$

Multiplication is

$$0 \times 0 = 0$$
$$0 \times 1 = 0$$
$$1 \times 1 = 1$$

The simplicity of these operations accounts for the use of the binary system in many computer systems. Obviously, decimal addition and multiplication would require more equipment.

Basic binary arithmetic operations are illustrated by the following examples. Note the use of a subscript to denote the base of the number system used. Multiplication of 26_{10} by 19_{10} results in

$$11010_2 = 26_{10}$$
$$10011_2 = 19_{10}$$
$$11010$$
$$11010$$
$$\underline{11010}$$
$$111101110_2 = 494_{10}$$

Similarly dividing 494_{10} by 19_{10} by the binary method gives

$$11010$$

$$10011\,\big|\,111101110$$
$$\underline{10011}$$
$$10111$$
$$\underline{10011}$$
$$10011$$
$$\underline{10011}$$

Octal Notation. Binary numbers require about $3\frac{1}{3}$ times as many digits to indicate a number as does a decimal system; the normal word size in binary computers is 30 to 40 binary digits. This is a large number of 1s and 0s in a row, and in practice it is rather cumbersome to handle such numbers. Although the addition and multiplication tables are simple for a machine, they are *too* simple for most humans trained in decimal arithmetic. Hence, human errors in handling and representing binary numbers result both from the relatively large number of digits required and from the monotony of the correspondingly large number of binary operations which need be performed for equivalent decimal operations.

To reduce such errors, an *octal* representation (to a base of 8) is frequently used in input-output units of binary digital computers. This is done by separating binary numbers into groups of three (each way from the binary point) and representing each group by the octal equivalent from the following table.

$$000 = 0 \quad 100 = 4$$
$$001 = 1 \quad 101 = 5$$
$$010 = 2 \quad 110 = 6$$
$$011 = 3 \quad 111 = 7$$

Thus 26_{10}, which is 11010_2 or $011\ 010_2$, becomes 32_8; and 19_{10} is $010\ 011_2$ or 23_8. Similarly 011.010_2 is 3.2_8 and 111.011_2 becomes 7.3_8.

Octal notation is more convenient than decimal for representing and manipulating binary numbers, since it requires only one-third as many marks as binary. Further, although it is not greatly less efficient than decimal notation, it retains for the machine the advantage of simple binary operation tables for addition and multiplication. The human operator using the octal system will find it necessary to learn octal addition and multiplication tables. These are almost as extensive as their decimal equivalents and certainly more difficult, because of the possible confusion with decimal. The derivation and use of such tables is left as an exercise.

It must be emphasized that the use of octal representation is external to the computer proper. The internal computer operation will remain binary whether the coder thinks in binary or octal terms. In many binary machines, however, the input-output equipment has been modified to take in or to put out octal numbers. Thus reading in a 0 through 7 will cause, for each input digit, the corresponding set of three binary digits to be put into the computer. Similarly, in the output, the binary digits in groups of threes are converted to octal digits.

Gray Code. The binary code considered above is sometimes called the *natural* binary. It is a positional notation system, which makes it convenient for arithmetic operations. However, there are other binary notation systems which do not possess this positional notation.

An example of this is the *Gray code* (a form of cyclic code also known as progressive binary and as reflex or reflected binary). Its basic advantage is that, as the number represented changes by one unit, only one of the bits in the Gray code will change. Table 4.6 illustrates the natural binary and Gray codes for decimal numbers 00 through 15. For example, 7_{10} is 0111_2 and 8_{10} is 1000_2 in natural binary. Note that all four bits change when changing from 7_{10} to 8_{10}. However, in the Gray code the representations are 0100_2 and 1100_2, respectively; only the first (most significant) digit is changed. All other numbers, differing by one count, are similarly formed by changing one and only one bit.

The advantage of the Gray code lies not in the computer itself but in certain kinds of peripheral input or output devices. For example, there are data systems in which the input is the amount of a shaft rotation. To convert such an input into information a binary computer can use, the shaft position at discrete positions causes switches to be opened or closed to represent 0 and 1, respectively. If the position is to be defined to only 1 of 16 discrete positions, four switches are sufficient. As the shaft turns from, for example, the 7 region to the 8 region, the four switches will not all necessarily change at the same time. Hence, intermediately between the definite 7 and 8 areas might be more than one of all the other four-bit combinations! Such ambiguity is avoided when using the Gray code.

Table 4.6. Natural Binary and Gray-code (Progressive-binary) Equivalents

Decimal number	Natural binary	Gray code
0	0000	0000
1	0001	0001
2	0010	0011
3	0011	0010
4	0100	0110
5	0101	0111
6	0110	0101
7	0111	0100
8	1000	1100
9	1001	1101
10	1010	1111
11	1011	1110
12	1100	1010
13	1101	1011
14	1110	1001
15	1111	1000

Obviously, to use the binary system in a computer requires that it be converted to the natural-position notational system. This and other aspects of the input output and converter aspects of a computer will be considered in more detail elsewhere in this text.

Binary Complements. Let us consider an example of the use of complements in a binary computer. For simplicity, assume that four binary digits in each of two numbers A and B are to be added and that the sum, S, register normally contains four digits (obviously the properties described will apply or can be extended to either larger or smaller registers). As shown in Table 4.7(A), these normally 16-position registers accommodate numbers from -7 to $+7$ inclusive, which, including the zero representation, is 15 positions. The use of end-around carry prevents the register from ever containing 0000, which would be the sixteenth position.

Notice that all positive numbers have a 0 in the most significant position, and all negative numbers have a 1 in that position. The left-most position is thus the *sign digit* and can be handled as any other digit in the word. Even in so-called decimal computers the concept of a 0 for positive and a 1 for negative in the most significant position is used. In some cases, however, the sign digit is not limited to just two values; it may have several states, but most of them serve other nonarithmetic

Table 4.7. Arithmetic Operations Involving Binary Complements

(A) Decimal	Binary			
+7	0111		+6	0110
+6	0110	(B)	−4	1011
+5	0101			⊂10001⟩
+4	0100		+2	0010
+3	0011			
+2	0010			
+1	0001			
0	1111			
−1	1110			
−2	1101		+3	0011
−3	1100	(C)	−4	1011
−4	1011		−1	1110
−5	1010			
−6	1001			
−7	1000			
			−2	1101
		(D)	−5	1010
				⊂10111⟩
			−7	1000
	+3	0011	+5	0101
(E)	−3	1100	−0	1111
	0	1111	(F)	⊂10100⟩
			+5	0101
	−0	1111	+5	0101
(G)	−0	1111	(H) +3	0011
		⊂11110⟩		1000
		1111		

purposes such as control. In one decimal computer,[3] + is indicated by a 9 in the sign digit and − by an 8.

Further, note that the complement representation of any binary number in Table 4.7 is derived from the normal one by interchanging 1s and 0s. This is particularly important, as later it will be noted that this *self-complementing* characteristic is relatively easily done electronically.

It will also be noted that this results in the *ones complement*,[7] that is, as if the binary number had been subtracted from 1111. If a 1 is added in the least significant position of a ones complement, the result is a *twos complement*,[16] for this is the same as subtracting from 10000, that is, 2^n. Hence, it is analogous to the so-called tens complement in the decimal system. This twos complement is sometimes called the *binary complement,* and the ones complement is called the *binary complement minus one.*

In the table we see that 0 is not 0000 but 1111, which by definition is negative. As in the decimal case, if a sign must be associated with 0, a negative sign is as good as a positive one. The complement system, especially for self-complementing, here makes it mandatory.

Examples will illustrate the validity of Table 4.7(A). We see that adding two positive numbers together presents no complications. However, let us add +6 and −4 [Table 4.7(B)]. Note the end-around-carry operation. Table 4.7(C) shows +3 added to −4 (or 4 subtracted from 3); here there is no end-around carry and the answer is obtained directly. When [Table 4.7(D)] −2 and −5 are added in binary form, carry to the right again occurs.

Manipulation of negative zero is also illustrated. Table 4.7(E), which is the addition of +3 and −3, shows how the self-complementing feature of this number system makes 1111 for 0 necessary. Table 4.7(F) illustrates how when 0 is added to +5 end-around carry produces the correct sum of +5. Table 4.7(G) shows −0 added to −0 to obtain −0.

Use of end-around carry changes our concept of overflow (exceeding register capacity). In our previous considerations overflow was generally to be avoided. But with end-around carry a digit lost from the most significant position is reintroduced at the far right in the least significant position. Detecting that the capacity of the S register has been exceeded obviously cannot be done by sensing a carry from the most significant position. What can be used is shown in Table 4.7(H). Here +5 and +3 are added and the sum, +8, is outside the register capacity of +7 to −7 inclusive. The indicated sum in this case is 1000, which, since it indicates −7, is obviously wrong. We say "obviously" because two positive numbers added together (0s in the most significant positions) cannot result in a negative sum (a 1 in the most significant position); hence the answer is obviously wrong and implies overflow. Similarly, the addition of two negative numbers resulting in a sum with a positive sign again means that the capacity of the register has been exceeded.

BINARY-CODED DECIMAL SYSTEMS

As indicated previously, humans are trained to think decimally, but computers operate in a binary mode. This gap is bridged by the use of *binary-coded decimal (bcd)* systems. Since a group of four binary bits (a *tetrad*) can represent 16 states or conditions, such a group can be so arranged as to represent the 10 states (numbers) in the decimal system. The specific arrangement chosen from the variety of possible four-bit (or even five- or seven-bit) combinations depends on several factors, and this has resulted in the use of different *bcd* systems in different computers. Three of these factors are (1) ease of arithmetic operations, (2) ease of complementing, and (3) facility for checking.

1-2-4-8. An obvious system for *bcd* representation is one using four bits in a straightforward manner (1, 2, 4, 8 in relative value from right to left), with each set of four bits equal to one decimal digit. Note that this is *not* a grouping of a natural binary number in sets of four bits comparable to the grouping of three bits for the octal system. For example, 78_{10} is 1001110_2 or 116_8, but as two 1-2-4-8 binary-coded groups it would be 0111 1000 in which from right to left the positional values are 1, 2, 4, 8, 10, 20, 40, 80 rather than the 1, 2, 4, 8, 16, 32, 64, and 128 in a natural binary.

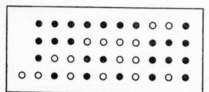

Fig. 4.1. Display of the number -123 456 7890 in a register of a computer having a 10-digit word and using a straight binary-coded-decimal system.

The 1-2-4-8 system is widely used.[4,5] It facilitates arithmetic operations both because, within each set of four representing a single decimal digit, the arithmetic is binary and because from decimal digit to decimal digit the value obviously varies by powers of 10. As shown in Fig. 4.1, the four bits for each digit are frequently displayed in a vertical column and the corresponding decimal digits in horizontal rows. The number -123 456 7890 is taken as an example.

Since any *bcd* system is a *mixed-base notation* (that is, binary within each decimal digit, but decimal from one digit to another), it is necessary to convert from one base to another. For example, when adding 7_{10} (0111_2) in the 1-2-4-8 system to 6_{10} (0110_2), the addition is

$$
\begin{array}{r}
0111 \\
0110 \\
\hline
1101
\end{array}
$$

The sum, 1101_2, which is 13_{10}, must be *decimal-converted* to 0011_2, which represents the 3 to be retained in that position as the sum. Also there must be a *decimal carry* of a 1 to represent the 1010_2 (10_{10}) carried to the next most significant position (the next tetrad). The propagation of a decimal carry is an important aspect of the arithmetic-handling capabilities of a *bcd* system. Obviously such a carry is not inherent in the 1-2-4-8 system, but it can and must be especially provided for by the equipment used for adding.

An important characteristic of any *bcd* system is the ability to form the nines complement of the digit. This should be done by a process simpler than actual subtraction. The straight binary-coded system is somewhat involved in this regard. Table 4.8 shows the binary

Table 4.8. Representation of the Decimal Digits and Their Nines Complements by the 1-2-4-8 Binary-coded-decimal System

Decimal	1-2-4-8 binary	Nines complement
0	0000	1001
1	0001	1000
2	0010	0111
3	0011	0110
4	0100	0101
5	0101	0100
6	0110	0011
7	0111	0010
8	1000	0001
9	1001	0000

equivalent plus its nines complement for each decimal digit. A regular pattern for translating to the complement form is present and can be summarized as follows.

1. There is a 1 in the *one* position of the complement if there was 0 in the *one* position of the number. Similarly, there is a 0 in the complement when a 1 is present in the number.

2. There is a 1 in the *two* position of the complement when there is a 1 in the *two* position of the number. Similarly, a 0 is a 0.

3. There is a 1 in the *four* position of the complement if there is a 1 in either the *two* or *four* position of the number, but not if a 1 is present in both the *two* and *four* position.

4. There is a 1 in the *eight* position of the complement if the *eight, four,* and *two* positions of the number are all 0.

Building the ability to make this conversion into a digital computer is not so difficult as it may appear at first, and later we will take up how it is done.

With respect to checking, the 1-2-4-8 system uses a *forbidden-combination* type of check. Since only 10 of the possible 16 states of a four-bit code are used, the redundancy of the extra six states can be used as a check. Thus, if any of the six combinations of four bits which represent 10 − 15 are present, an error has occurred. Note, however, that this is a limited check. Although it would detect that 8 and 2 indicated an unallowed 10, when actually an 8 and a 1 for a 9 was intended, it would not detect that there were erroneously a 4 and 2 (6) when a 4 and 1 (5) was the correct number.

Excess-three. Another four-bit code is the *excess-three* system,[6] as shown in Table 4.9. The binary representation progresses in the expected

Table 4.9. Excess-three Representation of the Decimal Digits and Their Complements

Decimal	Excess-three binary	Nines complement
0	0011	1100
1	0100	1011
2	0101	1010
3	0110	1001
4	0111	1000
5	1000	0111
6	1001	0110
7	1010	0101
8	1011	0100
9	1100	0011

manner except that all numbers are 3 more than the usual binary number. For example, 4 is represented by 0111, which naturally represents a 7.

The first advantage of excess-three notation is that it is self-complementing; all bits are changed to the opposite state in complementing or decomplementing when a nines complement is required. Even when a tens complement is used (as it is in some excess-three *bcd* computers), this is accomplished by self-complementing to obtain a nines complement and then adding 1 in the least significant position. This adding of 1 of course can cause a carry to the left in the register, but this doesn't create the problem that borrowing a tens complement normally implies.

Arithmetic operations, although not as straightforward as in the 1-2-4-8 system, are not too difficult; as a matter of fact, there are some arithmetic advantages. Adding two excess-three numbers, for example, will result in an excess-six sum, which exists immediately after the initial addition and provides directly the decimal carry to the next-higher decimal position. However, a disadvantage of the excess-three system is that after each such addition the equivalent of subtracting 3 must be done to reduce the excess-six sum to the excess-three required for subsequent operations. Actually, if there is no decimal carry in an addition, it is necessary to subtract 3 from the sum to get the proper excess-three answer. If a decimal carry occurs, then 3 must be added. It is suggested that examples be worked out to demonstrate this.

Table 4.10. Representation of the Decimal Digits and Their Nines Complement by the 1-2-4-2* System

Decimal	1-2-4-2* number	Nines complement
0	0000	1111
1	0001	1110
2	0010	1101
3	0011	1100
4	1010	0101
5	0101	1010
6	1100	0011
7	1101	0010
8	1110	0001
9	1111	0000

1-2-4-2*. As shown in Table 4.10, in this system the four bits (from right to left) have values 1, 2, 4, 2, respectively, instead of the 1, 2, 4, 8 of the previous system. Note that the maximum amount which can be indicated is 9, and that the 2* is used in forming the representation for 4, 6, 7, 8, and 9.

Although this system has the obvious disadvantage of making it difficult to perform arithmetic operations, its forte is the ease with which it forms a nines complement. A 1 in any position is exchanged for a 0 and vice versa; hence it is also self-complementing. This operation is very easy to do in the electronic devices which represent each of these bits.

Checking comparable to the forbidden combination can also be done. The combinations 0100, 0110, 0111, 1000, 1001, and 1011 are not used. Circuitry to indicate if such unused combinations were formed erroneously could be used. Again, however, it would permit only a limited check.

0-1-2-3-6 System.   Heretofore, the binary-coded-decimal systems considered do not permit complete checking for errors. Where emphasis is placed on error checking, it is generally necessary to use five or more bits to represent a single decimal digit.

An example is 0-1-2-3-6 code.[3]   Table 4.11 illustrates this five-bit code

Table 4.11. Table of the Five-bit Binary-coded-decimal 0-1-2-3-6 System

(Note: all digits have two 1s and 0 has a somewhat unusual value.)

No.	Five-bit code				
	0	1	2	3	6
0	0	1	1	0	0
1	1	1	0	0	0
2	1	0	1	0	0
3	1	0	0	1	0
4	0	1	0	1	0
5	0	0	1	1	0
6	1	0	0	0	1
7	0	1	0	0	1
8	0	0	1	0	1
9	0	0	0	1	1

in which any and all decimal numbers are represented by two 1s and three 0s. Further, only 10 ways exist for having two 1s and three 0s in a group of five bits, and all are used here. This permits a very exacting check. Relatively simple checking circuits will detect the absence of two 1s in any number representation. Any single error (a 0 for a 1 or vice versa) will be detected. Although two simultaneous errors could go undetected, the probability of this is too remote for general consideration.

This system is not straightforward for mathematical operations but has been adapted for use in one computer.[1]   It is also widely used for storage of information where each bit is one track of a magnetic-drum storage device.[3]

Biquinary.   The advantages of relatively easy arithmetic operations (including complementing) and of complete checking are generally obtained with a seven-bit biquinary system.[3]   As shown in Table 4.12, this system consists of five bits, for 0, 1, 2, 3, and 4, and two other bits to indicate whether a 0 or 5 is to be added to the previous figures. Such representation is quite ancient (it is used in the abacus, in fact) and

Table 4.12. Biquinary System for Representing Decimal Digits by a Seven-bit Code; in All Cases, the Digit Has Two and Only Two 1s

No.	Biquinary representation							Nines complement						
	B_0	B_5	Q_0	Q_1	Q_2	Q_3	Q_4	B_0	B_5	Q_0	Q_1	Q_2	Q_3	Q_4
0	1	0	1	0	0	0	0	0	1	0	0	0	0	1
1	1	0	0	1	0	0	0	0	1	0	0	0	1	0
2	1	0	0	0	1	0	0	0	1	0	0	1	0	0
3	1	0	0	0	0	1	0	0	1	0	1	0	0	0
4	1	0	0	0	0	0	1	0	1	1	0	0	0	0
5	0	1	1	0	0	0	0	1	0	0	0	0	0	1
6	0	1	0	1	0	0	0	1	0	0	0	0	1	0
7	0	1	0	0	1	0	0	1	0	0	0	1	0	0
8	0	1	0	0	0	1	0	1	0	0	1	0	0	0
9	0	1	0	0	0	0	1	1	0	1	0	0	0	0

is analogous to the two-hand five-finger system of number representation. This code has the advantage that for any decimal digit one and only one of the *bi* bits (B_0 and B_5) and one and only one of the *quinary* bits (Q_0, Q_1, Q_2, Q_3, Q_4) is a 1. Thus a powerful check is possible.

Further, this system is orderly with respect to arithmetic operations and complementing. These and other aspects of *bcd* systems will be discussed in more detail in Chapter 7.

PROBLEMS

1. Make a table of other possible four-bit binary-coded decimal systems.
2. Make a table corresponding to Table 4.3, where the basic operation is subtraction and end-around-borrow is used. Work out some examples as in Table 4.5. Why is there no need for a table corresponding to Table 4.4?
3. Derive the addition and multiplication table for a ternary-base number system (0, 1, and 2).
4. Take various decimal numbers, convert to binary, and perform multiplication in binary. Check the answer by converting the answer back to decimal.
5. Try various division examples in binary. For example, express ⅓, ⅕, ⅐, and ⅑ as binary repeating fractions.
6. Derive the octal addition and multiplication table. Express the octal numbers in binary form, perform the operation, and convert the output back to octal.

BIBLIOGRAPHY

The following material covers number systems and their digital computer representations.

Chapin, N.: "An Introduction to Automatic Digital Computers," pp. 254–293, D. Van Nostrand Company, Inc., Princeton, N.J., 1957.

Culbertson, J. T.: "Mathematics and Logic for Digital Devices," pp. 45–86, D. Van Nostrand Company, Inc., Princeton, N.J., 1958.

Eckert, W. J., and R. Jones: "Faster, Faster," pp. 112–121, McGraw-Hill Book Company, Inc., New York, 1956.

Engineering Research Associates: "High-speed Computing Devices," pp. 74–99, McGraw-Hill Book Company, Inc., New York, 1950.

Goode, H. H., and R. E. Machol: "System Engineering," pp. 203–213, McGraw-Hill Book Company, Inc., New York, 1957.

Gotlieb, C. C., and J. N. P. Hume: "High-speed Data Processing," pp. 13–31 and 310–314, McGraw-Hill Book Company, Inc., New York, 1958.

Humphrey, W. S.: "Switching Circuits," pp. 1–9 and 64–77, McGraw-Hill Book Company, Inc., New York, 1958.

Ivall, T. E., ed.: "Electronic Computers," pp. 13–25, Philosophical Library, Inc., New York, 1956.

Lerner, I. S.: Digital Computers Need Orderly Number Systems, *Control Eng.*, vol. 2, no. 11, pp. 82–89, November, 1955.

McCracken, D. D.: "Digital Computer Programming," pp. 30–51, John Wiley & Sons, Inc., New York, 1957.

Phister, M.: "Logical Design of Digital Computers," pp. 13–29 and 399–401, John Wiley & Sons, Inc., New York, 1958.

Richards, R. K.: "Arithmetic Operations in Digital Computers," pp. 1–25 and 177–192, D. Van Nostrand Company, Inc., Princeton, N.J., 1955.

CHAPTER 5

Logic of Computers

The word "logical" is applied to computers in several different but basically similar ways. Even if computers were merely arithmetic devices we would find that an understanding of logic is necessary to an understanding of arithmetic operations. Moreover, since computers are *not* limited solely to arithmetic operations, an understanding of logical analysis is even more pertinent.

We will consider an intuitive, nonmathematical approach to computer logic and take up how this is related to the "logic" of programming, the logic of flow charts, and the organization of basic "logical" elements to form computers. Basic "logical" operations and their representation, as well as more widely known applications of "logic" to game-playing devices and parlor puzzles, are a part of this approach. The concept of two states—true or false, yes or no, high or low, on or off—the requirements for two-state devices, and the usefulness of the "logic" associated with two-state conditions will also be considered.

LOGIC?

Much of what is referred to as "logical" in a computer or its applications is not in the strict sense formally logical. This is especially true with respect to computer "hardware." However, since computer equipment operates analogously to true logical operations, and since the techniques of logical manipulations thus are applicable, the equipment is called *logical.*

PROGRAMMING LOGIC

One aspect of logic as applied to computers has already been discussed in Chapter 3. It pertains to the logical flow diagram for a problem. A computer's ability to solve complete nontrivial problems means, in general, that the computer must make decisions as it progresses through the solution. A flow diagram specifies the requirements for making these decisions, i.e., for *branching* or *choice* (*bifurcation*) operations. The purpose of a flow diagram is to organize all parts of the problem logically before determining the minute coding details.

If the basic flow diagram does not allow for all possibilities or calls for the wrong operations, it is generally said that "its *logic* is wrong." Also, branching or choice instructions in a computer are sometimes called *logical* instructions.

LOGICAL DESIGN

The use of the term logical with respect to a computer itself and associated equipment implies that the whole device acts "in accordance with the inferences reasonably to be drawn from events or circumstances." As we will note in greater detail later, the functioning of a computer requires that a very large number of events occur in sequence in a manner which is precisely and completely predetermined. From one point of view, a computer may be regarded as a large number of *logical devices interconnected in networks in such a way that inputs will result in predetermined outputs*. Although many devices operate logically, the sophistication of computers and the intricate relationship between the input (problem statement) and the output (problem solution) makes basic logical units a necessity. Of course, many computer parts exist for technical or engineering reasons, and these change as new physical devices and phenomena are developed to implement the basic logic of the entire computer. Thus the same logical design can, in different computers, result in very different sets of equipment, depending upon whether the equipment is engineered around vacuum tubes, transistors, or ferromagnetic or ferroelectric devices. We will avoid as much as possible references to specific implementation of parts of a computer.

Two-state Logic. To achieve the reliability required of computers, a two-state representation of information is used. Information is broken down into elementary *bits*, with each bit being in either one of the two states. In computer logic these two states will be designated 0 and 1. This means only that the two states are the opposites one of the other, not that they necessarily represent the numerical values of 0 or 1, although they frequently do. Logically, 0 and 1 are defined to be anything and its opposite. Thus 0 actually could represent the value 1 and 1 the value 0. However, this situation should be avoided for obvious reasons. A 1 could mean *yes, good, true,* and *presence,* and hence 0 would mean *no, bad, false,* and *absence,* respectively. Physically, in the computer, 1 might be represented by a tube conducting, a magnetic material being magnetized with a certain polarity, a hole being punched in a card, or any of a large number of other phenomena. Similarly, a 0 would be a tube cut off (nonconducting), a magnetic material being magnetized with the opposite polarity, or a hole not being punched in a card, etc.

We will not be concerned in this chapter as to precisely what 0 or 1 represents in a given problem nor how they are represented in a computer. It is important to know, however, that, no matter what it means, the 1 state is normally the *desired condition,* is used for comparison purposes, and represents the presence of a certain attribute or quality. The 0 state, on the other hand, represents normally the negation of the desired condition.

LOGICAL PROBLEMS

Actually many problems solved on digital computers are essentially logical rather than arithmetic. Looking through abstracts of technical papers for specified categories of information, choosing names for new chemical compounds (and eliminating names with bad connotations), or making a concordance of the Bible are examples of logical problems solved by computers. Although arithmetic instructions may be used in the program, they are generally a part of the necessary *red tape.*

In this chapter only logical problems will be taken up. In Chapter 7, however, we will see that the arithmetic of computers is also considered in terms of basic logical operations.

Tick-Tack-Toe. An example of logical problems which can be solved on a logical computer is the game of *tick-tack-toe* (*tit-tat-toe,* or *naughts and crosses*). This ancient child's game is simple enough to be thoroughly analyzed, and many devices for playing it have been built. It is played (if anyone need be told) by two people, who alternately place naughts (0) and crosses (X) on a 3 × 3 grid. The game is won by the player who gets three marks in a row. In game-theory parlance, the game is *finite* (comes to a definite end) and if played *rationally* will result in a draw (a cat's game).

Its rules are simple enough so that its logic can be shown completely in a simple schematic. Such a general block diagram is given in Fig. 5.1, which shows the manner in which one tick-tack-toe–playing machine has been built. The input is a voltage which, each time it is the machine's turn to play, is diverted to operate an 0 light to indicate the machine's response. The machine's opponent plays Xs. The logic of deciding what to play is done by the machine in much the same way as it would be done by a human.

Although the voltage is always present at the input to the *turn* portion of the logic, an output occurs only when it is the machine's turn to
play. Play is controlled by switches which keep account of the number
of plays that have been made, and assuming that the machine and its
opponent alternate in taking turns, the input voltage is diverted to the
output only when it is logical for the machine to play.

How does it know what to play? The first possibility is, "Is there any
place where the machine has two 0s in a row of three, and the third position is not occupied by the opponent?" If so, "indicate the third position
as the machine play." This is the logic of the *offensive* switching circuits

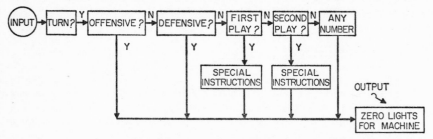

Fig. 5.1. Basic logical organization of a Tick-Tack-Toe playing machine.

of Fig. 5.1. There are eight such sets of switches, for there are eight
possible ways of getting three marks in a row. This kind of *force play*
is obviously considered first, for it is the way to win the game.

However, suppose that it is the machine's turn to play but that there
is no *offensive* combination to permit it to play. The input voltage will
then be diverted to the *defensive* switching circuits. Here the logical
operations are, "Is there any place where the machine's opponent has
two X marks in a row of three and the third position is not occupied by
the machine? If so, play this third position." This is the obvious *defensive* consideration where, again, the machine is forced to play, in this
case to prevent getting beat. Thus the combination of *offensive* and *defensive* circuits provides for many of the plays which this special-purpose
logical computer must consider.

Such a machine must be capable of providing a good response for other
situations as well. Obviously there are no force plays in response to the
opponent's first move. Further, the response in nonforced situations
would be different if the opponent had made two moves or three or more.
Thus the input voltage is diverted to one of three outputs depending on
whether the opponent has made (1) only one play (2) two plays or (3)
three or more plays. In case of (1) or (2) the voltage is diverted to
the *special-instructions* switching. Here special instructions are given

for all situations which the *offensive* and *defensive* circuits do not cover. For example, if the machine's opponent takes the center position on his first play, the machine's response is to play a corner position, for those who have investigated realize that to play any of the four mid-side positions could result in the machine's losing in forced plays.

If, however, the game has progressed to where the opponent has made three or more plays, then only a limited set of instructions need be given the machine, as represented by the *any number* switches. Basically, the logic is, "Play any unoccupied position left considering them in this order, center, outside corner, and last, mid-side positions." This is sufficient to permit the game to be played to its logical conclusion, the *offensive* and *defensive* logic will provide the correct response for most situations.

Schoolboy Curriculum. Many aspects of another type of a logical problem are illustrated by the following example. A schoolboy is considering what subjects to take. Seven are available—English, history, mathematics, science, Latin, German, and French and there are six restrictions:

(1) History is available only at a time when he cannot take it.

(2) If he takes science then he must also take mathematics.

(3) If he takes Latin, then he cannot take German.

(4) If either science or French is taken, then the other must also be taken.

(5) A total of either five or six subjects must be taken.

(6) English is required.

What courses will he take?

Reflection on this problem will reveal that it is almost trivial and the answers obvious and independently verifiable. Therefore it is a useful problem to take as an example.

Truth Table. The approach illustrated in Table 5.1 is a *truth-table* representation of the problem. Each column represents one subject—English, history, mathematics, science, Latin, German, and French, respectively. Each row contains a series of 1s and 0s, a 1 if that subject is taken, a 0 if it is not. Since there are seven subjects, 128 different combinations are possible, ranging from 0000000 (meaning no subjects taken) to 1111111 (indicating that all seven would be taken). Obviously these two cases as well as others of the 128 combinations violate at least one of the six basic restrictions.

To examine all possibilities there would have to be 128 rows in the table. However, notice that restrictions (1) and (6) permit no choice. Thus we have only five *decision variables;* hence, we need only consider the 32 possible cases where there is some choice between mathematics, science, Latin, German, and French. In Table 5.1, in all rows the first two columns contain a 10, since English will be taken and history will not. The systematic arrangement in the last five columns is the same as the binary representation of the decimal numbers 00 through 31.

Table 5.1 thus represents all possible choices. Let us examine them in view of the restrictions. Restriction 5, that a total of five or six subjects must be taken, eliminates all but possibilities 16, 24, 28, 30, 31, and 32. Considering restriction 3, that if one takes Latin he cannot take German, eliminates 24, 31, and 32. Examination of 16 reveals that it violates restriction 2, that is, it would indicate that science is taken but mathematics is not. The only other restriction is 4. Examining the only remaining combinations, 28 and 30, reveals that they do not violate it, thus, 28 and 30 are solutions to the problem. The student must take English, mathematics, science, either (but not both) Latin or German, and French.

Logical Connectives. It is possible to state logical problems in terms of basic AND, OR, and NOT logical connectives. Thus condition 2 of the schoolboy problem can be stated: Science AND mathematics OR NOT science AND mathematics OR NOT science AND NOT mathematics. Condition 3 becomes: Latin AND NOT German OR NOT Latin AND NOT German OR NOT Latin AND German. Condition 4 becomes science AND French OR NOT science AND NOT French.

The ability to break down logical problems into statements with these connectives is used extensively in digital-computer design. It is possible to have electronic, mechanical, and electromechanical devices perform these connective operations. Further, systems of shorthand symbolism and notation as well as mathematical tools for manipulating these models (*propositional calculus*) make the use of AND, OR, and NOT helpful in computer analysis and synthesis. (The propositional calculus, as it applies to the mathematics of two-state logic, is considered in the appendix. Logical diagrams of computer components are considered in Chapter 6 and following chapters.) Sometimes, however, the word statements become tedious. For example, condition 5, which is five or six subjects must be taken, becomes: English AND mathematics AND science AND Latin AND German OR English AND mathematics AND science AND Latin AND French OR English AND mathematics AND science AND German AND French OR English AND mathematics AND Latin AND German AND French OR English AND science AND Latin AND German AND French OR English AND mathematics AND science AND Latin AND German AND French.

Table 5.1. Truth-table Approach to the Schoolboy-curriculum Problem

	E	H	M	S	L	G	F	Violates
1	1	0	0	0	0	0	0	5
2	1	0	0	0	0	0	1	5
3	1	0	0	0	0	1	0	5
4	1	0	0	0	0	1	.1	5
5	1	0	0	0	1	0	0	5
6	1	0	0	0	1	0	1	5
7	1	0	0	0	1	1	0	5
8	1	0	0	0	1	1	1	5
9	1	0	0	1	0	0	0	5
10	1	0	0	1	0	0	1	5
11	1	0	0	1	0	1	0	5
12	1	0	0	1	0	1	1	5
13	1	0	0	1	1	0	0	5
14	1	0	0	1	1	0	1	5
15	1	0	0	1	1	1	0	5
16	1	0	0	1	1	1	1	2
17	1	0	1	0	0	0	0	5
18	1	0	1	0	0	0	1	5
19	1	0	1	0	0	1	0	5
20	1	0	1	0	0	1	1	5
21	1	0	1	0	1	0	0	5
22	1	0	1	0	1	0	1	5
23	1	0	1	0	1	1	0	5
24	1	0	1	0	1	1	1	3
25	1	0	1	1	0	0	0	5
26	1	0	1	1	0	0	1	5
27	1	0	1	1	0	1	0	5
28	1	0	1	1	0	1	1	None
29	1	0	1	1	1	0	0	5
30	1	0	1	1	1	0	1	None
31	1	0	1	1	1	1	0	3
32	1	0	1	1	1	1	1	3

AND **CONNECTIVE**

A logical AND (*conjunction, both*) device is one which will produce a 1 output only if all inputs are 1s. Thus whatever 1 represents must be present at all inputs to get a 1 out; if any one of the inputs is a 0 the output is 0 no matter how many others are 1s.

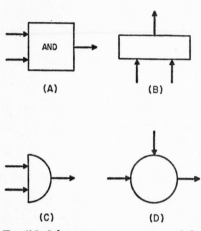

(A)   (B)

(C)   (D)

FIG. 5.2. Schematic representations of the logical AND operation.

There are many electronic, electrical, and mechanical devices which can be made to have this property. (It can be done quite simply with unilateral devices such as diodes, but we will not consider specific circuits here.) Because it is equivalent to an electronic device called a *gate*, the AND operation is sometimes simply referred to as *gating* or as an AND *gate*.

Schematic representations of AND are given in Fig. 5.2. Note the wide variations used. As a matter of policy, all logical elements in this text will be represented by a rectangle labeled as to type of element.

INHIBIT **CONNECTIVE**

Another widely used gating logical device is an INHIBIT. An INHIBIT is similar to an AND gate except that one of the inputs performs an inhibiting function. Thus, if there is a 0 at this input, an INHIBIT acts exactly like an AND with respect to the other inputs and the output. However, if the inhibiting input is a 1, then there is no output. If an INHIBIT has only one other input in addition to the inhibiting input, 0

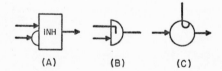

(A)   (B)   (C)

FIG. 5.3. Schematic representations of the INHIBIT logical operation.

on the inhibiting element allows the output to be the same as the other input; with 1 on the input, the output is always 0. This logical device is also called an UNLESS; that is, "the output is determined by the noninhibiting inputs *unless* the inhibiting input has a 1 input."

Schematic representations of inhibitors are given in Fig. 5.3. Note that they resemble AND devices except that the inhibiting input is marked in some distinct manner, generally a circle instead of an arrow head.

Some devices used in computers generate the INHIBIT function readily; hence, in some computer designs they are used extensively.

OR CONNECTIVE

The OR operation most generally used is the INCLUSIVE OR (alteration, inclusive disjunction, either or both), in that, if any one or more of the inputs are 1, the output of the device is a 1. The output can be 0 only if all inputs are 0.

A frequent use of OR devices is in combining logical operations in computers. Thus an OR with its two inputs connected to two devices, *A* and *B*, will produce a 1 output if either *A* or *B* or both have a 1 output. It would appear possible to dispense with the OR device and simply connect the output of *A* and *B* together. Sometimes this can be done, but frequently it cannot. If there is a 1 output, for

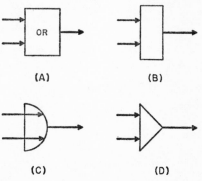

Fig. 5.4. Schematic representations of the OR logical operation.

example, from *A* this could produce the desired 1 output, but it could also affect the *B* device which was trying to produce a 0 output at the same time. In practical logical networks, where a large number of logical elements are interconnected to perform a specific function, this can adversely affect the operation and produce spurious and incorrect results by "feeding back" into other circuits. Thus an OR device actually performs a very useful function in *buffering* its inputs one from another, that is, in preventing interaction between them. This eliminates unwanted *back circuits*. For this reason the OR operation is frequently called a *buffer*.

Fig. 5.5. Schematic representations of the logical NOT operation.

Schematic forms for OR are given in Fig. 5.4, with the version of Fig. 5.4(A) being used elsewhere in this text.

Duality. INCLUSIVE OR and AND are duals. Thus OR will produce a 1 output if *any* input is a 1, but will have a 0 output if *all* inputs are 0. Thus it is actually an AND device with respect to 0 but an OR device with respect to 1. Similarly, an AND device for 1 is an OR device for 0. Since the significance associated with 0 and 1 is arbitrary, a switch in this meaning is the same as changing all OR elements into AND elements and vice versa. Although of interest to a logical designer, since it sometimes permits simplification, we will not consider duality further here; it is discussed further in the appendix.

NOT CONNECTIVE

The NOT logical operation (*negation*) results in an output which is opposite to its single input. If the input is 1, the output is 0; if the input is 0, the output is 1. Thus a NOT *inverts* the sense of the output as compared to the input; hence it is frequently referred to as an *inverter*.

Schematic representations are given in Fig. 5.5. The version of Fig. 5.5(A) will be used here.

SYMBOLISM

It is convenient to use a set of symbols to represent computer logical elements. Since AND, OR, and NOT are most widely used, a convenient method of expressing them is desirable and for our present purpose will be sufficient. The usual method appears to be mathematical, but need not be used mathematically. It is intended, and can be used, only as a "short-cut" representation. Those who wish to consider the mathematical manipulations are referred to the appendix.

Take the logical problem of a hall light operated by two-way switches which permit it to be turned on or off from either the top or the bottom of the stairs. Let us call the switch at the top of the stairs A, the one at the bottom B, and the light itself C. This light is either on or off, glowing or not. We will call *on* 1, *off* 0. The switches A and B are considered to be 1s in the *up* position and 0s in the *down* position.

We know that the hall light C is on when the top switch A is up AND the bottom switch B is up OR the top switch is down AND the bottom switch is down. For convenience, let us assume that

$$AB$$

means

$$A \text{ AND } B$$

and that

$$A + B$$

means

$$A \text{ OR } B$$

Further, let

$$\bar{A}$$

mean

$$\text{NOT } A$$

that is, the condition opposite to A. Specifically, if A represents the A switch being up, then $\bar{A}$ means the A switch is down. Thus our statement about the hall light becomes

$$C = AB + \bar{A}\bar{B}$$

Repeating this means literally and in order, the hall light C is on when the top switch A is up AND the bottom switch B is up OR when the top switch A is down AND the bottom switch B is down.

Take as another example, "We will buy a new car if I get a raise and if your mother does not come to live with us." If C represents buying a new car, A getting a raise, and B the mother-in-law's arrival, then

$$C = A\bar{B}$$

is a succinct manner of writing this statement. Note that this employs an INHIBIT function.

As another example, reconsider the rules given in Chapter 4 for obtaining the nines complement of a decimal digit using the 1-2-4-8 binary-coded-decimal system. This system of notation for logical statements permits writing them in briefer form. Let us use T to represent the binary bits of the *true* number with T_8 being the 8s position, T_4 the 4s position, etc. Similarly, C will be used for the complement. The rules of page 49 now become

1. $C_1 = \bar{T}_1$
2. $C_2 = T_2$
3. $C_4 = (T_2 + T_4)(\overline{T_2 T_4})$
4. $C_8 = \overline{T_8 + T_4 + T_2}$

Later we will see how this complementing can be implemented directly from these equations.

The above symbolism is not consistent with that used by some groups. The symbolism used here is useful in terms of mathematically manipulating logical networks as considered in the appendix. However, some groups use ∩ for AND, ∪ for OR, and ' for NOT. Likewise, two other connectives which are yet to be considered are represented by → for IF . . . THEN and ↔ for IF AND ONLY IF. Incidentally, AND is sometimes called *intersection*, OR is *union*, and NOT is *complementation*.

Matrix Representation. Concise methods of representing information are frequently used. For the two-input logical element, a two-dimensional matrix serves the purpose and is the equivalent of a truth table. For example, consider the statement A AND B written simply

$$AB$$

This can also be represented as shown in Fig. 5.6(A), which indicates that both A and B inputs must have a value of 1 to obtain an output value of 1. Although not efficient in this case, this sort of representation is useful in more complicated cases. For example, INCLUSIVE OR, which is

$$AB + A\bar{B} + \bar{A}B$$

is shown in Fig. 5.6(B). We recognize by its position in the matrix which input is represented and its state; thus there is no need to write this down. This matrix representation is convenient and useful. Similarly, NEITHER . . . NOR . . . is illustrated in Fig. 5.6(C) and NOT BOTH in Fig. 5.6(D).

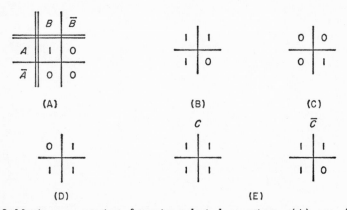

FIG. 5.6. Matrix representation of two-input logical operations. (A) AND, (B) OR, (C) NEITHER . . . NOR, (D) NOT BOTH, and (E) Three-input OR.

This sort of representation becomes somewhat impractical for three or more inputs; for example, the INCLUSIVE OR for three inputs is $ABC + AB\bar{C} + A\bar{B}C + \bar{A}BC + A\bar{B}\bar{C} + \bar{A}B\bar{C} + \bar{A}\bar{B}C$, as shown in Fig. 5.6(E).

In any event this is merely a scheme for representation. Manipulation generally requires that the terms in the mathematical notation be written out.

OTHER LOGICAL CONNECTIVES

The use of AND, OR, and NOT as the basic elements in computers is rather general, probably because they are simple concepts and easy to mechanize. However, other logical connectives can be used in a computer. For two inputs there are 16 possibilities for logical connectives, as given in Table 5.2. A 1 indicates that an output exists corresponding to the circumstances at the top of the column.

Table 5.2. Table of the 16 Possible Logical Connectives Involving Two Inputs, A and B

Item	$AB + A\overline{B} + \overline{A}B + \overline{A}\overline{B}$				Connective
1	0	0	0	0	0
2	0	0	0	1	NEITHER A NOR B
3	0	0	1	0	B AND NOT A, B UNLESS A
4	0	0	1	1	NOT A
5	0	1	0	0	A AND NOT B, A UNLESS B
6	0	1	0	1	NOT B
7	0	1	1	0	A OR else B (EXCLUSIVE OR)
8	0	1	1	1	NOT BOTH A AND B
9	1	0	0	0	A AND B
10	1	0	0	1	A IF AND ONLY IF B
11	1	0	1	0	B
12	1	0	1	1	IF A, THEN B
13	1	1	0	0	A
14	1	1	0	1	IF B, THEN A
15	1	1	1	0	A OR B (INCLUSIVE OR)
16	1	1	1	1	1

Notice that AND is ninth in the list. EXCLUSIVE OR (also called exclusive disjunction, material inequivalence, one and only one, or simply or else, to distinguish it from the usual OR) is seventh. The NOT logical connective is illustrated in the fourth and sixth. The first and sixteenth cases are trivial; the first shows no output no matter what the inputs may be; the sixteenth always shows a 1 output. The eleventh and thirteenth also have no useful function.

The other seven combinations, however, represent five other possible logical connectives. The second combination is NEITHER . . . NOR. . . . The combinations of 3 and 5 represent the AND NOT, UNLESS, or INHIBIT operation. Combination 8 is the NOT BOTH concept. The tenth illustrates the logical IF AND ONLY IF (also known as compare, biconditional, or material equivalence). And last, 12 and 14 represent IF . . . THEN . . . , which is also termed conditional, material implication, or implicative. These other connectives are used in some general-purpose automatic digital computers, and also in special-purpose logical computers.

Three of these other connectives were encountered in the schoolboy problem. Condition 2 of that problem could be given as "IF science THEN mathematics," which is the same as "science AND mathematics OR NOT science AND mathematics OR NOT science AND NOT mathematics." This corresponds to case 12 in Table 5.2, where A is science and B is mathematics. Condition 3 of the schoolboy problem is actually NOT BOTH, case 8 in Table 5.2, that is, "NOT BOTH Latin *and* German." The next condition, 4, is a form of IF AND ONLY IF, that is, "French IF AND ONLY IF science," which is another way of saying "French AND science OR NOT French AND NOT science."

Primitives. AND, OR, and NOT form a useful set of logical connectives. However, it is not possible to synthesize all possible logical connectives from any one of them. However, two connectives in Table 5.2 (case 2, NEITHER . . . NOR . . . , and case 8, NOT BOTH) are each *primitives* and are the only primitives. Thus it is possible to build a computer using only NOR devices, since they can be arranged to provide any desired logical operation. Similarly, NOT BOTH could be used as the logical element of a computer. Incidentally, this primitive is also known as a *Sheffer stroke*. A good exercise would be to synthesize the other logical connectives from either of these.

PROBLEMS

1. Which logical connective (Table 5.2) is "and/or" equivalent to?

2. Indicate how AND, OR, and NOT operations can be performed for two inputs A and B using NOR devices only; that is, perform (1) AB, (2) $A + B$, and (3) $\overline{A}$.

3. Assume A, B, C, and D represent the verses of a song and E is the chorus. Represent the case where one of the verses and the chorus are sung.

4. A three-way switching system permits turning a light (L) on or off from any of three switches, A, B, and C. (A indicates the A switch in the *up* position, $\overline{A}$ the A switch in the *down* position.) The light is on if all three switches are in the *up* position. It is off if any one switch is *down*, on if two are *down*, etc. Write the logical expression for the light being on.

BIBLIOGRAPHY

In the following references either the basic principles of symbolic logic are presented or specific logical computers of various types are considered. References to Boolean algebra are given in the Appendix.

Berkeley, E. C.: "Giant Brains," pp. 144–166, John Wiley & Sons, Inc., New York, 1949.

Bowden, B. V., ed.: "Faster than Thought," pp. 181–202 and 286–310, Pitman Publishing Corporation, New York, 1953.

Carnap, R.: "Introduction to Symbolic Logic and Its Applications," Dover Publications, New York, 1958.

Culbertson, J. T.: "Mathematics and Logic for Digital Devices," pp. 87–114, D. Van Nostrand Company, Inc., Princeton, N.J., 1958.

Erickson, R. S.: Logistics Computer, *Proc. IRE*, vol. 41, p. 1325, 1953.

Gardner, M.: "Logic Machines and Diagrams," McGraw-Hill Book Company, Inc., New York, 1958.

Goode, H. H., and R. E. Machol: "System Engineering," pp. 319–327, McGraw-Hill Book Company, Inc., New York, 1957.

Koppel, H.: Digital Computer Plays NIM, *Electronics*, vol. 25, pp. 155–157, November, 1952.

McCallum, D. M., and J. B. Smith: Feedback Logical Computers, *Electronic Eng.*, vol. 23, p. 458, 1951.

McCormick, E. M.: Tick-Tack-Toe Computer, *Electronics*, vol. 25, p. 154, August, 1952.

May, W., and D. G. Printz: Relay Machine for Demonstration of Symbolic Logic, *Nature*, vol. 165, 1950.

Miehle, W.: Burrows Truth Function Evaluator, *J. Assoc. Computing Machinery*, vol. 4, pp. 189–192, 1957.

Newman, J. R., ed.: "The World of Mathematics," vol. 3, pp. 1856–1931, Simon and Schuster, Inc., New York, 1956.

CHAPTER 6

Control in Computers

The control unit is the heart of a computer. It essentially directs all computer operations, including the arithmetic unit, storage, and input-output. Actually control is so intimately associated with the other parts of a computer system that it is often difficult to separate it from them.

To perform a complete operation, the functions required of control are (1) to select instructions to be performed, (2) to interpret these instructions, and (3) to cause the other elements of the computer to carry out their functions.

Before these control functions can be examined in detail, it is necessary to consider certain concepts of timing and sequencing which are basic in digital computers.

TIMING

Digital computers solve problems by executing the steps of programs in sequence. The time it takes to do various operations is an important factor in comparing computers. For every operation (ADD, SUBTRACT, etc.) that the coder uses in his routine, the computer must perform a large number of individual *suboperations;* and in control, where time is measured in *microseconds* (millionths of a second), timing is important.

Clock. In most computers all the myriad operations are timed and sequenced by a device called a *clock, master clock,* or *pulse generator.* The "clock" consists of a series of electrical signals occurring at a rather fixed rate, which can be of a megacycle (1 million cycles) or more per second. In a 3-hour period a clock with a 1-megacycle rate would produce 10^{10} (10 billion) cycles, each of which could be used to control certain operations of the computer.

The clock in a computer can be a fixed-frequency oscillator such as a crystal-controlled oscillator. Often, however, the storage device is used to generate the clock. In a magnetic-drum computer, for example, where

70

the timing and sequencing of operations must be done exactly in phase with the rotation of the drum, the clock is generated from the drum as the information on the drum becomes available. Thus if the speed of the drum varies somewhat it will not matter, since the computer determines its own sequence and "time" by counting the cycles of its clock. When the timing of computer operations is determined by a clock, it is called *synchronous* or *fixed-cycle* operation.

A basic unit of computer time is the time to process one digit of information, that is, one *digit time*, sometimes called *minor-cycle time*. Digit time is frequently related to the basic clock operation; i.e., if the clock has a 1-megacycle rate, the digit time would be 1 microsecond. If a computer is serial, i.e., if it handles the digits in a word one at a time in sequence, the *word time* or *major-cycle time* is also an important unit in timing. As an example, a computer with a 125-kilocycle master clock rate and a 12-digit word time (10 digits, sign digit, and a space between words) would have a digit time of 8 microseconds and a word time of 96 microseconds.

Most computers also have other timing signals, which are generated after a fixed number of word times or whenever other operations in the computer or computer system occur.

Since many computer output devices require much longer than a word time to operate and since the operation time is variable, it is often impractical to determine the end of the operation by counting a fixed number of word times. In such cases, *asynchronous* (*nonsynchronous*) operation may be used, in which the output device indicates asynchronously to the computer when an operation has been completed. In asynchronous operation the sequence starts after receipt of a signal indicating that the previous operation has been completed. Such operations would therefore not necessarily be dependent on the master clock. It is also known as *variable-cycle operation*. In a few computers asynchronous control is also used for internal operations, but most computers are synchronously controlled.

Pulse. As previously noted, the basic unit of information, a bit, is represented by a two-state device being in either of its two states, corresponding to 1 or 0, true or false, yes and no, etc. When information is sent from one part of a computer system to another at the high rates of speed generally required, a single bit is represented by the absence or presence of an electrical pulse. A *pulse* is a short-time change of voltage level from one value to another, with a return to the original value. Pulse duration is usually measured in microseconds. A time sequence of pulses (a *pulse train*) is quite widely used to convey information dynamically for control or other purposes in computers.

An idealized pulse train is shown in Fig. 6.1(A), while Fig. 6.1(B) indi-cates an actual pulse train. Many of the engineering problems in com-puters are associated with the limitations of the devices used in handling pulses, especially as pulses deviate from the ideal. We will be con-cerned only with ideal pulse wave-forms.

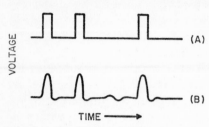

Delay. The use of logical de-vices in time sequence in the con-trol unit and other parts of com-puters also requires a *delay* concept. Control, arithmetic, and logical de-vices generally convey information from one part of a computer to another through pulses, and even

FIG. 6.1. (A) Idealized form of a series of pulses representing 1101, and (B) an actual waveform of a pulse train in a computer.

in the same part of a computer, it is often necessary to delay a pulse, say, one digit time from the time it is produced to the time it is used. Exam-ples will be given later.

These *logical delays* are quite important. They can be produced by, or are inherent in, various electronic logical devices used in computers. For very short delays, *delay lines* may be used. Logical delays are an integral number of digit times in duration. Various symbolic representa-tions are shown in Fig. 6.2.

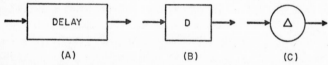

(A)   (B)   (C)

FIG. 6.2. Various symbolic representations of the DELAY function as used in computers.

A second type of delay in computers is that required to assure syn-chronous arrival of pulses at a given point in the computer. The speed of operation is so great in most computers that two pulses generated at the same time but having a different distance to travel to reach a given point (even though the difference in distance is but a few feet) will arrive at different times. This is avoided by putting enough delay in the path of one pulse to assure simultaneity of arrival. These delays are used only to overcome this practical engineering problem. The delay time would only by chance be a multiple of a basic timing cycle of the computer. They are not the logical delays whose use is necessary in dynamic logical devices. Unless stated otherwise, the term DELAY will be used here to mean logical delays.

CONTROL CYCLE

The basic control operations involved in executing the instructions in the academic computer of Chapter 3 are shown in Fig. 6.3. The figure has been simplified to eliminate multiplication and division, which can

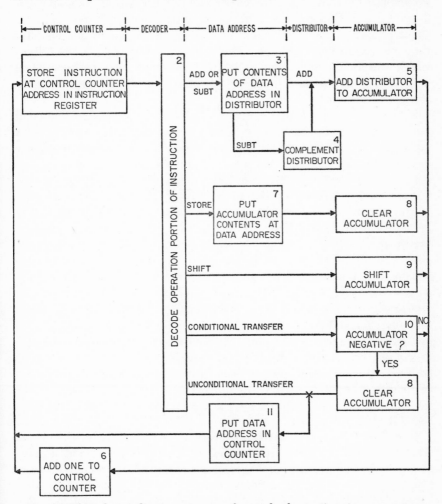

Fig. 6.3. Flow chart indicating sequence of control suboperations in a computer.

be performed by combinations of the other operations given. The operations considered are (1) ADD, (2) SUBTRACT, (3) SHIFT, (4) CONDITIONAL TRANSFER and (5) UNCONDITIONAL TRANSFER. Numerically these were designated in Chapter 3 as 1, 2, 8, and 9, 7, and 6. Notice further in

Fig. 6.3 that the two shift instructions are not considered separately as they would be in practice.

Single-address Complete Operation. In performing each step of a program, all single-address stored-program computers have much in common. The control unit embraces (1) a register which contains the storage address of the next instruction and is called a *control counter* (or instruction location counter, address register, memory address register, counter register, and similar terms) and (2) a register which contains the instruction to be executed. The latter will, of course, contain digits which specify the operation to be performed and the address (data address) of the operand involved. Thus it is generally called the *instruction register*.

Let us assume that one instruction has been completed and the computer is ready to execute another. The control counter will contain digits indicating the address of the new instruction. The instruction register will contain the instruction just executed. (The control counter will generally contain a number one digit higher than the address of the last instruction. However, the address specified by the counter could be the data address specified in the previous instruction if it had been a branch or jump instruction.) As indicated by the corresponding numbers in the blocks of Fig. 6.3, (1) the computer control unit would first go to the control counter address and put the contents of that storage location into the instruction register. This is sometimes called the *fetch* part of the cycle; then (2) the contents of the instruction register are *interpreted* and—from the operation digits part of the instruction register— the computer is instructed as to the operation to be performed. For example, if the operation requires the contents of a specific data address in storage, the digits in the instruction register are interpreted as that address. However, if it were a *nonaddress* instruction such as SHIFT, the digits would be interpreted as the number of shifts. When the digits in the data address do refer to a specific storage location, the computer refers to that address as the operand.

Next, for all instructions, the operation is executed; that is, the operation digits are *decoded* to produce the proper sequence of events to perform the desired action. The *execute* phase would, for an ADD instruction (5), for example, cause the contents of the distributor to be added to the accumulator and the result would remain in the accumulator. For a SUBTRACT (4) the contents of the distributor would be complemented before being added to the accumulator contents. If it were a SHIFT instruction (9), the execution would involve shifting the digits in the specified arithmetic register (usually the accumulator) as required.

Lastly the control counter (6) would advance one count to the address for the next instruction. However, the operation just performed may cause the address in that instruction to be substituted for the contents of the control counter. An example of this is the CONDITIONAL TRANSFER instruction (10): If the contents of the accumulator are negative (8), clear the accumulator and (11) go to the given address specified for the next instruction; if zero or positive (6), go to the next storage location in sequence for the next instruction. The execution of this instruction involves examining the sign digit of the accumulator. If the sign digit is negative, the accumulator is cleared and the control counter reset to the address specified; otherwise, 1 is added to the control counter.

Just as various computers differ in the details of performing a complete operation, so the terminology used to describe operations also differs. The time for the complete operation is often considered in two parts, (1) *instruction time* (the reading and interpreting of the instruction) and (2) *execution time* [12] (the actual execution). These are sometimes called the *fetch* and *execute* portions of the cycle.[4,14] Further, it is possible to consider either three or four phases in the complete operation rather than two, taking any of the following operations as separate and distinct: (1) the search for the instruction, (2) the search for the data address, (3) the placing of the data address in the instruction register, and (4) the operations performed on the operand. Further, some portions of the complete cycle may be combined. It is possible, for example, to eliminate block (3) of Fig. 6.3 if the computer will add the operand to the accumulator as the operand is being read from storage, without there being an intermediate storage of the operand.

As shown in Fig. 6.3, this simple computer executes the various instructions by performing in sequence several of the basic 11 suboperations which are summarized in Table 6.1. The portions of the computer

Table 6.1. List of the 11 Suboperations in the Control System of Fig. 6.3

1. Store instruction at control counter address in instruction register
2. Decode for operation portion of instruction
3. Put contents of data address in distributor
4. Complement distributor
5. Add distributor to accumulator
6. Add one to control counter
7. Put accumulator contents at address
8. Clear accumulator
9. Shift accumulator
10. Accumulator negative?
11. Put data address in control counter

Table 6.2. Sections of a Computer Involved in the Various Suboperations

Portion of computer involved	Suboperation										
	1	2	3	4	5	6	7	8	9	10	11
Control counter	x					x					x
Instruction register	x	x	x				x				x
Operation		x									
Data address			x				x				x
Distributor			x	x	x						
Accumulator					x		x	x	x	x	

involved in each suboperation are given in Table 6.2. *It is the purpose of control to select and sequence the suboperations.*

In practical computers, the control function is much more complicated than that shown in Fig. 6.3. The number of instructions would be much larger, and the number of suboperations also larger and more detailed.

Although suboperations generally occur in accordance with instructions derived from the operation code, the coder does not directly specify the suboperations. However, in some computers it is possible in the instruction to select and control the individual suboperations directly to form new operations. This permits extreme flexibility in forming special instructions and, hence, instructions which are more efficient or faster than those for general-purpose machines. Such detailed coding is generally called *microcoding* or *microprogramming*. One computer [16] using this general technique has over 1300 different possible instructions available.

Modified One-address Operation. A computer which utilizes an instruction which contains not only a data address as considered above but also always specifies the next instruction address, has a somewhat different control sequence.[3] In it, the address register specifies the location of the instruction to be executed. The first half cycle (data half cycle) is concerned with (1) putting the contents of the address specified by the address register into the program register, (2) putting the operation digits in the operation register and the data address of the instruction in the address register, and (3) obtaining the contents of the data address and placing it in the arithmetic distributor register, if necessary, and executing the instruction. During the next, *instruction,* half cycle, the instruction address is read into the address register and the next instruction brought into the program register.

CONTROL DEVICES

The above review of the functions of a computer in executing a program indicates that there are many operations involved in control, some of

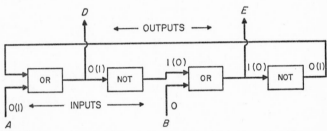

Fig. 6.4. Logical diagram of a two-input bistable element. This device stores one bit of information.

which we will consider now (others will be considered in subsequent chapters).

As has been previously indicated, a digital computer consists of many logical elements which operate time-sequentially to perform the various functions required to solve a problem. A basic element for this purpose is one which will store one bit of information, that is, will assume one of two different states (be *bistable*) in response to external signals such as voltage pulses.

Two-input Bistable Element. First consider the logical circuit of Fig. 6.4. Note that it consists of two OR devices and two NOT devices. Assume that there is no input on *A*, that is, it is at the 0 state, and that the output from the right-hand NOT device is also 0. In this case the output of the left OR device is 0 and thus the output from the left NOT device is 1. Whether or not there is an input on *B*, the output of the right OR device is 1. This being applied to the right NOT device produces the 0 output we had presumed. Hence the device is stable under these conditions. All states will remain the same indefinitely. Further, the application of 1s to *B* or of 0s to *A* will not affect this state.

However, assume that in some interval of time a pulse representing 1 is applied to *A*. This, as shown by the states enclosed in parentheses,

results in a 1 to the left NOT device and hence a 0 as one input to the right OR device. Assuming no input simultaneously on B (only one input at any given time), the input to the right NOT device is 0; hence its output is 1. The output of the left OR device will continue to be 1 even after the single input pulse is applied to A. Further, it will remain stable in this second condition with all 1s and 0s interchanged from the original states until a 1 pulse is applied at B. If a 1 is applied to B, the device will return to the original conditions. Such a device is called a *two-input bistable element*.

Application of a pulse at one input results in the device switching to one state; application of a pulse at the other input causes a switch to the

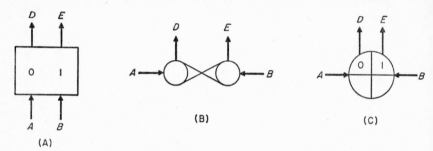

(A)

(B)

(C)

FIG. 6.5. Schematic representations of a two-input bistable device.

other stable condition. Basically, this device "remembers" one binary bit of information, this being which of the two inputs last received a pulse. Schematic representations are given in Fig. 6.5. It will be recognized by those familiar with electronics as a form of *flip-flop*, the OR devices being the input networks and the NOT devices the inverting normally obtained in a single-stage vacuum-tube amplifier. Because it statically stores information, that is, stays in any given state indefinitely with respect to time, it is sometimes known as a *staticisor*.

Single-input Bistable Element. Another fundamental device useful in binary operations is one that counts by 2s (*scale of 2*). Thus, for two input signal pulses, one output pulse would be produced. (Remember that, in the general sense used here, a pulse merely represents an output condition which is normally at the 0 state but which will for a portion of the time during the pulse go to and remain at the 1 state. It must return to 0 when the pulse is complete.) Hence the basic mechanism is one which will go to the 1 output state for a pulse at one input and to 0 for a pulse at a second input. This change from 0 to 1 and from 1 to 0 in the output would represent one output for two inputs.

The basic bistable device of Fig. 6.4 is not sufficient for *binary counting* or *scaling*, however. A system for taking a series of input pulses

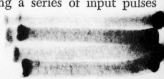

and alternately applying them to the two inputs of a bistable device is required. The logical circuit for such a single-input binary counter is shown in Fig. 6.6. Consider that the state initially is that shown without parentheses. The input *C* is applied to one terminal of each of the AND devices; however, only the right-hand AND device is conditioned to give a 1 output. Hence, through the DELAY element (a nonlogical delay whose function will be explained later) a 1 is applied to the *B* input of the basic bistable device. It will therefore *flip* to the condition shown in the parentheses. When the next input pulse occurs, only the left AND device

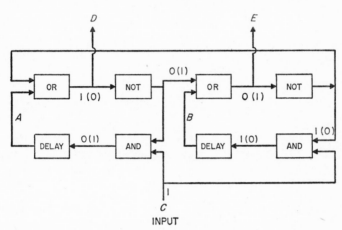

FIG. 6.6. The basic logical circuit for a single-input bistable element.

produces a 1 output, so that it will cause a *flop* to the alternate condition, that is, to the condition shown without parentheses.

The added circuitry thus does the job of applying the input pulses alternately to the two sides of a bistable device.

DELAYS are essential to this binary counter, as they are to many other digital-computer components. They are used essentially to assure that the switching occurs only in response to the input signal *C*. To avoid any possible instable condition due to some logical devices operating faster than others or *during* the pulse on *C*, the DELAYS assure that the switching occurs *after* the pulse on *C*.

Again, those familiar with the electronics of a binary counter will recognize the logical elements shown. There are a variety of electronic devices and circuits for these purposes, but the essentials of all are shown in Fig. 6.6. Alternate representations are given in Fig. 6.7.

The schematic representation of Fig. 6.7(A) will be used for bistable elements. Such a device is said to contain a 1 if the right-hand output is at a voltage level which represents a 1 and a 0 if the left output is at the 1 level. Being symmetrical in this sense and with two outputs D and E which are the inverse of each other, it is particularly useful. Likewise a two-input bistable element requires a 1 input at its right input line to store a 1. It will store a 0 if the left input is a 1.

Bistable elements of this general type have several names, *flip-flop, multivibrator, toggle,* or *trigger* being ones commonly used. The term *Eccles-Jordan* is also used. Also, as noted, the single-input type is referred to as a *binary counter* or *scaler.* Because of its expressiveness, the term *flip-flop* will be used in this text.

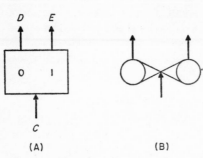

(A)   (B)

Fig. 6.7. Alternate schematic form of single-input bistable element.

Relays. Electromagnetic relays are also used to store bits of information for control, arithmetic, storage, and input-output operations. One schematic representation is given in Fig. 6.8. The basic operation involves switching an input applied to the C (*common*) input terminal to either the N (*normal*) output or to the T (*transferred*) output. With no input to the device, any input to C is available at N, but an input pulse will cause C to be connected to T. One relay may control a large number of switches simultaneously, so that it is possible to cause them to perform logical operations. (The appendix considers how this is done.) Thus relays can also be made equivalent to the bistable elements considered. Relays are versatile devices. Indeed, complete computers have been built using just relays. However, because of their slow speed, they are now used primarily in relatively slow input-output equipment where relatively large currents for motors and solenoid-operated devices need to be switched. They are used extensively in electric accounting machines.

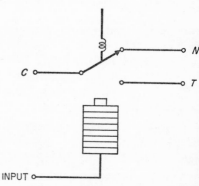

Fig. 6.8. Representation of a relay for one bit of storage.

Registers. Registers, as their use considered above has indicated, are devices for storing information. Generally they are one-word-length devices, the basic elements of which are flip-flops or their equivalent. Thus a **36-binary-digit-word** computer would require 36 flip-flops for each one-word register. A 10-digit binary-coded-decimal computer (if a four-bit code is used) would require 40 flip-flops per word. In addition, the sign digit would require another flip-flop.

When information is stored in a register consisting of physical devices such as flip-flops, the storage is said to be *static*. This means that the magnitude of the number is indicated by the *space* position of the device which stores it. Thus one flip-flop stores a 1, the next a 2, the next a 4, etc. (Fig. 4.1 is an example of such a system). Further, the information is available at any time; hence static registers are frequently referred to as *zero-access-time* devices. On the other hand, *dynamic* storage and trans-fer of information is also widely used in computers. Dynamic stor-age consists of a series of pulses (as for example in Fig. 6.1) where the magnitude of the number repre-sented is indicated by its position in *time*. Obviously, one word time is required to know the value of a dynamically stored word. However, this is not a limitation in many computers.

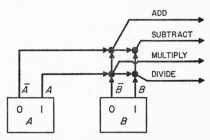

Fig. 6.9. Decoder for interpreting the contents of two flip-flops in terms of four operations: ADD, SUBTRACT, MULTIPLY, and DIVIDE.

Function Table. The control in a digital computer obviously must perform a different sequence of suboperations for each different type of operation specified. Thus the control in a computer must include this function of causing the proper sequence of suboperations to occur ac-cording to the digits in the operation code.

For any specific combination of digits in the operation code, one and only one operation is implied. A device which will take the many in-puts from the flip-flops containing the operation digits and produce an output for the specific operation is a *decoding function table*. On the other hand, an *encoding* (or simply *coding*) function table would take a single input (specifying a particular operation) and produce a number of outputs to control the suboperations required to perform that operation. The control unit of a computer generally does both operations.

An elementary decoder is shown in Fig. 6.9. Let us assume two flip-flops, A and B, which can have a combination of four states, 00, 01, 10, and 11. Further, assume that 00 is used to designate ADD, 01 SUBTRACT, 10 MULTIPLY, and 11 DIVIDE. The decoder must for any of these condi-tions provide an output on one and only one of four output lines.

Since flip-flops were assumed as inputs, both A and $\overline{A}$ as well as B and $\overline{B}$ are available as outputs from each flip-flop. If connected as shown, and with the dots at the intersections of lines being two input AND devices, the desired outputs are obtained from these four AND devices. For example, the upper left AND device (whose inputs are $\overline{A}\overline{B}$) produces an output only if the operation is ADD. The upper right AND device, with $\overline{A}B$ as inputs, corresponds to SUBTRACT, etc.

This technique can be turned around to encode as well. Where there is systematic arraying of the elements in decoders and encoders, such devices are sometimes called *matrices*. Also, for obvious schematic reasons, other similar control circuits are called *pyramids* or *Christmas trees*.

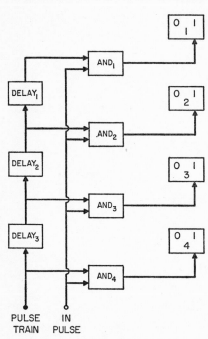

As was indicated in Table 6.2, suboperations involve various portions of the control counter, the instruction register, the distributor, and the accumulator, and each suboperation may involve more than one of these devices. Thus the techniques for transferring information and control signals between various parts of the control unit and arithmetic and logic unit are of interest.

Distributors and Collectors. Information in a computer exists either dynamically, as a series of pulses in time sequence, or statically, in a series of basic bistable elements (toggles, triggers, flip-flops). One bit of information is represented by the presence or absence of a pulse at a given time interval in a time sequence which is analogous to a specific flip-flop being either in the 1 or 0 state.

Fig. 6.10. Basic distribution device for converting dynamic information in a pulse train to static storage in flip-flops.

Dynamically, information exists only as long as the pulse itself, but this is sufficient for many purposes. In contrast, information stored statically in toggle registers exists indefinitely. Many control, arithmetic, and logical operations require that dynamic information be stored statically and, likewise, that static information sometimes be converted to dynamic form.

A circuit for distributing the information in a series of pulses to flip-flops is shown in Fig. 6.10. This *distributor* is used for only four bits of

nformation, although obviously it could be extended. In the input pulse
rain the presence of a pulse indicates a 1, the absence a 0.

The delay times in Fig. 6.10 are equal to the time between pulses.
Thus the first pulse of the series (if it exists) will initially be one input
o AND₄; but until there is also an *in* pulse, there will be no output and
flip-flop₄ will remain in its initial (0) state. At the time for the second
pulse the first pulse would have
passed through DELAY₃ and would
be applied to one input of AND₃,
and the second pulse itself would
be applied to AND₄. Again nothing
happens until an *in* pulse occurs.
Similarly, the time for pulse 3 will
find pulse 1 at AND₂, etc. At the
time of pulse 4, pulse 4 will be an
input to AND₄, pulse 3 will be at
AND₃, pulse 2 at AND₂, and pulse 1
at AND₁. If at this time an *in* pulse
is applied to the other input of all
the AND devices, their outputs will
correspond to the absence or presence of a pulse at the corresponding pulse times in the original pulse
train. If the binary equivalent of
decimal 9 were transmitted, this
would result in a pulse, no pulse,
no pulse, pulse, i.e., in 1001. Thus
AND devices 1 and 4 would have
both inputs as 1, and the corre-

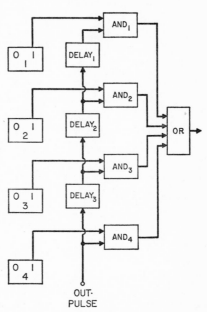

Fig. 6.11. A collector device for converting static information into dynamic form
in a pulse train.

sponding flip-flops would be set to 1. The other two flip-flops would
remain at 0 to provide the desired static storage, 1001.

This distributing of dynamic information into static storage devices is
sometimes called *staticizing*, and the time for doing it, as in reading an
instruction into a register, is *instruction staticizing time.*[17]

The process of collecting the information in a series of flip-flops into
a pulse train is shown in Fig. 6.11. Note that the elements in such a
collector are the same as in a distributor, but that an OR device has been
added. Actually this is done here only for completeness. In practice,
it may be done by a simple interconnection of the outputs of the AND
devices.

There will be no output until an *out* pulse is applied to AND₄. A
single *out* pulse will cause a pulse train of output pulses. If at the time

of the initial *out* pulse flip-flop$_4$ contains a 1, the output from AND$_4$ would be a pulse; if not, there would be no pulse. At the time for the second pulse, the original *out* pulse would be at AND$_3$ because of the presence of DELAY$_3$. Hence, at this time there would be a pulse or not depending on the condition of flip-flop$_3$. Similarly, the presence or absence of a pulse at the time for pulse 3 depends on flip-flop$_2$, and pulse$_4$ on flip-flop$_1$. Notice that the information is read out in a sequence inverse to the read-in sequence of Fig. 6.10.

Obviously, this same general technique can be used for control of information between the storage and arithmetic units. If the information in storage is available as a pulse train, a distributor-like arrangement could be used to place it in the distributor register, as in suboperation 3 of Table 6.1. Note that this process of placing information into a static register requires that the previous information be erased.

Similarly, a collector-like arrangement could be used to transfer information from a register into storage. This could be used for suboperation 7 in Table 6.1. Reading information out of a static register does not necessarily destroy the register contents.

Other Control Considerations. In considering the details of control and its implementation, it is desirable and in many cases practically necessary to have certain control elements to do more than one job. This is practical when they would not be required to do separate functions at the same time. This *time-sharing* of functions makes it possible to save cost, weight, and heat, and it increases reliability. However, it sometimes makes it more difficult to analyze and, hence, "trouble-shoot" and maintain the equipment.

Another very important function of control is in input and output. Since such devices frequently operate asynchronously to the computer itself, control is thereby complicated. Detailed aspects of control in input-output and in storage will be considered in chapters devoted to those subjects. However, one aspect of control of interest here involves an *interrupt* feature.[7] This permits a computer, upon demand of an input device, to interrupt the normal sequence of interpreting and executing instructions and to store or otherwise handle the information from that input device. After the interruption the computer can continue the original problem (having lost nothing but the time used in performing the alternate operation). Such a feature is particularly important in certain *on-line* operations, as in process control (see Chapter 9).

The scope of this book does not permit minute examination of the details of the control function, but its great importance cannot be overstated.

ROBLEM

1. The student should be able to mark for each box in any logical diagram such as Figs. 6.10, 6.11, 7.1, 7.2, 7.3, 7.4, etc.) which have 0 and which have outputs for any possible input conditions. Of course, many will have so any input conditions that it will be impossible to try them all. However, is essential that the student be able to know how to do this. Simple examples are given in Figs. 6.4 and 6.6 where the 0s and 1s are marked for each f the two conditions possible.

IBLIOGRAPHY

The following references generally contain material on the control in digital omputers. The paper of Burks *et al.* is a classic and is not limited to the ibject in this chapter.

olles, E. E., and H. L. Engel: Control Elements in the Computer, *Control Eng.*, vol. 3, no. 8, pp. 93–98, August, 1956.

ooth, A. D., and K. H. V. Booth: "Automatic Digital Calculators," pp. 22–34 and 90–112, Academic Press, Inc., New York, 1953.

urks, A. W., H. H. Goldstine, and J. Von Neumann: "Preliminary Discussion of the Logical Design of an Electronic Computing Instrument," Institute for Advanced Study, Princeton, N.J., September, 1947.

hapin, N.: "An Introduction to Automatic Digital Computers," pp. 350–363, D. Van Nostrand Company, Inc., Princeton, N.J., 1957.

ckert, W. J., and R. Jones: "Faster, Faster," p. 154, McGraw-Hill Book Company, Inc., New York, 1956.

ngineering Research Associates: "High-speed Computing Devices," pp. 12–55, McGraw-Hill Book Company, Inc., New York, 1950.

vall, T. E., ed.: "Electronic Computers," pp. 85–97, Philosophical Library, Inc., New York, 1956.

Jelson, E.: Digital Computers Need Logical Design, *Control Eng.*, vol. 2, no. 12, pp. 60–66, December, 1955.

hister, M.: "Logical Design of Digital Computers," pp. 112–173 and 340–388, John Wiley & Sons, Inc., New York, 1958.

Richards, R. K.: "Arithmetic Operations in Digital Computers," pp. 193–208 and 312–353, D. Van Nostrand Company, Inc., Princeton, N.J., 1955.

cott, N. R.: Practical Circuits for Gating in Digital Computers, *Control Eng.*, vol. 3, no. 2, pp. 93–98, February, 1956.

tibitz, G. R., and J. A. Larrivee: "Mathematics and Computers," pp. 128–149 McGraw-Hill Book Company, Inc., New York, 1956.

CHAPTER 7

Arithmetic and Logical Units

The arithmetic unit of a computer performs the mathematical operation of addition, subtraction, multiplication, and division. The performance of these operations is perhaps the first thing one expects from a computer. However, since computers perform logical operations as well, and since such operations are frequently either tied in with arithmetic operations or use the same equipment, arithmetic and logical operations must be taken together.

The arithmetic and logical unit (*alu*) of a computer is generally the only one that operates on and modifies information. The input-output and storage units handle information but do not modify it. The control unit, acting on instructions from storage and on the contents of the arithmetic unit, causes the information modification to occur in the arithmetic unit.

The heart of an arithmetic unit is the *adder*. The adder not only performs addition but, as we have seen, does subtraction as well, through complements. Further, as will be considered later, with the additional facility to shift numbers an adder can also be used for multiplication and division.

BINARY ADDITION

The simplest adder is a binary adder. The binary addition table for two numbers is

A	B	S	C
0	0	0	0
0	1	1	0
1	0	1	0
1	1	0	1

A and *B* are the two binary numbers to be added, *S* is the sum, and *C* is the carry.

Examining the logic of the binary addition table, we note that "there is a 1 in *S* when either *A* or *B* is a 1 but NOT when both *A* AND *B* are 1." Symbolically, this is written

$$S = (A + B)(\overline{AB})$$

The condition for a carry *C* is that there be "a 1 in *C* when both *A* AND *B* are 1," that is,

$$C = AB$$

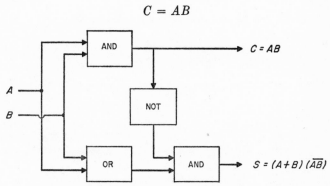

FIG. 7.1. Logical circuit for a half adder using AND, OR, and NOT elements.

Two-input Adder. The corresponding arrangement of logical AND, OR, and NOT elements to perform this two-input adding function is shown in Fig. 7.1. Again, the means for mechanizing the logical operation of each block will vary from one computer to another, but all must perform this basic logic.

Alternately the condition for *S* for the binary two-input adder is "a 1 in *S* if *A* is 1 and *B* is not 1, OR if *A* is not 1 AND *B* is 1," that is,

$$S = A\bar{B} + \bar{A}B$$

The equivalent logical circuitry for this is given in Fig. 7.2. It is more complicated than that of Fig. 7.1. Note in Fig. 7.1, two AND, one OR, and one NOT devices were used, while in Fig. 7.2 three AND, one OR, and two NOT devices are required.

A third form for this adder is given in Fig. 7.3 where INHIBIT, OR, and AND devices are used. The basic definition of an INHIBIT is such that two of them, with an OR device connected as shown, result in the second logical statement for *S*. There are circumstances that make this type of adder advantageous.

In general, an adder must accommodate not only the two numbers

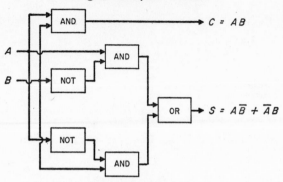

Fig. 7.2. Alternate half-adder logical circuit.

to be added but also a third input, which would be the carry from the previous position. Three-input addition can be done with 2 two-input

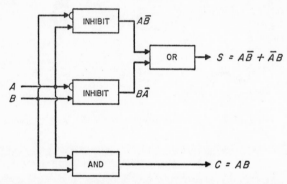

Fig. 7.3. Binary half adder using INHIBITOR, AND, and OR elements.

adders, but a three-input adder is also used. The latter is generally called a *full adder*, the former a *half adder*.

Full Adder. A full adder (FA) will have three inputs, the two numbers to be added A and B and the carry C' from the previous (less significant)

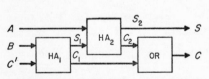

position. The eight combinations of these three inputs and the corresponding sum-and-carry outputs are shown in Table 7.1, both in truth-table and logical-statement form.

Fig. 7.4. Binary full adder using two half adders and an OR device.

Another way of performing three-input addition (see Fig. 7.4) involves two *half adders* (HA) and an OR device. Addition can also be done by logical elements arranged as the equations in Table 7.1 indicate.

Table 7.1. (A) Truth Table and (B) the Logical Equations for Full Binary Addition

A	B	C'	S	C
0	0	0	0	0
0	0	1	1	0
0	1	0	1	0
0	1	1	0	1
1	0	0	1	0
1	0	1	0	1
1	1	0	0	1
1	1	1	1	1

(A)

(B)

$$S = ABC' + (A + B + C')(\overline{AB + AC' + BC'})$$
$$= ABC' + (A + B + C')(\overline{C})$$
$$C = AB + AC' + BC'$$

Serial Binary Addition. Addition is frequently done serially with the bits representing each number occurring as pulses in a pulse train. Thus the pair of pulses representing the least significant digits of the numbers to be added are first presented to the adder. One digit time later the inputs for the next most significant digits are the inputs to the adder along with the carry from the previous addition. This carry requires a logical delay of one digit time.

An example of this is given in Fig. 7.5, where pulse train A represents 7_2, pulse train B 5_2, and the output pulse train S, the sum, which is 12_2. In addition, the carry formed at each digit time (C) is shown as well as the delayed form (C'), which is the third input to the adder at each digit time.

This dynamic binary full adder is shown in Fig. 7.6 in terms of basic logical elements (AND, OR, NOT, and DELAY). This is equivalent to the logical statements of Table 7.1 and obviously could be implemented in other equivalent arrangements.

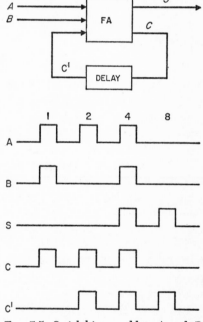

FIG. 7.5. Serial binary adder, A and B are input pulse trains and S is the output.

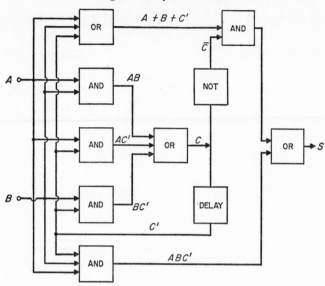

Fɪɢ. 7.6. One logical form of a serial binary full adder.

DECIMAL ADDITION

Decimal addition generally involves some parallel operations. Even in the majority of decimal computers, which are serial digit-by-digit, general practice is to operate in parallel on the bits for each of the decimal digits. Thus the four (or five or seven) coded binary digits for each decimal digit are handled simultaneously.

Decimal Correction. An adder for the 1-2-4-8 code is shown in Fig. 7.7. Notice that it involves more than simply one full adder for each of the four bits in the code. This happens because the addition within a decimal digit is binary but the carry to the next most significant position must be decimal. In other words, the four binary bits which would normally count 16 positions before overflow must be caused to overflow and reset to 0 after 10 counts. This is necessary because the fifth digit is 10 (1, 2, 4, 8, 10, 20, 40, 80, 100, etc.) rather than 16 in the binary sequence (1, 2, 4, 8, 16, 32, 64, etc.). Hence *decimal correction* is required, which accounts for the additional circuitry.

In Fig. 7.7 the subscripts indicate the 1, 2, 4, and 8 binary-bit components of the decimal digits A and B being added to form a sum S. C' indicates the carry (least significant digit) from the previous addition, and C_{10} is the carry from this addition, which, after a digit time delay, will be the C' for the next (more significant) addition.

The four full adders (FA_1 through FA_4) add the four binary bits from A and B to form the sum S. If the sum is less than 10, the sum outputs of FA_1 through FA_4 will appear as S_1, S_2, S_4, and S_8 as desired, and HA_1, FA_2, and HA_2 will not affect them. However, if the sum is 10 or more, a decimal carry must be generated and the S digits decimal-corrected. For example, if 6 (0110_2) and 7 (0111_2) are added, the sum from FA_1 through FA_4

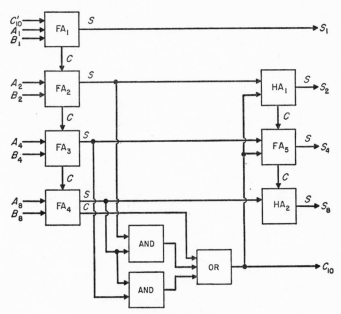

FIG. 7.7. Basic adder for 1-2-4-8 code.

would be thirteen (1101_2). Actually, however, this should be a decimal carry (C_{10}) and an S of 3 (0011_2). The decimal carry is accomplished by the OR and two AND devices. A decimal carry will occur "if the sum as indicated by the C output from FA_4 is 16 or more OR if there is both an 8 AND a 4 in the sum OR an 8 AND a 2 in the sum." The subtracting of 10 in the sum as required for decimal correcting is accomplished by HA_1, FA_5, and HA_2. This involves subtracting 16, by ignoring the C output from HA_2 and by adding six to FA_5 and HA_1 from the decimal carry. The outputs S_1 through S_4 would be 0011 as required.

All other binary-coded-decimal systems must cope with the problems of decimal carry and correction. In the excess-three system the decimal carry coincides with a carry from the eights digit.

PARALLEL ADDITION

Instead of adding time-serially, it is possible to add in parallel. If the two numbers A and B are stored in static registers, logical circuitry can be devised which will cause the addition to occur essentially simultaneously in one digit time. This is obviously much faster than serial addition, which requires as many digit times as digits in the numbers for the addition itself with a repeat for end-around carry. However, parallel addition requires more than a half adder for each digit and hence involves much more logical circuitry than serial addition. We will not consider such complicated logic here. Even where parallel addition is used to obtain the advantage of speed, addition is not attempted in one digit time. To make the problem manageable, especially with regard to the propagation of the carry, more than one minor cycle (digit time) is normally used.

ACCUMULATOR

Our consideration of adders has heretofore involved two inputs A and B (either binary or decimal) added to form a sum S which is not stored but is available as an output. The inputs and outputs can exist dynamically in a series of pulses or statically in flip-flop registers.

An *accumulator*, on the other hand, normally stores a number statically and, when a second number is added to it, will retain the sum in itself. An example of one bit in a binary accumulator is shown in Fig. 7.8, where the bit of the *addend* register is also stored statically in a bistable element. A pulse on the *add* line will cause the contents of the addend flip-flop and the *in* carry from the next least significant position to be added into and left in the accumulator. A subsequent pulse on the carry line will cause the binary carry to propagate out to the next most significant position.

All arithmetic units have an accumulator or equivalent device. The basic adding function is done either in or in conjunction with the accumulator.

COMPLEMENTING

In many computers negative numbers are handled in the adder by a complement representation. In others, where the basic arithmetic device is a subtractor, complement systems are used for adding. Some computers can add and subtract and handle signs, so that complement systems are not needed.

Complements as such have been considered in Chapter 4; however, some means for complementing in arithmetic units will be considered now.

Binary Complements. The ones complement of a binary number is obtained by interchanging 0s and 1s. If the number exists in single-input

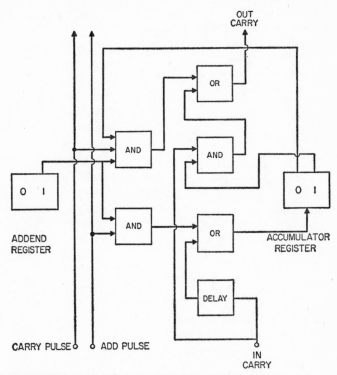

OUT
CARRY

ADDEND
REGISTER

ACCUMULATOR
REGISTER

CARRY PULSE   ADD PULSE

IN
CARRY

Fig. 7.8. A binary accumulator where the contents of the addend register are added to and left in the accumulator.

bistable elements, complementing can be done by simply applying a pulse to the input of each element. Each element then changes state, 0s becoming 1s and vice versa. If a twos complement is desired, a 1 is added to the ones complement obtained in the above manner.

Frequently the binary number to be complemented exists dynamically as a train of pulses. If this is applied as one input to a half adder while a train of 1 pulses (clock) is applied to the other input, the sum output from the half adder will be the ones complement of the number. This is a frequently used complementing method in binary computers. Another method is to use the output from an INHIBIT device with the number to be complemented at the inhibiting input while a series of 1 pulses (clock) is applied to the other input. This also will produce a ones complement.

Decimal Complements. In some binary-coded-decimal systems the decimal nines complement is obtained by self-complementing each of the binary digits. The same or equivalent methods can be used as were used for binary complementing.

Some binary-coded-decimal systems, however, require additional logical circuitry for complementing. Complementing for the 1-2-4-8 system, for example, is illustrated in Fig. 7.9. This figure shows how the verbal statement of the conditions for complementing, as given in Chapter 4, and the equivalent symbolic statements of Chapter 5 could be built from basic logical devices. The complement output is C and the true number input is T; the subscripts indicate the weight of the four binary digits for each decimal digit.

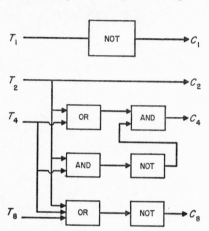

Fig. 7.9. Logic of obtaining the nines complement with the 1-2-4-8 code.

Digit complementing in the biquinary system is shown in Fig. 7.10. The seven inputs are at the left. The outputs are at the right. Individual combinations and how they are complemented can be investigated by those interested. It will be noted from Table 4.12 on page 53 that in the nines complement in the biquinary system a 1 in Q_2 always means that there is a 1 in Q_2 of the output. Also, it will be noted from Fig. 7.10 that O_7 will always have a 1 output, so that the output Q_2 from A_5 will always be the same as the input Q_2.

This logical circuit also illustrates *logical switching*. Either the *true* or *complement* control input (not both) must be a 1. If the true input is 1, the output will be the same as the input. This, too, can be verified by example. A complement is obtained only if the complement input is 1. Switching from true to complement is done simply by applying a pulse to one or the other of these inputs. Most computers use logical switching, since it is compatible with their speed and other characteristics.

SHIFTING

Shifting may be considered an arithmetic operation, since the position of the digits of a number indicates the number's magnitude. A shift to the left is equivalent to multiplication by the base; thus 230_{10} is 10 times 23_{10} and 0110_2 is two times 0011_2. A shift to the right is equivalent to dividing by the base. Shifting is essential to multiplication and division operations.

Shifting can be done in various ways. For example, if the number to be shifted is being distributed into a static register, the time of the *in* pulse determines the position of the number in the register and hence can be used to control the shift. A method of shifting in each bit of a binary static register is shown in Fig. 7.11. If the bistable element represents 0, the left side will have a value of 1 and AND$_2$ will have a 1 output. The two DELAY devices are nonlogical and are long enough to prevent the output from one position reaching the next position during the time of the shift pulse. However, the delays are shorter than the time between shift pulses. Thus the output of DELAY$_1$ will cause the flip-flop to the right to set to zero before the time for another shifting pulse. Any flip-flop which contains a 1 will result in AND$_1$ sending a 1 to the next position to the right. Although only

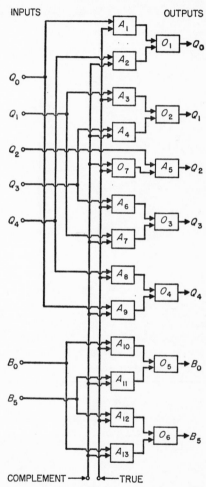

Fig. 7.10. Biquinary nines-complementing circuit.

one register position is shown in Fig. 7.11, the shifting pulse will be applied to all positions of a register simultaneously and will cause all positions to shift one place to the right before a second shift pulse can occur. To shift two positions, two pulses are required, etc.

A similar arrangement could be used for shifting left. The many computers that can shift in one direction only accomplish virtual shifting in both directions by a simple device. Assume, for example, a 10-decimal-digit register which can shift right only but in which whatever is shifted off on the right reenters at the left end of another 10-digit register. Digits shifted off the right of this second register enter the left of the original

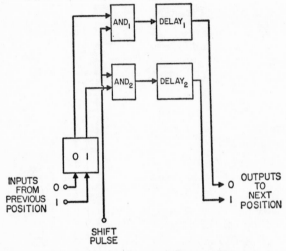

Fɪɢ. 7.11. Basic binary shifting register.

register. A right shift of 10 or fewer places of the quantity in the original register will simply be a right shift. However, a right shift of 11 places will leave the contents of the original register the same as if it had been shifted left 9 places. Similarly, a right shift of 12 is the same as a left shift of 8, etc. A left shift of 1 requires a right shift of 19. A right shift of 20 is the same as no shift at all, etc. The coder need not know in his use of separate right and left shift instructions that the computer can actually shift in one direction only.

MULTIPLICATION AND DIVISION

As already stated, in automatic digital computers multiplication is done by a successive adding and shifting process and division by subtracting and shifting. For illustrative purposes let us take positive numbers and assume four-decimal-digit words and a nine-decimal-position accumulator with the sequence running from A_1 (the most significant position) down to A_9 (the least significant position). Furthermore, assume a *shift counter* initially set to zero.

Multiplication. Table 7.2 considers the multiplication of 7596 by 3514, yielding a product of 26,692,344. In step 1, the multiplier (3514) is initially in positions A_2–A_5 of the accumulator; positions A_6–A_9 are zero. (These multiplication and division systems are similar to ones widely used.[3])

Table 7.2. The Sequence of ADD and SHIFT Operations Which Can Be Used in Multiplication

		A_1	A_2	A_3	A_4	A_5	A_6 7	A_7 5	A_8 9	A_9 6 (multiplicand)	Shift counter
1	Multiplier	0	3	5	1	4	0	0	0	0	0
2	Shift	3	5	1	4	0	0	0	0	0	1
3	Add	2	5	1	4	0	7	5	9	6	1
4	Add	1	5	1	4	1	5	1	9	2	1
5	Add	0	5	1	4	2	2	7	8	8	1
6	Shift	5	1	4	2	2	7	8	8	0	2
7	Add	4	1	4	2	3	5	4	7	6	2
8	Add	3	1	4	2	4	3	0	7	2	2
9	Add	2	1	4	2	5	0	6	6	8	2
10	Add	1	1	4	2	5	8	2	6	4	2
11	Add	0	1	4	2	6	5	8	6	0	2
12	Shift	1	4	2	6	5	8	6	0	0	3
13	Add	0	4	2	6	6	6	1	9	6	3
14	Shift	4	2	6	6	6	1	9	6	0	4
15	Add	3	2	6	6	6	9	5	5	6	4
16	Add	2	2	6	6	7	7	1	5	2	4
17	Add	1	2	6	6	8	4	7	4	8	4
18	Add	0	2	6	6	9	2	3	4	4	4

First the control unit must (step 2) shift the contents of the accumulator one position to the left. A zero will enter A_5. The shift counter will increase by 1. Step 3 involves adding the multiplicand into positions A_6–A_9 with carry to A_2–A_5 positions. But in this example there can be no carry from A_2 to A_1, since this is fractional multiplication, with the decimal point in the product implicit between A_2 and A_1. In step 3 A_1 is decreased by 1. If A_1 is not zero then, as shown in steps 4 and 5, the adding process repeats. However, when A_1 becomes zero (in step 5), the control (in step 6) will cause the contents of the accumulator again to be shifted left one position and the shift count increased by 1. This process repeats until A_1 again becomes 0 and the shift count is at the maximum

of 4.   At that time the process stops.   The product 26,692,344 exists in
positions A_2–A_9 of the accumulator.   Obviously, if two 10-digit numbers
are to be multiplied, a 21-digit accumulator would be used and the maximum shift count would be 10.

The flow diagram of this multiplication operation is given in Fig. 7.12.
The operations shown there are built into the computer.   However, if

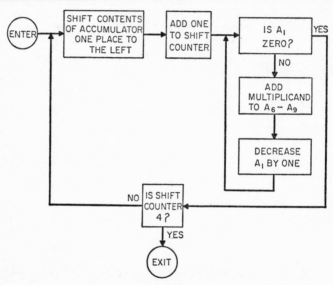

Fig. 7.12. Flow chart of the multiply operation of Table 7.2.

multiplication were not available as an operation, it could still be coded
by means of this flow diagram, the number of steps to accomplish it
depending on the sum of the digits in the multiplier.   In this case, for
example, there were 13 add operations $(3 + 5 + 1 + 4)$ as well as four
shift operations.   The maximum number of add operations for a four-
decimal-digit multiplier would be 36, the minimum 0.

Division.   The division example given in Table 7.3 involves dividing
an eight-decimal-digit dividend (26,693,578) by a four-decimal-digit divisor (7596) to obtain the four-digit quotient (3514) and four-digit remainder (1234).   The flow diagram of the sequence of operations is
given in Fig. 7.13; note that is similar to (some boxes are, in fact, identical
with) the multiplication flow diagram of Fig. 7.12.

Initially the dividend is in positions A_2–A_9 of the accumulator and the
shift count is 0.   The first operation (step 2) involves a left shift of
one position of the accumulator contents and an increase of 1 in the

Table 7.3. A Sequence of SHIFT, ADD, and SUBTRACT Operations for Division

		A_1	A_2 7	A_5 5	A_4 9	A_5 6	A_6	A_7	A_8	A_9	Shift counter
				(divisor)							
1	Dividend	0	2	6	6	9	3	5	7	8	0
2	Shift	2	6	6	9	3	5	7	8	0	1
3	Subtract	1	9	0	9	7	5	7	8	1	1
4	Subtract	1	1	5	0	1	5	7	8	2	1
5	Subtract	0	3	9	0	5	5	7	8	3	1
6	Subtract	−0	3	6	9	0	4	2	1	7	1
7	Add	0	3	9	0	5	5	7	8	3	1
8	Shift	3	9	0	5	5	7	8	3	0	2
9	Subtract	3	1	4	5	9	7	8	3	1	2
10	Subtract	2	3	8	6	3	7	8	3	2	2
11	Subtract	1	6	2	6	7	7	8	3	3	2
12	Subtract	0	8	6	7	1	7	8	3	4	2
13	Subtract	0	1	0	7	5	7	8	3	5	2
14	Subtract	−0	6	5	2	0	2	1	6	5	2
15	Add	0	1	0	7	5	7	8	3	5	2
16	Shift	1	0	7	5	7	8	3	5	0	3
17	Subtract	0	3	1	6	1	8	3	5	1	3
18	Subtract	−0	4	4	3	5	1	6	4	9	3
19	Add	0	3	1	6	1	8	3	5	1	3
20	Shift	3	1	6	1	8	3	5	1	0	4
21	Subtract	2	4	0	2	2	3	5	1	1	4
22	Subtract	1	6	4	2	6	3	5	1	2	4
23	Subtract	0	8	8	3	0	3	5	1	3	4
24	Subtract	0	1	2	3	4	3	5	1	4	4
25	Subtract	−0	6	3	6	2	6	4	8	5	4
26	Add	0	1	2	3	4	3	5	1	4	4

shift count. In step 3, the divisor is subtracted from positions A_2–A_5 of the accumulator and there will be borrowing operations from A_2 to A_1 as required. The flow diagram indicates that the sign of the contents of the accumulator is next examined. When positive, a 1 is added to A_9 and the subtracting of the divisor is repeated. In the example this occurs in steps 3, 4, 5, and 6. However, after step 6, the content of the accumulator is negative; hence, in steps 7 and 8 it is necessary to add the divisor into A_2–A_5 and then repeat the process of shifting and increasing the value in the shift counter. This continues until, after a negative balance and restoration (steps 25 and 26), the shift counter is found to be 4. The process is then complete. The quotient, 3514, will be in positions A_6–A_9 of the accumulator; the remainder, 1234, will be in positions A_2–A_5.

The number of steps depends on the sum of the digits in the quotient. The number of subtract operations will be four more than the sum of $(3 + 5 + 1 + 4)$, that is, 17. In addition, there will always be (for four-decimal digits) four add and four shift operations. Including the initial step, the maximum number of steps would be 49 for a 9,999 quotient and 13 for a 0000 quotient.

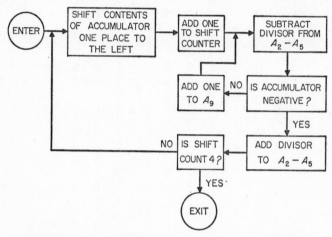

Fig. 7.13. Flow chart of the division operation of Table 7.3.

Both the multiplication and division processes are analogous to mechanical-calculator methods. In computer division, however, it is customary to have the control operation skip this procedure if the quotient would be greater than 1, i.e., if the divisor is smaller than the dividend where the decimal point between A_1 and A_2 applies to both. Otherwise, division by zero would result (as it does in mechanical calculators) in a divide cycle which would never stop. The divide stop control on mechanical calculators serves the same purpose.

Sign in Multiplication and Division. Although complements permit subtraction and handling negative numbers, they are generally not used in multiplication and division. These operations are generally performed with the absolute value of the given two numbers, that is, as if both were positive. The sign associated with the answer is determined separately. This, of course, is the grade-school method.

Thus, if a computer is to multiply two numbers together, it must (1) examine each of the two numbers and decomplement either or both if negative, (2) determine the sign of the product, (3) perform the multiply or divide operation, and (4) complement the result if negative or leave the same if positive. The manner and the order in which these operations are accomplished depend on the specific design of the computer.

The second operation, determining the sign of the result, is a simple logical problem. Remember the product (quotient) is negative if *either* the multiplier (or dividend) or the multiplicand (or divisor) is negative; the product is positive if *both* are negative or both are positive. Obviously, the logic for determining the sum in a binary half adder can be used for this function.

LOGICAL OPERATIONS

Logical operations in computers may be considered as branching or decision operations. The basis for decision can take any of many forms. We will consider only two, one requiring an examination of the sign of a word such as the content of an accumulator and the second depending on a comparison of the magnitude of two words.

Branch on Sign. One example of a logical decision operation is illustrated in Fig. 7.14. The conditional change of control instruction previously considered in Chapters 3 and 6 depended on the sign of the contents of the accumulator. If positive, one course of action was indicated; if negative, another.

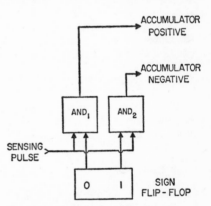

Fig. 7.14. Logical circuit for CONDITIONAL TRANSFER depending on the sign of the contents of an accumulator.

Figure 7.14 shows logical circuitry which could be used for this. The flip-flop shown contains the sign digit of the accumulator. If the accumulator is positive, the flip-flop contains a 0 and the left side is at a 1 level; hence, on receipt of the sensing or interrogating pulse, AND₁ will produce an output pulse indicating that the content of the accumulator is positive. If the accumulator contents are negative, AND₂ will produce the output. Thus a different sequence of events can be caused to occur depending on the accumulator sign.

Comparing. Another usual basis for a decision instruction requires the comparison of the magnitude of one word with that of another. This can be done by determining whether one word is identical with another. If both exist as simultaneous pulse trains, a half adder can be used for comparing. The binary addition table on page 86 shows that if both digits A and B are alike (either both 0 or both 1) there is no S output. However, if A and B are not the same, there is an output from S; hence the words to be compared would be the two inputs to a half adder. If there is an output from S during the word time in which the two pulse trains are being read in, the two words differ; if not, they are identical.

Other logical circuits are used if, for example, branching one way is desired when the first word is larger than the second but not when the second is larger.

PROBLEMS

1. Devise a routine for multiplication, using the flow chart of Fig. 7.12 and assuming the instructions of Chapter 3 except those for multiplication or division. It would probably be best to use three words, one for A_1, another for A_2–A_9, and a third for the shift counter.

2. Similarly, devise a division routine.

3. Devise a logical circuit for a half adder using NOR devices only.

4. Consider the complementing circuit of Fig. 7.10. If the input is 6, list the AND or OR devices which will have a 1 output. Similarly, consider other values of input.

5. Refer to Fig. 7.7. Assume the A input is decimal 8 and the B input is decimal 9. Further, assume a carry from the previous position. Indicate for each of the boxes (full adders, half adders, and OR device) whether the output is a 1 or 0. Also do this for inputs of 8 and 6 and of 6 and 3.

BIBLIOGRAPHY

Blankenbaker, J.: How Computers Do Arithmetic, *Control Eng.*, vol. 3, no. 4, pp. 93–99, April, 1956.

Booth, A. D., and K. H. V. Booth: "Automatic Digital Calculators," pp. 35–56, Academic Press, Inc., New York, 1953.

Chapin, N.: "An Introduction to Automatic Digital Computers," pp. 254–293, D. Van Nostrand Company, Inc., Princeton, N.J., 1957.

Eckert, W. J., and R. Jones: "Faster, Faster," pp. 19–42, McGraw-Hill Book Company, Inc., New York, 1956.

Ivall, T. E., ed.: "Electronic Computers," pp. 69–84, Philosophical Library, Inc., New York, 1956.

Phister, M.: "Logical Design of Digital Computers," pp. 242–325, John Wiley & Sons, Inc., New York, 1958.

Richards, R. K.: "Arithmetic Operations in Digital Computers," pp. 81–176 and 209–285, D. Van Nostrand Company, Inc., Princeton, N.J., 1955.

CHAPTER 8

Storage

The storage unit of an automatic digital computer is an important part of the system. However, the relatively large size of the unit and the ease with which information is available from it are recent developments; the development of arithmetic or even control devices for obvious reasons has normally preceded the complete development of information storage devices.

Our study of storage devices will include the concept of access time, levels of storage, size of memory, and device classifications. Some mention will be made of specific physical characteristics employed in storage units; however, as usual, basic principles will be emphasized. Although specific methods for implementing storage vary rapidly with the state of the electronics art, the principles remain much the same.

BASIC TERMS

The storage in a computer is frequently referred to as "memory" or simply as *store*. Several characteristics distinguish the storage of one computer from that of another. The most frequently used characteristic is the word capacity, which varies from a few thousand in smaller computers to millions in large systems. However, the usefulness of the storage depends not only on its size but also on *access time*, the time required to transfer information or make it available from storage. It is also called *latency time*.

The time required to perform a complete operation depends, therefore, not only on the speed of the arithmetic unit but on the access time. As will be noted in specific cases, the nature of the storage device used determines the access time. When access time to any storage location does not depend on the storage address of the previous word, the storage is said to have *random access*. In contrast, in a *cyclic* storage system such as a rotating magnetic drum (in which the addresses available de-

103

pend on the instantaneous drum position), the access time to a stated storage location does depend on the location of the previous storage references. This factor, insofar as it affects optimum programming, is considered later in this chapter.

Another important characteristic of storage is whether it is *dynamic* or *static*, that is, whether it exists in time as a sequence of pulses or in space as the condition of bistable elements.

Storage is also classified as *erasable* or *nonerasable*. Erasable storage is widely used in computers, since the ability to store different words at different times in the same storage location is essential. Nonerasable storage is also used in most computer systems, either in the form of punched cards or as punched paper tape. However, only erasable storage will be considered here; nonerasable storage will be considered as a part of input-output in the next chapter, since it comes thereunder logically.

Whether information in storage requires electrical energy to remain in storage is also important. If removal or loss of power destroys or alters the contents, the storage is said to be *volatile;* if not, it is *nonvolatile.* Volatility is related to *regeneration,* which is the periodic application of power to the electronic circuitry to regenerate information. Many types of dynamic storage require regeneration and hence are volatile.

Storage is also either *serial* or *parallel* in access; that is, information is either read or written with each digit occurring serially in time sequence or else more than one bit is simultaneously transferred in parallel to or from storage. A storage system in which all bits of a word are transferred in the same cycle is said to be parallel. Only the smaller binary computers are entirely serial in storage access. Most decimal computers are series-parallel; that is, the binary digits within a decimal digit are handled in parallel but the decimal digits in a word are transferred time-serially. Very few computers use parallel storage systems.

LEVELS OF STORAGE

Information is stored at various places in a computer, and the storage unit itself can be divided into different levels of accessibility. We will consider three levels of storage, *internal, secondary,* and *external.*

Internal Storage. There is some storage in arithmetic units. Single- and double-input bistable elements have been used for storing information during arithmetic operations. Here, registers hold information much as do the counter wheels on hand-operated calculators. This type of storage is said to be *zero access;* that is, access time is always negligible. Such storage, however, is generally expensive and used only to a limited extent. Normally a computer will have only a few words of zero-access internal storage. Again the comparison to hand-operated calculators is instructive; the amount of storage in the wheel counters is quite small compared to the amount of information which is stored externally.

Since instructions are interchangeable with data, there may be similar registers in computers which store instructions or other control information. However, we will not consider these registers as storage, since we consider storage to be specific locations of words or instructions or data which are directly addressable or otherwise available to the coder using the computer.

The storage at the next level of availability is the main storage of a computer. This is a relatively large (thousands of words) storage which is available to operate to and from the arithmetic unit, but where the time for access to any specific word is not negligible but is compatible with the speed of operation of the arithmetic unit. It is obviously out of line to have a computer with an arithmetic unit capable of multiplying two numbers together in 1 millisecond when the computer must wait 10 milliseconds to store the product. Magnetic drums or magnetic cores are examples of compatible storage.

This storage may not all be of the same level. In some computers a small portion of the storage may be available with relatively rapid access while the bulk of the storage is slower. Nevertheless, all of this storage is available and useful without too serious a slowdown of the over-all operation.

Secondary Storage. Secondary storage is characterized by being cheap in cost per word of storage but slow in access. However, it is generally quite large, storing hundreds of thousands or millions of words. It is not the kind of storage which the coder would normally refer to directly. Rather, *blocks* of secondary storage are brought out and referred to the arithmetic unit as required.

Secondary storage is not an integral part of the computers, although it is directly connected to and controlled by it. For example, it would consist of magnetic-tape units in computers with magnetic drums for main storage, or would be both tapes and drums for computers using magnetic cores or their equivalents for main storage.

The secondary-storage access time to any specific word is frequently quite slow. The computer may be able to do a large number of other operations in the time required to get a word in secondary storage. Some magnetic-tape units may take minutes for average access, while others require a few seconds or even less and a drum only a few milliseconds. Secondary storage may have a capacity hundreds or thousands of times greater than that of the internal storage. Another measure for comparison is the amount of time for the contents of the internal storage to go to or from a portion of the secondary storage. This is a few seconds or may be even less than one second for tapes; down to milliseconds for drums. Secondary storage is one step removed from that storage which the coder refers to in setting up the specific operations for the control and arithmetic units.

External Storage. The last general level is external storage, which, although entirely divorced from the computer, holds information in the form prescribed for it. Punched cards, punched paper tape, and magnetic tapes stored in files or cabinets are examples. Obviously external storage can be even larger than secondary storage, but the latency time can also be large, since the computer has no direct access to the former.

MAGNETIC STORAGE

Many devices of differing physical properties are used for computer storage. Perhaps the most widely used device is a form of the familiar tape recording. In this process, sections of magnetic material existing by or moving close to a magnetic recording or reading head are magnetized. The magnetic field formed by an electric current passing through the wire coiled in such a head will cause different areas of the magnetic material to be magnetized with opposite polarities, each area thus representing one bit of information. The information may be recorded on magnetic tapes, drums, disks, or cores. This technique is widely used because it makes it easy to read, write, and erase information; yet magnetically recorded data is permanent and nonvolatile. Further, the reliability, low cost, and ability to store large quantities of data contribute to the wide use of magnetic storage.

MAGNETIC CORES

One popular magnetic storage device is the *coincident-current magnetic core*. This consists of a series of small ferromagnetic rings. Each bit of information is stored as the magnetization of one ring. Such a core can be magnetized by the magnetic field created by a pulse of current flowing through a wire threaded through its center. One polarity of current will cause magnetization in one direction; the opposite polarity will cause magnetization in the opposite direction. These two states can then be used to represent binary 0 and 1.

The magnetic core is a static storage system; the information is stored in a fixed space position. Further, such a core has random access, access time to any bit in the matrix being the same as to any other bit. Access time is very low in such a storage system, which in part accounts for its popularity.

Magnetic-core storage is not volatile. No power is required to maintain the information. A core will remain magnetized in one direction until deliberately set to the other state. It is therefore also quite reliable.

Selection. The magnetization characteristic of these cores is such that current up to half the amplitude required to magnetize will not affect the existing magnetization. This is a useful characteristic, since two wires each carrying half current will thus not affect the magnetism of a core unless the magnetic fields associated with their respective current pulses coincide. Since the core is ring shaped, the magnetic effects from each wire add to the other's, even when the wires are at right angles.

This property permits using magnetic cores in a matrix-type storage, as illustrated in a very simple case in Fig. 8.1. Half-current pulses through any one of the four wires, X_1, X_2, Y_1, or Y_2, will not affect the

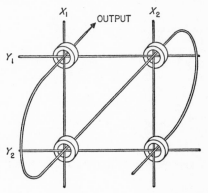

Fig. 8.1. Basic matrix of magnetic cores used for storage.

magnetization of any of the four cores. However, as an example, assume that current pulses in lines X_2 and Y_1 are made to coincide. Only the upper-right core will be affected, and it will be magnetized according to the polarity of the current pulses. It is thus possible to communicate with any core simply by *selecting* the proper pair of wires.

In a magnetic core used to store, say, 4096 words of 36 binary bits each, there would be 36 sets (planes) of cores, and each plane would contain 4096 cores arranged with 64 on each side of a square. Thus the address of the word depends on which pair of the 64 X lines and 64 Y lines are used. Each plane provides a different digit of the word.

Reading information out of any core requires that information also be read into it. For example, if a specific core is sensed to determine whether it contains a 0 or 1, a 1 is read into it. If it had contained 1, the 1 would remain unchanged. The rapid reversal of magnetic field when changing from 0 to 1 causes a voltage to be introduced in the *output* or *sensing* line which is common to all cores. The presence of an output pulse indicates that the core had contained a 0; lack of an output pulse indicates a 1 had been, and is, stored.

Read-out may therefore be destructive. Thus the read cycle must also include time to permit a subsequent resetting of the core to its original state. The output pulse which indicated that the information in the core was 0 would then be used to reset it to 0. Lack of an output pulse means that the core should remain in the 1 condition.

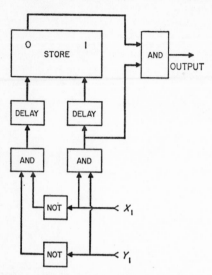

The logical equivalent circuit for one bit of magnetic-core storage is given in Fig. 8.2. This involves only basic AND, OR, NOT, DELAY, and bistable storage elements. However, note the complication of trying to represent it logically as compared to the actual device itself. Thus Fig. 8.2 is of academic interest only and perhaps serves its most useful purpose in pointing out the

Fɪɢ. 8.2. Equivalent logical circuit for one-bit magnetic-core storage.

danger of trying to devise logical equivalent circuits for everything.

DIODE-CAPACITOR STORAGE

Another type of internal storage is the diode-capacitor type,[3] in which the fact that a capacitor is charged or not charged is used to record one bit of information. By using pulses to record and to interrogate such a device, very fast access can be obtained. The equipment is relatively expensive, however.

The operation of a diode-capacitor storage device presupposes more knowledge of electronics than has previously been required. Those who do not readily understand the electronic schematics on Figs. 8.3 and 8.4 should lean more heavily on the equivalent logical circuit of Fig. 8.5. Again the actual circuit is simpler than the logical circuit, but the latter may be useful as a supplement to the electronic explanation.

Fɪɢ. 8.3. Schematic representation of one bit of diode-capacitor storage.

Figure 8.3 shows the electronic schematic of a circuit for one bit of diode-capacitor storage. In it a 1 is indicated if the capacitor is discharged and a 0 if the capacitor is charged. *A* is normally at −50 volts and *B* at +50 volts. Terminal *A* is used to initiate read-out by a pulse which momentarily drops its voltage to zero. The read-out itself is a pulse which causes it to go to zero. *D* is the input terminal in this case.

The action of this device is shown in Fig. 8.4. All four cases, read-out 0, read-out 1, read-in 0, and read-in 1 are considered. Note that read-out is destructive; it always results in the capacitor being charged, that is, set to 0. If the information stored were a 1 before read-out, this 0 must be

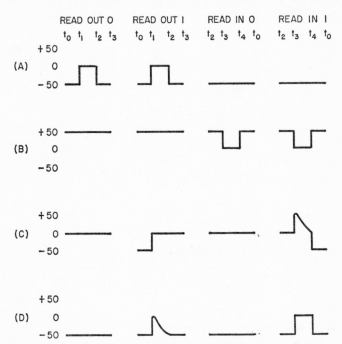

Fig. 8.4. Waveforms in a diode-capacitor storage device for the reading in and out of 0s and 1s.

changed back to a 1 by discharging the condenser by a read-in following each read-out.

Diode-capacitor storage is essentially zero-access and is static, but it also can be volatile. It can be selected in the manner considered for magnetic cores.

MAGNETIC DRUM

Magnetic drums are widely used for storage in computers because of the relatively low cost for the amount of storage. As shown in Fig. 8.6, a drum is physically cylindrical, rotates about its axis, and has sets of read/write heads which read and/or write bits of information onto or off from the thin magnetic coating of the drum.

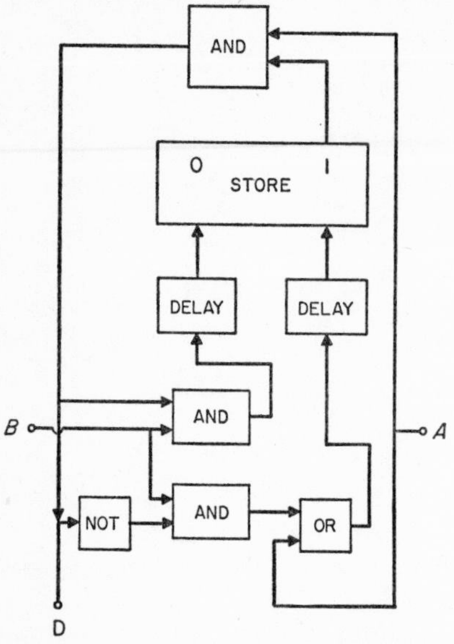

Information on a magnetic drum is stored on a set of *bands* or *tracks*. For example, a 2000-word drum could have 40 tracks along the length of the drum with 50 words on the periphery of the drum for each track. Thus, as the drum rotates, information is available at the same time from the 40 tracks. In a serial computer only one read/write head is required for each band. Frequently, however, in decimal computers each band or track will have four or five heads operating in parallel on the four or five binary bits for binary-coded-decimal representation. In addition to the storage tracks, magnetic drums have control tracks which generate timing signals such as clock pulses.

Fig. 8.5. Equivalent logical circuit for one-bit of diode-capacitor storage.

Magnetic-drum storage is dynamic, since the information contained on the rotating drum is not fixed in space and is available only at certain times as the drum rotates. Although the information is available cyclically, it does not require regeneration and is not volatile. The information stored on a magnetic drum remains on the drum until it is replaced, and need not be lost when the power is removed.

Selection. Since the information is available on a cyclic time basis, the selection technique differs from that used for such static-storage devices as magnetic cores. Assume a magnetic drum containing 2000 words on 40 tracks of 50 words each. The control function of the computer will interpret any given address as pertaining to one of the 40

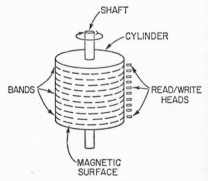

Fig. 8.6. Magnetic-drum storage.

heads. However, it is necessary to wait until the specific one of that set of 50 words comes under the read/write head before its contents are available. To know what addresses are available at any instant of time, the computer has a *current-address* or similar register which operates in synchronism with the drum rotation. It could do this by counting the word pulses and resetting to 0 after each 50 count. Thus any given address specifies not only a certain track but a word number from 00 to 49 on that track. This word number is compared to the current-address register, and when coincidence is detected, the contents of the given address are available under the read/write heads and the transfer between the arithmetic unit and storage is effected.

The current-address register counts continuously as the drum revolves. To permit initial alignment of the current address with the position of the drum, and to check on possible errors in this counting, another pulse, which occurs only once every drum revolution, can also be detected. If the second pulse coincides with the changeover from 49 to 00, the current-address count is known to be in step; if not, an error has occurred. Basically the same kind of check is also called a *sector alarm*.[4]

Optimum Programming. In a magnetic-drum computer, access time to data can be long in comparison to arithmetic operation times. If a drum rotates at 3500 rpm, the average time required for access to a random location on the drum is one-half drum revolution, that is, about 8 milliseconds. It is obviously wasteful for the computer to wait this time unable to perform any other function.

For example, consider a program in which, in one drum revolution, 100 words of storage are available on one track. Further assume that the first instruction is in 00, the next in 01, etc., and that the data is in 50, 51, etc. After the computer acquires the instruction in 00, it will have to wait one-half a drum revolution before it has access to 50 in order to execute the instruction. Further, about one-half drum revolution is generally wasted in waiting for the next instruction in 01. After that, the computer again will have to wait until location 51 is available before it can execute this next instruction, etc. In general, the computer takes one drum revolution for each instruction, even though the actual execution requires only a small fraction of drum revolution time. Obviously, the storage access time limits the speed of operations.

To overcome this difficulty, the information may be so distributed on the drum as to minimize the access time.[3,14] A general technique for doing this is variously called *optimum programming* or *coding*, or *minimum access* (or *latency* or *time*) *coding*. It is generally used in a synchronous computer, where the time to execute an operation can be expressed in terms of a specific number of word times. For example, if the first instruction in 00 takes two additional word times to be ready to procure the operand, then this operand should be in storage location 03 instead of 50 to minimize the access time. Further, if the operation performed requires eight word times, then the next instruction should be in 12, not 01, etc. Hence by (1) knowing the amount of time for each operation and (2) designing the computer to use any storage location for the next instruction, wasted time can be minimized. Notice that item 2 would rule out optimum programming for computers where the next instruction is normally taken from the next storage location in sequence. Being able to minimize access time to operand addresses is only half the problem; minimum access to the instructions is the other half.

The programming of such an optimum routine is complex, in that (1) the time for various operations must be carefully accounted for and (2) the routine is difficult to follow as it "jumps around" from one storage location to another. Fortunately, the computer itself can be used to locate instructions and data in an optimum way.

Interlacing. Another means of optimum programming involves staggering the location of the addresses around the drum in a manner which provides a useful interlacing.[2] (Actually many drums have physical interlacing of the heads even when the numerical equivalent storage locations are available at the same time from different heads.) Thus, considering a 64-word track, each consecutive address could be placed one-seventh drum revolution from the previous one. For example, between 00 and 01, storage locations 57, 50, 43, 36, 29, 22, 15 would occur, in that order. Thus the operand could be located at one of these addresses and the entire operation including both accesses could be done in one-seventh drum revolution. Actually only the middle six addresses are used, because of timing restrictions. This, of course, presumes that the operation can be done in the time available between access to sequentially numbered storage locations. The full advantages of such a system require careful coding, even though interlacing facilitates minimum-access-time coding. In such a system it is sometimes necessary to introduce deliberate delays to obtain advantageous optimum-coded instructions later in the routine.

MAGNETIC TAPES

Magnetic-tape storage is widely used in computers for the bulk storage at the secondary level. Information is stored on reels of magnetic tape, and each reel will hold millions of digits. One reel can contain, for example, 100 times the storage in main memory. The tape may be metallic, although a plastic base is also popular. The information is recorded on and read from a thin film of magnetic material coated on the magnetic-tape base.

The speed of tape movement (60 inches per second is a low value), the information-recording density (more than 100 bits per longitudinal inch), and the number of heads operating in parallel (seven heads is a minimum) of each tape unit make it possible to store very large volumes of information on magnetic tapes. Millions of digits may be stored on one reel; thus the storage volume required is less than 1 per cent of that required for punched-card storage. Further, from 10 to 100 tape units can be used with a computer where required.

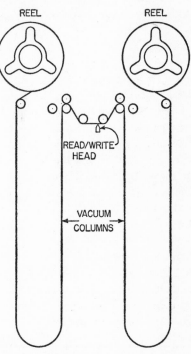

The transport mechanisms used in tape units (Fig. 8.7) are generally capable of starting, stopping, or reversing direction of tape motion in a few milliseconds. This is done by controlling the direction of motion of a loop of tape which passes under the read/write heads, but with enough slack to allow the more sluggish tape reels enough time to follow the direction of tape motion.

Blocks. The large volume of data which can be stored on magnetic tapes frequently requires that the information be stored in manageable units called *blocks*. Each block would in turn contain, as examples, 20, 60, or 100 words, etc.

Fig. 8.7. Magnetic-tape transport device.

Two hundred thousand words at 20 words per block is 10,000 blocks. Instructions pertaining to internal storage refer to the addresses of individual words; in secondary storage they refer to blocks.

The blocks on a magnetic tape can be searched in either an *absolute* or *relative* manner. If each block has associated with it a set of digits which uniquely identifies it, it is said to be addressable, and execution of a search instruction will cause the tape unit to search until it finds this absolute block address. However, many tape systems have no block addresses; the computer can search forward or backward a specified number of blocks but can do so only relative to its previous location on the tape. This is not a handicap, however, for many applications of magnetic tapes. In a record-updating operation, for example, new information is added to the tape as the tape unit progresses through the records which are already filed in order. The average access time for information on magnetic tapes can be of the order of minutes. This slow access makes it imperative that the information be organized to minimize the time in storing and retrieving information. This results in designs where the magnetic-tape operations are performed in parallel with other computer operations, even in an otherwise serial system. Thus tape units on a computer will generally search, move forward or backward, or rewind at the same time as computations are being performed by the main computer.

In an addressable system, the instructions for reading or writing information must be separate from the search or comparable instructions, to permit this parallel operation. Thus a tape unit can be instructed to go to a specific location and then, later in the program (after time for such a search), be instructed to read or write as required. Since it is quite possible that the tape will not have reached the desired position at the time of the instruction, a *tape-ready* test is frequently used. If the tape is still in motion at the time of the instruction, this not-ready status could be used to transfer control to an alternate storage location for its next instruction. Thus the coder can instruct the machine in an alternate course of action (if any) when the tape unit is not ready to handle data. When the tape unit is ready, the read or write operation is executed and the rest of the program follows in sequence.

Of course, in a nonaddressable system, which presumes organization of data in a manner that requires relatively small access time, there is no need for a search instruction as such. READ, WRITE, BACKSPACE, or REWIND instructions can provide basic operations required.

The long access time needed to search a reel of magnetic tape has resulted in alternate methods to reduce this time. One method is to use a multiplicity of short reels. If 50 short tapes are used,[4] the average access time is reduced by a factor of 10, even though the total length of the 50 short tapes is five times that of a single long reel.

MAGNETIC DISK

Storing information on magnetic disks permits storing a large number of short records with random access to each record.[8] For example, as shown in Fig. 8.8, 50,000 records of 100 characters each are available on 50 disks, each having 100 tracks and 10 records per track. The access-arm mechanical arrangement causes magnetic read/write heads to be moved to the designated track and disk in a few tenths of a second. The disks rotate similarly to a magnetic drum, but their large area permits many more tracks to be available than on a drum.

The advantage of this type of storage is that it permits *in-line* processing of accounting data. This means that, with the entire file stored in the computer, accounting transactions can be processed in order of occurrence, without having to sort them before processing. If the file is kept in a storage (for example, externally in a file of punched cards or magnetic tapes) where the average access time is long, it is necessary to store the file in order. Furthermore, all transactions must also be sorted in the same order so that a minimum amount of file access time is involved in updating. However, with random access to a large-capacity storage, the transaction records need not be put in order before processing. Even the file itself no longer need be in order, and indeed random distribution of the items in the file is sometimes used.

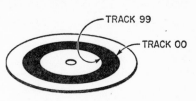

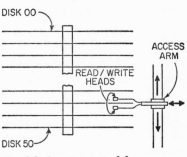

Fig. 8.8. Arrangement of data on magnetic disks.

Of course, the same in-line techniques can be used with other rapid-access storage such as magnetic-core storage; however, it is generally impractically expensive to obtain the very large storage business accounting records require.

DYNAMIC STORAGE

In dynamic storage devices information exists as a series of pulses which occur in time sequence. In static storage, information exists as the condition of various bistable elements, each representing one bit. Dynamic storage is characterized by the need to regenerate the information, since pulses exist for only short periods of time, generally in the order of microseconds. Thus dynamic storage is usually volatile with respect to power and cyclic with respect to access time. We will consider first a one-bit dynamic storage device and larger-capacity storage later.

Dynamic Latch. A basic type of dynamic storage element is the logical store shown in Fig. 8.9.[3] It is a dynamic device and is also referred to as a *latch*.

The function of a latch is to provide a series of output pulses occurring at the clock rate of the computer, with the facility for turning the pulses on and off as required. Thus the application of a *start* signal will be stored or remembered by the device in that it will continue to produce pulses which represent dynamically the 1 condition. Similarly, a *stop* pulse causes the device to switch to and remain at the 0 state, that is, producing no output pulses, until receipt of the next *start* pulse.

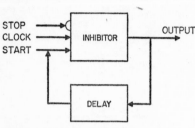

FIG. 8.9. Basic dynamic-latch storage device.

This device is sometimes called a latch because once it has been triggered to one condition or the other it will remain latched to that condition until unlatched by a definite subsequent action. It is another form of the basic one-binary-bit storage device.

It consists of INHIBIT and DELAY elements, and it illustrates the basic characteristics of a dynamic element. First, the prime information is the presence or absence of a series of pulses, which are required to perform a sequence of logical, control, arithmetic, and other operations, and second, a DELAY is used to convey information (again in the absence or presence of a series of pulses) from one timing cycle (clock pulse) to another.

Consider that initially there is no signal on the *stop* input to the INHIBIT; hence it acts only as an AND device. Thus, although clock pulses are applied to one input, there will be no output. However, now consider that a pulse occurs on the *start* input simultaneously with a clock pulse. This will then produce an output pulse. Further, this output passing through the DELAY device will cause (if the delay time is equal to the time between clock pulses) a pulse at the *start* input to the INHIBIT to coincide with the next clock pulse. Hence, there will be another output pulse, etc. Thus this device will produce a train of output pulses after only one input pulse is used to start it.

This condition will continue as long as there is no signal on the *stop* line. However, as inherent in an inhibiting device, the presence of a pulse on the *stop* input will inhibit an output. Thus, although a pulse occurs simultaneously on the other two inputs, the presence of a pulse on this third input results in no output. Further, the device remains in this no-output condition (0 state) until the next *start* pulse.

Recirculating Storage. To obtain relatively cheap, large-capacity dynamic storage, recirculating techniques are used. The basic schematic given in Fig. 8.10. This type of storage requires a logical delay device having a time delay equal to the total of a large number of computer digit times. This permits a corresponding number of bits of information to be continuously circulating. As a pulse comes out of the delay device, is connected to one input of the AND device while the clock timing pulses re applied to the other. If the pulse is a 1, the output from the AND evice is a 1 pulse, which will be reintroduced into the DELAY. However,

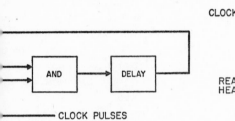

CLOCK PULSES

FIG. 8.10. Basic dynamic storage device such as used in mercury delay line or recirculating magnetic-drum loop.

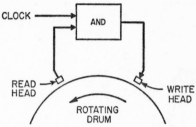

FIG. 8.11. Recirculating loop on a magnetic drum.

the output at some clock time is 0 instead of 1, then the 0 is reintroduced. The DELAY may hold hundreds or thousands of digits which are onstantly being circulated. Hence, a relatively large number of digits an be stored for the amount of equipment required.

The DELAY itself can be of several different types. For example, it may be a tube of mercury in which the 1s and 0s are ultrasonic pulses which propagate through the length of the tube. The delay time using such a system may be only 250 microseconds, but at a 4-megacycle clock rate, his results in 1000 bits constantly being in storage. Or the DELAY may be a recirculating loop on a magnetic drum (Fig. 8.11). In this case the information is read off a rotating magnetic drum and then reintroduced forward on the drum. The storage is on the drum in the space between the read/write heads. The delay time is the time for a given position on the drum to move from the reading head to the rewriting head. Such a system is sometimes called a *revolver* or a *quick-access* loop. Twenty-word storage in the loop is obtained in one computer by having the heads spaced one-tenth of the drum periphery apart in a 200-word-track drum.[4]

RECORDING LEVELS

In a binary system only 0 and 1 need be represented. Idealized representations of binary 10110 are shown in Fig. 8.12.

Two-level. The two-level form is shown in Fig. 8.12A. Vertically there are the two levels that represent 0 and 1, respectively, by having the tube in a certain half of a flip-flop, for example, either nonconducting or conducting. Or an ideal form of a train of pulses may be used, where a pulse is 1 and the absence of a pulse is 0. Actual pulses are not and need not be as flat as shown in this figure. Thus the horizontal axis of Fig. 8.12 would be space position for static storage and time for dynamic storage.

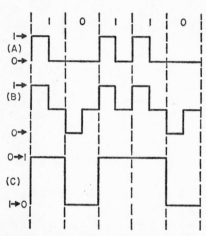

FIG. 8.12. Idealized representation of the binary number 10110 by (A) the two-level system, (B) the three-level and, (C) the nonreturn-to-zero system of recording data.

Three-level. However, note that the 0 level in Fig. 8.12A could result either from the binary number being 0 or from its actually being because of pulse failure due to malfunction. To guard against this possibility, many storage systems have three levels, as shown in Fig. 8.12B. A 1 is represented by a pulse in the upward direction (a positive pulse) and 0 by a negative pulse. All bits of a binary number are represented by pulses; the absence of a pulse would be easily recognized as the result of a malfunction. This then provides a useful check. In static storage, the 1 level could be magnetization in one direction, the 0 level magnetization in the opposite direction. The center (nonnumeric) level would be no magnetization.

In Fig. 8.12A the information is contained in the presence of a pulse which exists for only a part of the time between pulses. Thus even between two 1s, the level returns to 0. Similarly, in Fig. 8.12B the time between pulses is at a 0 level. A 1 is represented by a positive pulse, a 0 by a negative pulse, and the time between by no pulse.

Nonreturn to Zero. In contrast to this there are storage systems which use *nonreturn to zero* (*nrz*). Figure 8.12C shows this where the two levels represent changes in the sequence of information (1) from 0 to 1 or (2) from 1 to 0. Thus assuming 0 level initially, the first digit of 10110 (a 1) requires an upper-level representation; the second digit (being a 0) requires a change to the lower level; the third (a 1) requires a shift back to the upper level; the fourth (another 1) remains at the upper level, and the last (a 0) requires a shift to the lower level. In practice, the information recorded in the storage medium, such as a magnetic drum, is the change of the *nrz* levels, since it is neither practical nor necessary to record a long-sustained level as would be encountered in a series of 1s or 0s.

There are sometimes simplifications in the computer design which result from using an *nrz* system; hence it is popular. However, the use of *nrz* does not affect the coding; in fact, the coder may be unaware that it is being used.

VARIABLE-LENGTH RECORDS

It has been assumed up to now that all words in any specific computer are of the same length, i.e., 10 decimal digits, 36 binary digits, etc. This use of words to designate a fixed number of digits is satisfactory for scientific computation. However, it is *not* satisfactory for many business applications.

Business records vary in length. For example, the number of digits or characters (Chapter 9) to represent the amount of a sale is not the same used to designate the customer's firm name, the salesman's initials, the credit rating of the firm, the stock part designation, etc. In a fixed-word-length computer, it is necessary to *pack* information in order to avoid wasting storage space. For example, if a two-digit code designates the salesman, three digits the customer's code, and five digits the amount of sale, all this information could be stored in one 10-digit word. However, this is fortuitous; in practice it is not easy to fit variable-length records into fixed-word-length units. Even when it is done, it is tedious to code the packing and unpacking of information. Considerable red tape is involved. A 12-digit stock number would have to be split between two 10-digit words, for example.

These difficulties are avoided in many business computers by organizing the storage to accommodate variable-length records. One method is to have many word lengths but each one of a fixed length. Thus, in any problem, the stock identification number would always be 12 digits, the credit status two digits, etc.

Also, the concept of "word" is often eliminated, and storage is taken to consist of records of various lengths. Thus, instead of organizing a storage unit to contain 10,000 words each containing 12 characters, it would simply be a storage for 120,000 characters. This total storage could be used as required for various record lengths. In this case the location of a unit record in storage is generally given as the location of the least significant digit in that record. Thus it is necessary to specify the length of the record, as the unit record exists as a field of digits and/or characters which are handled from right to left.

The length of the field can be specified in the instruction pertaining to it. However, it is possible to provide a special mark or character to de fine the left end of the field.[5] Thus only the address of the digit farthest right need be given. The computer automatically scans until it encoun ters this mark and considers this to be one unit record.

When arithmetic operations are to be performed on such data, these operations must be serial. Thus, in adding two such records together as in updating a file, the least significant digits are added first, the next least second, etc., until the end-of-record mark is encountered. Multipli cation and division, which cannot be done entirely serially, are more restrictive with regard to record lengths than other operations. Variable length-record computers can, while performing arithmetic operations also recognize nonnumeric digits as they scan to the left, and they use this ability to define the left limit of a field. In general, there is no meaning associated with arithmetic operations on nonnumeric data.

At secondary storage levels variable-length records are similar to those in the internal storage of the arithmetic unit. In tape units the number of fixed-length words which form a block may simply be allowed to vary. On the other hand, record lengths may not be related to words but to a fixed number of characters which can vary from one record to another. Again *end-of-record* or *end-of-file* marks may be used in tape storage; sometimes merely a gap between records is used to separate unit records.[8] It will be noted that, with variable-length records, the con cept of addressable fixed blocks is not feasible. Nonaddressable tape storage and relative search are used instead.

BIBLIOGRAPHY

Booth, A. D., and K. H. V. Booth: "Automatic Digital Calculators," pp. 113–135, Academic Press, Inc., New York, 1953.
Canning, R. G.: "Electronic Data Processing for Business and Industry," pp. 88–95, John Wiley & Sons, Inc., New York, 1957.
Chapin, N.: "An Introduction to Automatic Digital Computers," pp. 294–320, D. Van Nostrand Company, Inc., Princeton, N.J., 1957.
Eckert, W. J., and R. Jones: "Faster, Faster," pp. 43–59, McGraw-Hill Book Company, Inc., New York, 1956.
Engineering Research Associates: "High-speed Computing Devices," pp. 302–384, McGraw-Hill Book Company, Inc., New York, 1950.

Fowler, F.: The Computer's Memory, *Control Eng.*, vol. 3, no. 5, pp. 93–101, May, 1956.

vall, T. E., ed.: "Electronic Computers," pp. 98–111, Philosophical Library, Inc., New York, 1956.

McCracken, D. D.: "Digital Computer Programming," pp. 150–158, John Wiley & Sons, Inc., New York, 1957.

Phister, M.: "Logical Design of Digital Computers," pp. 174–211, John Wiley & Sons, Inc., New York, 1958.

Richards, R. K.: "Digital Computer Components and Circuits," pp. 263–396, D. Van Nostrand Company, Inc., Princeton, N.J., 1957.

Ridenour, L. P.: Computing Memories, *Sci. American*, vol. 192, p. 92, June, 1955.

Scott, N. R.: Temporary Storage Elements and Special-purpose Tubes, *Control Eng.*, vol. 3, no. 3, pp. 93–98, March, 1956.

CHAPTER 9

Input-Output

Input-output characteristics very largely define an entire computing system. Communication to and from the outside world and the computer is accomplished through the input-output system. Whether a computer is considered to be "business" or "scientific" is largely dependent on this characteristic. If the input on a computer is limited as compared to its internal data-handling capabilities, then it is more likely to be used for "scientific" computation. If the system is capable of maintaining a very high input-output information rate while processing data, this would help classify it as a "business" computer.

The input-output equipment is the means of communication between the user and the machine. In general, it is used to translate the coder's marks and symbols into the internal machine language and vice versa. The coder or operator causes a series of numbers and/or alphabetic information to be inserted into the input device, which results in bits of information being stored in the storage unit. Similarly, the information in storage is changed by the output device to symbols which the user can interpret directly.

Various basic devices for translating information from one medium to another will be considered. These include typewriter, punched-tape, magnetic-tape, and punched-card systems. Of particular importance are the methods used to represent numbers, letters, punctuation marks, and special symbols in terms of the limited language of a computer. Especially in considering input-output equipments and systems does one become aware of the great potentialities for employing automatic-digital-computing systems in a general language sense as well as in a mathematical sense.

Formulating a problem in the specific terms which a computer can use is frequently quite a chore. Man expresses himself by means not at all suited for an electronic computer; much of the normal information exchange between humans is verbal, but we are quite a long way from being able to tell a computer verbally what needs to be done. (However, progress *is* being made both on this and the somewhat easier task of causing computers to "speak.")

Aside from verbal communications, written records are part and parcel of our modern day and age. Interestingly, computer systems are being used to reduce the "paper-work problem" these voluminous written records have produced. Here, again, the visual record is not suitable as direct input. The problem of reading typewritten or printed material is very difficult; a system for reading handwriting is well nigh impossible. Fortunately other media for communication are better suited to be input-output devices.

BASIC DEVICES

The input of a computer requires information which is, or can be converted into, electrical signals for each bit of information. Similarly, the output of a computer will be sets and/or sequences of electrical signals representing bits of information.

Fortunately, several devices and systems which were developed for other purposes meet these requirements. For example, the development of the telegraph required that information be broken down into elementary signals. These dots and dashes were transmitted over telegraph lines as electrical signals to operate recording equipment. The development of telegraphy resulted in teletype and associated equipment for transmitting and receiving information as electrical pulses. It is interesting to note that the punched paper tape as used for storage of information in telegraphy was invented by Samuel F. B. Morse over one hundred years ago.

Another information-handling system, which developed independently of computers but is now widely used in them, is that developed for business accounting and records which uses punched paper cards for information storage. Punched cards seem to have been first used by Jacquard, in 1801, to control mechanically the designs produced on weaving looms. The work of Hollerith and many others has resulted in electromechanical business accounting machines which, fortunately, can be used in modern computers.

The third general type of input-output is magnetic tape, which was discussed in Chapter 8. However, a complete computer system still requires that final communication between human and computer be through a typewriter (or similar device) or through business accounting machines. Magnetic tape as used for input-output will not be considered here, since the system is generally the same as any described in Chapter 8.

SERIES AND PARALLEL

As in other parts of a computer, the speed of operation and the com plexity of input-output devices depends on whether operation is seria or parallel. The telegraph system is essentially serial in nature; that is, each character is sent in time sequence, and the dots and dashes for each character are also transmitted serially. However, modern telegraph equipment has many improvements to facilitate expressing information in electrical form. Since a typewriter-like device is frequently used to record information, the telegraph is limited mechanically to relatively slow rates.

In contrast, business accounting practice is generally to use a paralle system. The unit record is a punched card which can contain a large number of bits of information in its 80 or 90 columns. The associated equipment generally handles all columns simultaneously. Thus the card-reading and -punching devices handle columnar information in a parallel manner. The printers developed to list and/or tabulate information from punched cards also are parallel; all columns of one card will be read and printed simultaneously. The result is a line printer with each line corresponding to the information on one punched-card unit record.

As will be noted later, special input-output devices are being de veloped for use in computers. These are high-speed devices that permit rapid information interchange. Many are serial from, especially, digit to digit (or character to character) but likely to be parallel for the bits within a digit or character. However, the much higher speed of internal operations as compared to the speed of input-output devices often makes the distinction between series and parallel operation not too meaningful.

ALPHANUMERIC SYSTEMS

One should not restrict automatic digital computers to numeric opera tions only. The development of communications resulted first in symbols to represent the spoken word and eventually in languages and alphabets. In contrast, computers were first applied to the manipulation of numbers. After a while, it became apparent that the advantages of such computer systems could be applied to the manipulation of alphabetic information as well. The large storage capacity, the rapidity of information inter change, and the ability to perform operations on the data are some of the advantages useful in handling alphanumeric data. Hence the recent trend in business and industry to adapt and use computers in data-proc essing problems.

Characters. To understand alphanumeric applications we must enlarge our concept of a "word" and define a new term, character. *Character* is a general term for symbols, including not only numbers but also the letters of the alphabet and punctuation, that is, a full facility for communication.

The 26 letters of the alphabet and 10 digits are used in all alphanumeric computer systems. However, the punctuation and special symbols differ from one system to another. The total number of such symbols in one working system is 11, and in another 15, giving, respectively, totals of 47 and 51 characters over-all. The total set of characters available on a computer are sometimes referred to as its language.

2 ND AND 3 RD DIGITS	LAST FOUR DIGITS															
	0000	0001	0010	0011	0100	0101	0110	0111	1000	1001	1010	1011	1100	1101	1110	1111
00	i	Δ	—	0	1	2	3	4	5	6	7	8	9	'	&	(
01	r	,	.	;	A	B	C	D	E	F	G	H	I	#	¢	@
10	t	"	∣	)	J	K	L	M	N	O	P	Q	R	$	*	?
11	Σ	β	:	+	/	S	T	U	V	W	X	Y	Z	%	=	

FIG. 9.1. Characters representable on UNIVAC.

Since the total number of characters normally is less than 64, six bits can be used to represent each alphanumeric symbol. In general, however, computers use an extra bit for checking, for a total of seven.

One such system is given in Fig. 9.1.[6] The 16 columns represent the last four bits of the six-bit code, the first two bits are represented by the four rows, and the numbers are excess-three. Thus 0 is 000011, 1 is 000100, etc. In addition, the letters A–I are on the second row with 01 as the first two bits of the six-bit code. The letters J–R are in the 10 row and S–Z in the 11 row. Fifteen other symbols are interspersed on the ends of the rows. Only the characters in the outline are normally available on a line printer. The others are, however, available on typewriter output devices.

In this system, checking is accomplished by a seventh bit, which is 1 if it is necessary to make an odd number of 1s in the code. Thus the full seven-bit representation for 1 is 0000100, for 9 1001100; D is 1010111, P is 0101010, T is 1110110, and % is 0111101. Circuitry for error checking will be considered later.

Another seven-bit system is shown in Fig. 9.2.[8] The numerical (digit) part of the code is a 1-2-4-8 binary representation. The top two rows (0 and X) correspond to *zones* which will be considered later in connection with punched cards. Notice that there are 11 special symbols.

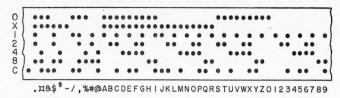

FIG. 9.2. The alphanumeric special-symbols system used in some IBM equipment.

Checking by means of the seventh bit (C row) assures that there is an odd number of 1s in each code.

PUNCHED PAPER TAPE

The first general application of punched paper tape to communications also was as a part of the development of telegraphy.

Although telegraph signals can be transmitted directly to the receiving device, it is generally preferable to store the information intermediately on punched paper tape. This permits more efficient use of the telegraph line, since information can be transmitted to and from punched paper devices at a rate higher than that which direct transmitting or receiving devices can handle.

Holes punched in a moving strip of paper permit two contacts to close and thus complete an electrical circuit. Otherwise the circuit is open. A sequence of electrical signals so produced can obviously be used to represent the 0 and 1 required for storing binary information in a computer. Communication services, especially the teletype, have developed extensive equipment for reading, transmitting, receiving, and interpreting information on punched paper tape. The familiar telegram is the final output form of such a system.

Teletype. Punched-paper-tape perforators and readers for teletype communications are necessarily designed for slower speeds of operation than are normally required by computers. Further, a standard communication system uses five holes which are sensed or punched in parallel (five *channels*); this, with a normal reading rate of about 10 rows of punches (*frames*) per second, results in a relatively slow input device.

A widely used teletype code is shown in Fig. 9.3. The five channels permit 32 different combinations to be transmitted. Six of these are used for control, including two to shift between letters and figures. In the *letter* position all 26 alphabetic characters are available; the 10 digits, 15 symbols, and an additional signal are available in the *figure* position of the carriage.

This or a similar five-channel code are sometimes referred to as a *common language system.* However, the five-channel system is limited in that there is no redundancy for error checking.

Computer Adaptations. Punched paper tapes with six, seven, or eight channels are widely used with computers. A six-channel system can be used to obtain all upper- and lower-case characters of a typewriter. As direct input to computers, seven channels are used, with the seventh used for checking purposes. The width of usual punched paper tape permits eight channels, and eight-channel systems are in use. One makes extensive use of checking by having all characters including numbers, letters, and symbols represented by four channels being punched.[10] Any

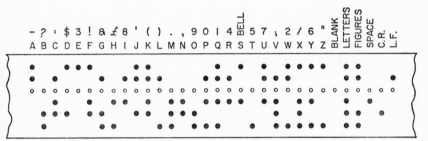

Fig. 9.3. A five-channel teletype code.

more or less than four channels of the eight being punched (or corresponding four pulses existing at one time) indicates an error. Seventy characters are possible in this system.

The multiple channels on paper tape, which are read simultaneously, permit several methods of reading information into the computer. In a binary computer three channels could be used for an octal input. Generally, however, four channels are used for a *hexadecimal* or *sexadecimal* input. These four bits represent 16 conditions or states. Thus, as the paper tape advances frame by frame (a frame is a single column of position across the width of a paper tape), four bits would be read in for each frame. This process uses only four of the five to eight possible channels in a frame; the other channels can be used to mark the end of words or serve some other control function. Another system uses six channels to read six bits into the computer for each frame. This *bioctal* system requires only six frames for a 36-bit word.

In a decimal computer, it is usual to let each frame contain one decimal digit. Thus, a four-bit binary-coded-decimal system uses four channels, with control on other channels.

Typewriter. A basic language device frequently used in conjunction with punched-paper-tape computer systems is the typewriter. An electrically operated typewriter provides a handy means to convert the symbols man uses to express himself into the electrical signals the computer needs. Likewise, the electrical output of the computer will, through such a typewriter, produce a printed form widely used and standardized long before computers existed. It is, therefore, logical that they are adapted for computer use.

Several kinds of electric typewriters are used. One is the type used for general office work. Another is a type developed to punch, and to read from, punched paper tape; it is widely used to produce automatically individually typed original letters. The third (which has already been discussed) is the kind used for teletype operation. Again the operation can involve punching and reading punched paper tape.

The main advantage of typewriter devices is the large number of symbols and characters available. Since the upper-case selection can be under computer control, it is possible to produce the same kind of copy as a typist would. Color control and backspacing for underlining are also possible. The relatively slow speed of the typewriter, however, limits its use to medium- or small-sized computers and for applications requiring a relatively small amount of input-output. Ten strokes per second is the usual limit.

PUNCHED CARDS

An important medium for input-output and external storage is the punched card. The punched card has been widely used in accounting operations and is also an important part of many automatic-digital-computer systems.

The widely used 80-column IBM punched card and the characters representable by it are shown in Fig. 9.4. Physically, the card is 7⅜ inches long by 3¼ inches wide and 0.0067 inch thick. It is divided into 80 columns 0.087 inch wide and into twelve ¼-inch rows. There are 960 positions on a card where a punch can exist.

The punched card well represents the *unit-record* concept. Each card contains 80 columns of information which can be altered without affecting the other cards in the complete record. The physical characteristics of the card facilitate sorting, collating, and other data-handling operations. Each card is generally divided into *fields* of several adjacent columns, with each field representing a set of data.

Card Characters. There are 47 symbols in the 80-column punched-card system, as shown in Fig. 9.4. Ten are the numbers 0–9; 26 the alphabet; and 11 special symbols. Note that the decimal digits are represented by single punches in the corresponding row of the card. Two special symbols (− and &) are single punches in the X (11) and Y (12) rows, respectively, and indicated in columns 14 and 11. The 12 row is sometimes used for the + sign.

All alphabetic characters are indicated by two punches in any column of a card. Columns 25 through 50 in the illustration contain the alphabet. One punch is a *digit punch*, 9–1. The other a *zone punch*, 0, 11, or 12. Note the regular manner in which the zone and digit punches are combined to represent the alphabet. Only the 0–1 combination is skipped. However, as shown in column 15, this combination is used for /. The

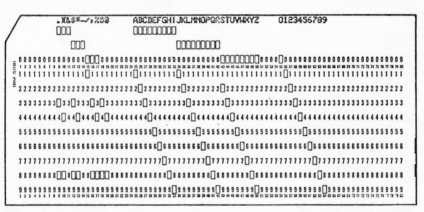

FIG. 9.4. An 80-column IBM card and the system of punches for representing its system of characters.

other eight special symbols all have an eight punch in common. Two, @ and #, consist of double punches only; the others are triple punches with zone punches, in addition to either three or four as digit punches.

It will be noted that the card system of information storage is decimal with regard to numbers. Although it thus requires translation for computer number systems, this system is obviously well suited to familiar types of card-handling equipment. Such equipment sorts, collates, reproduces, tabulates, and performs other handling and arithmetic operations on data stored on cards.

FORTRAN **Language.** The accounting language of Fig. 9.4 has been modified somewhat for mathematical purposes. The grand total, ampersand, per cent, number, and "at" signs have been replaced by closed (right) plus open (left) parentheses, equals, and minus sign, respectively. This system is used for the FORTRAN (FORmula TRANslating) automatic coding system (see Chapter 12).

Sequence. The order or sequence of alphanumeric characters is important for sorting, collating, and similar operations. All systems have the digits in numeric order. However, the digits may occur before or after the alphabet. Further, punctuation marks can occur in different places. The card system has punctuation, alphabet, and digits in that order. This assures, for example, that Smith, W. W. will be filed ahead of Smithfield, A. A. The characters in Figs. 9.2 and 9.4 are given in the sequence order.

IBM-ese. The IBM system for card handling and the equipment for such operation antedate most of the work done in the field of automatic computers. Further, they were developed for application in the general area of accounting. As a result, the nomenclature used in IBM systems

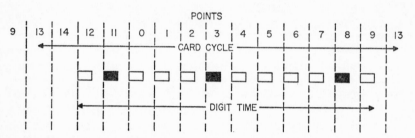

Fig. 9.5. The basic timing of an IBM-card device while reading a dollar sign from a card.

differs from that used in digital computers which were initially developed by electronic personnel for scientific computation. It is therefore necessary to know equivalent terms when dealing with combinations of IBM and other equipment.

To understand the punched-card system, one must know the basic timing cycle of card reading and punching. The time for such a *basic card operation* or *functional cycle* is divided into equal time intervals called *points*, corresponding to the time that a card is pulled laterally at a uniform rate under 80 reading brushes or punch magnets. The number of points varies between types of card equipment. Some use a 20- or 24-point system in which each point corresponds to 18° or 15° of a 360° complete cycle. In Fig. 9.5 we assume a 14-point system. If we assume a 100-card-per-minute rate (many card-handling devices operate at rates faster than this), each of these points is about 43 milliseconds in duration. Twelve of the 14 correspond to the 12 rows of the card. The electrical signals which can exist during this digit time are called *digit impulses*. In the example of Fig. 9.5, the solid blocks indicate the digit impulses which would represent the $ sign. The outlined blocks indicate the times that impulses may be present for other numbers or symbols. The other two points (13 and 14) correspond to the time between possible punches in cards. The rate of lateral card movement in this case would be ¼ inch per point, as the rows are ¼ inch apart and the 3¼-inch-wide cards are fed with a ¼-inch gap between each.

Since the point time during which a hole in the card is sensed defines the number which it represents, computer input equipment must translate this time of closure into the corresponding number representation used in the computer's storage system. Similarly, output equipment must translate the output digits into signals which will cause punches to be made in the appropriate row of the card as the card moves past the punch magnets. Further, since all 80 columns of the card are generally sensed at the same time by 80 individual brushes, it is necessary in reading to convert this parallel information to the serial type of digit handling so popular in computers.

The much greater speed of a computer as compared to most input-output devices permits serial reading or writing of data in a parallel input-output device. Each possible digit impulse in the card cycle may exist for 14 of the 43 milliseconds. This is normally ample to permit a computer to scan all 80 columns of a card to note which are 9s. Similarly, during the 8 time, all 80 columns can be scanned serially for 8s, etc.

The card cycle of a "twelves-edge-first" card device is shown. In other equipment the card may be read "nines edge first," with the points representing 9, 8, 7, 6, 5, 4, 3, 2, 1, 0, 11, and 12, respectively.

Some other IBM terminology will be considered. What IBM terms a *selector* is otherwise known as a relay. *Pilot selectors* and *coselectors* are relays with different holding or latching characteristics. A schematic representation of a relay was given in Fig. 6.8. Relay contacts are called *positions*.

The selectors and other devices in IBM equipment are electrically interconnected to do specific sequences of through wiring made on a removable *control panel* (jack panel, patch board, plugboard). Control-panel wiring corresponds to programming and coding of computers. The impulses are wired between *hubs* (terminals) on the panels. An impulse (also called "shot") can be used, for example, to *pick up* a selector. Before being picked up, each point of a selector provides an electrical contact between its *common* and *normal* hubs; after being picked up, between its *common* and *transferred* hubs.

The IBM designation *filter* is not that in the electrical engineer's concept but rather is a diode rectifier, that is, an electrically unilateral device. An *emitter* generates a train of impulses which correspond to the basic timing of the IBM device. A *digit selector* is effectively a stepping switch which, when connected to an *emitter,* will permit selection of designated timing signals corresponding to the rows of the card.

Knowing how to translate from one set of nomenclature to another is obviously advantageous. It is then possible to take techniques such as switching configurations from electrical engineering and apply them in using IBM card equipment. Further, many control-panel-wiring techniques can be applied to other fields.

Line Printers. The development of electromechanical devices for accounting purposes has resulted in equipment for faster read-in and read-out. The use of the punched card permits parallel operations, so that output devices (tabulators) for accounting purposes print a full line of 88 or 120 characters at one time. With the ability to print 1½ to 10 or more lines per second, the rate at which information can be recorded is considerably faster than with typewriter devices.

ALPHANUMERIC REPRESENTATION IN NUMERIC COMPUTERS

Instead of using a multibit system at each position in the word, some basically numeric computers simply use two decimal digits for alphanumeric characters. This permits 100 different symbols. The input and output information to the computer is, or can be, alphanumeric; however, the computer itself handles the information as pairs of normal decimal digits. Provision for numerical handling of this type of alphabetic information is made in coding. The input-output system does the translating. There are circumstances when the two-decimal-digit system is advantageous, especially because of its ability to use an existing numeric computer design.

Since each alphanumeric character is translated into two numeric decimal digits, a 10-decimal-digit-word machine can contain only five alphanumeric characters. Further, if a specific word position can be either alphabetic or numeric, then the translation may result in a two-decimal-digit representation for a single decimal digit of input.

A system used for representing punched-card characters in a decimal computer is given in Fig. 9.6.[3] Note that the alphanumeric portion consists of the lower (*digit*) punch of the card system as the least significant digit of the two, while the upper (*zone*) punch is changed to the most significant digit. Thus a 12 (Y) zone punch becomes a 6, an 11 (X) zone is 7, a 0 zone is an 8, and no zone (single numeric punch) is a 9. For example an A is 61, M is 74, Z is 89, and 7 is 97. Note that zero is 90 and that a completely blank card column is 00. The 11 punctuation and miscellaneous symbols are translated to the 10, 20, 30, and 40 series shown. In numeric order this decimal system follows the same order as given in Fig. 9.4. This alphanumeric data can be sorted in such a system simply by comparing the magnitude of the dual decimal numbers representing them.

SECOND DIGIT

FIRST DIGIT	0	1	2	3	4	5	6	7	8	9
0	BLNK									
1									•	¤
2	&								$	*
3	−	/							,	%
4									#	@
5										
6		A	B	C	D	E	F	G	H	I
7		J	K	L	M	N	O	P	Q	R
8			S	T	U	V	W	X	Y	Z
9	0	1	2	3	4	5	6	7	8	9

FIG. 9.6. Set of the two-decimal-digit numbers corresponding to the IBM characters.

BUFFERING

Most input-output devices operate at rates considerably slower than the computers with which they are associated. It is obviously undesirable to have the computer wait while the input device reads data or the output device writes it. This is generally avoided by buffer storage between the input-output and the computer.

With buffering, the immediate input-output for the computer is essentially this buffer whose access time is compatible with other storage in the computer. Thus, for output purposes, a card of information would be loaded into an output buffer and the computer would continue its computing. Meanwhile, and in parallel, the output punch could be activated and would punch the output into the card, thus leaving the buffer available to receive another card of data. Similarly, an input instruction would read the contents of an input buffer into the computer and computation would proceed. At the same time, the input device would operate, reading in other information for subsequent use.

Buffers are quite widely used in computers and are important for efficient input-output. Another example of their use is in transferring information to and from tape units and main memory. In one system [11] the time to transfer a word to or from storage is 12 microseconds and the time to read or write a word from or on magnetic tape is 400 microseconds. When the word is read, it is stored in a buffer until a 12-microsecond interval is available to effect the transfer. This buffer loads up with the next word in 400 microseconds, etc. Actually two buffers are used, to prevent the need for stopping the tape unit between words.

Buffering is another example of parallel operations which speed over-all computer operation.

OTHER INPUT-OUTPUT DEVICES

In addition to the input-output media and devices developed originally for other applications, new media are being developed specifically for computers, to produce more rapid input-output and to make it easier to communicate with a computer.

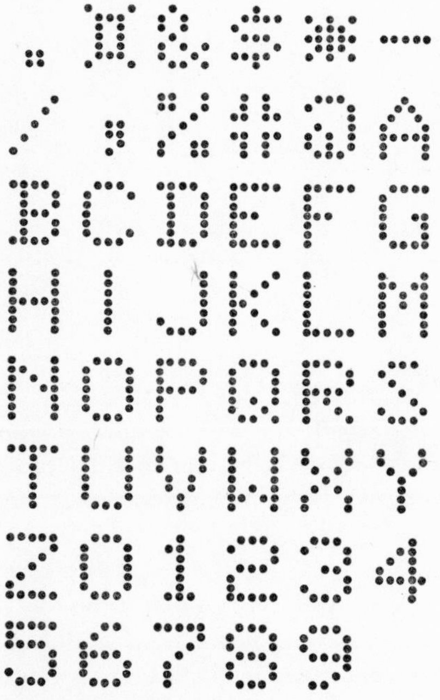

Cathode-ray Tube. Cathode-ray-tube devices are examples of this.[12] They permit a high rate of information display and are used in particular to provide a visual output display. Graphs or list data to be observed visually or photographed or otherwise reproduced for subsequent analysis are ideally displayed on cathode-ray tubes.

Another application is to project on the face of a cathode-ray tube numbers and characters to be photographically recorded.[13]

Optical. Other optical reading and display devices are being developed to provide rapid input and output. For example, optical devices are frequently used to read the holes in punched cards or punched paper tape at rates faster than mechanical switches would permit.

FIG. 9.7. 5-by-7 matrix representation of IBM characters.

Matrices. Many high-speed printing or data-presenting devices use a matrix of points to define characters. Examples of a 5-by-7 matrix representation is given in Fig. 9.7. The use of this system simplifies design problems and permits much faster rates of data presentation. Similarly, it can be used for storage of data for input to a computer or data-processing equipment. The Braille system used by the blind is simpler but not as easily recognized without special training. It will be noted that a 5-by-7 system uses 35 bits to represent a character in an easily recognized visual form and that over 34 billion combinations are possible. Only 46 of this number are used in Fig. 9.7.

Manual. Incidentally, most computers have some means for manual direct entry of information for editing or monitoring purposes. This may require use of a keyboard or the setting of switches, both obviously slow methods.

ON-LINE, OFF-LINE

The input-output equipment of a computer is sometimes referred to as *peripheral*. If operated and controlled by the computer itself, it is *in-line* or *on-line;* if operated independently of the computer, it is *off-line*. In relatively slow computer systems the input-output equipment is frequently on-line, even though such slow devices as typewriters are used for input-output. Others may use faster line printers.

However, to avoid holding up an expensive computer for time-consuming input operations, off-line input-output techniques are often used. For example, independent of the computer, a magnetic tape may be loaded with information from, say, punched cards. The tape is then connected into the computer system and the information read from it to the computer at a rate many times faster than the card-to-computer rate. The cost of using this technique is generally lower if there is a lot of input-output data. Similarly, output information, again on magnetic tapes, can be removed from the computer and unloaded off-line into punched cards, line printers, or typewriters. Indeed this use of magnetic tapes is essentially the only way of getting information into or out of some computers. It will be noted that magnetic-tape units actually are input-output devices in such a case, not merely secondary storage.

This off-line technique is the same as the use made of punched paper tape for off-line storage of information in the teletype system.

DECIMAL-TO-BINARY AND BINARY-TO-DECIMAL CONVERSION

We have noted that most number-handling systems use decimal numbers. All commerce, industry, and science is geared to this system. However, we noted further that although computers are basically binary, binary-coded-decimal representations are used to accommodate decimal numbers. Hence, although this now permits essentially decimal operation in binary computers, it is costly. It requires more equipment than a straight binary computer does. Further, a binary-coded-decimal computer is not as efficient as a binary computer, as each decimal digit requires four or more bits in the former while the latter uses an average of about 3⅓ bits per equivalent decimal digit.

For this and other reasons a number of binary computers are in use or in production. To permit such computers to accept decimal-data input, decimal-to-binary conversion is required. After the data is operated on in binary fashion in the computer, binary-to-decimal conversion is required to provide decimal output.

These conversions can be accomplished either (1) in the equipment used for input-output or (2) by the computer program. Generally a combination of both is used. For example, for each binary-coded-decimal digit read in a four-bit code, the equipment could store these four bits in a hexadecimal system. The computer program would convert this hexadecimal to binary. Assume that decimal 999 is read by the input device. Each 9 would be converted to 1001 for the 12-bit 1001 1001 1001 representation. This cannot be used directly but must be converted to 111 110 0111 before a binary computer can use it. Similarly, if such a number exists in a binary computer, the computer program must convert 111 110 0111 to 1001 1001 1001, which would then cause the output device to indicate 999. Obviously, binary-coded-decimal systems other than the 1-2-4-8 system could be used.

It would be possible to have all conversion done in the input-output equipment, and this is essentially what is done in so-called "decimal" computers in which four, five, or seven parallel bits form a binary-coded-decimal representation. However, in a binary computer general practice is to have decimal-to-binary and binary-to-decimal conversion routines. Computing time for such conversion must be taken into account when considering the use of a binary computer with decimal data. It is obviously most advantageous when the amount of input-output data is small and the amount of computing to be done relatively large. This is the case in many types of scientific and technical problems. However, where there is a large amount of input-output and a relatively small amount of computing involved, as in business data processing, this conversion becomes more inefficient. This is, of course, one of the reasons why computers intended for data processing or for both scientific and data-processing applications usually have decimal input-output. The design makes it unnecessary for the computer to convert to and from whatever internal binary system is used to true decimal and vice versa.

Of course, there are occasions when data is binary, such as that obtained from switch closures on an analog-to-digital converter. Generally, however, such data is converted within the equipment to computer form rather than through conversion routines.

PROBLEMS

1. Assume a computer capable of "reading" the letters, numbers, punctuation, etc., in this book. (Many computers have this ability.) Further, assume that these letters and punctuation marks are encountered serially in the same order that one would read them. Derive the logic involved in a program to distinguish the individual words in order. That is, if one or more letters are preceded and followed by a blank then those letters are a "word." If preceded by a blank and followed by a period or comma, then the word consists of the letters without the period or comma. Yet if a letter is followed by a hyphen, the hyphen is a part of the word, etc. This problem is not as trivial as it may appear.

2. One method of converting a natural binary to the usual 1-2-4-8 *bcd* uses a series of four-bit registers. The most significant digit of the binary number is shifted into the least significant of the right four-bit register. If the number in any register is 5 or more, 3 is added and the contents of the register is shifted left one place as the next least significant digit of the binary number is next shifted in. If less than 5, only the shifting takes place. The most significant digit of this four-bit register is the input to the least significant digit of the next four-bit register, etc. This process is repeated for each input digit. At any time the number in the four-bit registers will be the 1-2-4-8 *bcd* representation of the natural binary number. Try this out for yourself. How does it compare to the decimal conversion of Fig. 7.7? Can you devise a similar conversion system for some other *bcd* system, excess-three for example?

BIBLIOGRAPHY

The first three references and the Gruenberger reference are concerned primarily with punched-card operations. The other references generally consider other aspects of input-output equipment and techniques.

Anonymous: "Introduction to Data Processing," pp. 60–83, Haskin & Sells, New York, 1957.

Anonymous: "Machine Functions," Form 22-8208-2, International Business Machines, New York, 1954.

Berkeley, E. C.: "Giant Brains," pp. 42–64, John Wiley & Sons, Inc., New York, 1949.

Booth, A. D., and K. H. V. Booth: "Automatic Digital Calculators," pp. 61–74 and 175–179, Academic Press, Inc., New York, 1953.

Chapin, N.: "An Introduction to Automatic Digital Computers," pp. 73–105 and 321–349, D. Van Nostrand Company, Inc., Princeton, N.J., 1957.

Eckert, W. J., and R. Jones: "Faster, Faster," pp. 60–64 and 90–97, McGraw-Hill Book Company, Inc., New York, 1956.

Engineering Research Associates: "High-speed Computing Devices," pp. 385–418, McGraw-Hill Book Company, Inc., New York, 1950.

Gotlieb, C. C., and J. N. P. Hume: "High-speed Data Processing," pp. 171–187, McGraw-Hill Book Company, Inc., New York, 1958.

Gruenberger, F.: "Computing Manual," University of Wisconsin Press, Madison, Wis., 1952.

McCracken, D. D.: "Digital Computer Programming," pp. 132–149 and 227–230, John Wiley & Sons, Inc., New York, 1957.

Phister, M.: "Logical Design of Digital Computer," pp. 212–241, John Wiley & Sons, Inc., New York, 1958.

Richards, R. K.: "Arithmetic Operations in Digital Computers," pp. 286–290, D. Van Nostrand Company, Inc., Princeton, N.J., 1955.

Rubinoff, M., and R. H. Beter: Input and Output Equipment, *Control Eng.*, vol. 3, no. 11, pp. 115–123, November, 1956.

In many textbooks the components of an automatic digital computer are considered in an integrated manner. This makes it impractical to divide the material into the specific topics of this and the previous three chapters. For a review and different presentations on digital computer components refer to the following works.

Canning, R. G.: "Electronic Data Processing for Business and Industry," pp. 74–102, John Wiley & Sons, Inc., New York, 1957.

Engineering Research Associates, "High-speed Computing Devices," pp. 146–181, McGraw-Hill Book Company, Inc., New York, 1950.

Goode, H. H., and R. E. Machol: "System Engineering," pp. 214–243, McGraw-Hill Book Company, Inc., New York, 1957.

Gotlieb, C. C., and J. N. P. Hume: "High-speed Data Processing," pp. 32–61, McGraw-Hill Book Company, Inc., New York, 1958.

Livesley, R. K.: "Digital Computers," pp. 15–26, Cambridge University Press, New York, 1957.

Richards, R. K.: "Digital Computer Components and Circuits," pp. 36–262, D. Van Nostrand Company, Inc., Princeton, N.J., 1957.

Stibitz, G. R., and J. A. Larrivee: "Mathematics and Computers," pp. 95–127, McGraw-Hill Book Company, Inc., New York, 1956.

CHAPTER 10

Instructions

A digital computer requires a series of machine-language instructions to direct its operations. Each instruction consists of a set of digits or characters indicating the operation to be performed and the storage locations associated with that operation. Our consideration of instructions has to this point been meager. We have defined and used a minimum set of instructions as they may be used in a simple computer.

The number of instructions which can be executed by a computer represents a compromise between the designer's and user's requirements. The fewer the instructions, the easier it is to design and build the machine, but the more difficult (at least time-consuming) it is to code for it. Ease of coding is achieved with more instructions, but at the cost of more equipment in the computer. Simple computers generally have very few instructions in their repertory. The more sophisticated ones use a large number. For example, instead of the nine instructions of the academic set of Chapter 3, practical computers use 100 or more.

Although the nine or even fewer instructions are sufficient to perform all operations any larger set can do, it is not practical to use them. An operation which could be performed from a single instruction in a practical set might take many instructions if the limited academic set were used. This is not only wasteful of space for storing instructions but generally makes coding more difficult because of the likelihood of mistakes.

ADDRESS SYSTEMS

A one-address instruction system has been either explicit or implied in all previous discussion. Each instruction contained digits to indicate which of various possible operations was to be executed and one storage address to indicate the location of the word to be operated on. The definition of such instructions included reference to an accumulator as a storage register, for such a device is, in fact, present in the computer.

Although used almost exclusively, such a one-address instruction structure has limitations. In many problems the coding requires repetition of several single-address instructions. For example, using the operation code already presumed, the MULTIPLY operation "multiply the number in 21 by the number in 22 and put the product in 23" requires the following coding.

$$1 \ 0021$$
$$3 \ 0022$$
$$5 \ 0023$$

Multiple Addresses. A three-address instruction,[17] on the other hand, would have the form "take the number in a, operate on it with the number in b, and put the result in c." Obviously, this is well suited to the multiplication example given above. Assuming that the MULTIPLY operation is still representable by 3, this three-address instruction can be written

$$3 \ 021 \ 022 \ 023$$

in which the first digit refers to the operation to be performed and the three other sets refer to the three addresses. It will be noted that there is no need for the 1 and 5 instructions; they are implicit in the definition of the general three-address instruction. Further, no reference is made to an accumulator register, although the computer may continue to use one.

However, a three-address structure is not always so efficient. For example, if the operation required is simply to shift a number left or right, then the three-address instruction is wasteful. As another example, if it is desired to transfer a word from a to c, the general three-address instruction would be "take the number in a, add b to it, and put the result in c." The contents of b would be 0 and the addition would be useless.

The computer system heretofore considered is one in which, after one instruction is executed, the next instruction is taken from the next storage location in numerical order. The number of times that a deviation from this sequence is required has been assumed relatively small; hence specific instructions for conditional and unconditional transfer of control have been included in the instruction codes. However, there are cases (for example, *optimum coding*) for which it is advantageous to have each instruction include not only the data address but the address of the next instruction as well.[3] Such an instruction has the general form "take the word in address a and the word(s) in the accumulator, perform the operation indicated, leave the result in the accumulator, and go to b for the next instruction." Conditional transfer of control in such a system permits alternate branching to the next instruction in sequence. Although it contains two addresses, only one data address is referred to; hence this is generally called *modified one-address* operation, or a one-plus-one address, or augmented single-address instruction.

Some computers use *floating-reference addressing,* in which each instruction indicates the location of the next instruction not in an absolute sense, but relative to the present instruction. Thus it would include a number (*partial address*) to be added to the contents of the control counter, which would then indicate the location of the next instruction.

The concept of specifying in each instruction the location of the next instruction can be expanded to a four-address system, to wit: "Take the words from *a* and *b*, perform the operation indicated, transfer the result to *c*, and go to *d* for the next instruction." Again, conditional transfers can be used where required by considering the next storage location in sequence as the alternate address. This is sometimes called a *three-plus-one address* system.

Instruction and Word Size. In fixed-word-size computers the number of digits in an instruction is generally matched to the word size. For example, in a 10-decimal-digit machine, two digits can be used for the operation and four each for a data and an instruction address. However, two digits for the operation and four for the address would leave some *spare* positions, which could be used for special purposes such as control or input-output or peripheral-equipment designation.[4]

Some computers have two separate instructions in one word. This is practical, for example, in a 12-decimal-digit-word machine where each instruction contains two operation digits and one four-digit address.[6] It presents difficulties, however, when modifying instructions, for it is necessary to know if the desired instruction is on the left or on the right. Confusion and error can result. However, most computers, binary or decimal, use one instruction per word.

Address-modification Registers. Many programs for digital computers consist of a set of instructions in which the sequence of operations is repeated many times over; only the addresses of the information are altered. Frequently the information may come from or be sent to sequential storage locations. This may occur, for example, in doing the same processing on all items of a list.

A procedure for modifying addresses has already been illustrated as a portion of the red tape associated with preparing computer programs. However, the illustrated operation is so tedious, especially in one-address computers, that an alternate procedure involving special registers for address modification is often used instead. In this second method instructions in storage are not changed; rather, the contents of the special registers are used to modify them before the control unit receives and uses them. Different storage locations may be specified by changing the contents of the special registers. This makes coding easier, as one does not have to "worry through" the details of address modification.

The special registers used are called B (*base*) *registers* (B *box* is the English term) and *index registers* or *cycle counters*. In one computer the contents of the B *box* is added to the address in the instruction to obtain the address used by the control unit.[4] In other computers, the contents of *index registers* are subtracted to obtain the address actually used. The use of such devices naturally requires instructions for modifying the contents of the B or *index register*.[12]

Use of these registers provides not only means to count up or down (*cycle counting*) but usually also conditional transfers of control. For example, if an operation is to be repeated five times and involves information in five consecutive storage locations, B would be set to 4. After performing the first operation at location 4, the register would step down to 3 and repeat, etc., until the fifth storage location (0) had been used. Then the B box, in reducing one count further, would cause the program to switch away from this cycling and continue with the rest of the program. Index registers also can be modified by a single instruction by counts (*decrements*) other than one unit, making other kinds of conditional transfers possible.

The specific instructions to be so modified in executing a computer program must be identified in some unique manner. If there is only one special register, the simple device of modifying only negative instructions can be used. If there are more than one, the instruction itself must specify which register or registers are to modify the address. When the address is modified by more than one register, the resultant modification will be a combination of the contents of the registers specified.

MULTIPLE REGISTERS

Heretofore the arithmetic unit has been regarded as having only a single zero-access-time register. This is the accumulator, where, in general, one of the operands exists before the operation and where the result of the operation exists afterward. Further, the accumulator contains just one word. Such a single register, as far as coding is concerned, can be sufficient and indeed is so in some computers,[2] but it represents in many ways a minimum system.

Most computers have extra registers in the arithmetic unit to enhance the speed and versatility of the device. Although their number, type, use, and availability differ from one type of computer to another, some general characteristics may be given.

One-word-length accumulators are limited. For example, in a 10-digit-word computer, multiplication of a 10-digit number by a 10-digit number results in a 20-digit product; hence a two-word accumulator is required to store the full product. Of course, a single-word accumulator could be used if the 10 least significant digits are discarded. This would be the case when the arithmetic unit is *fractional;* if it is *integral,* the 10 least significant digits are retained.

Most computers, however, use a double-length accumulator (in effect, two registers) to retain the full product in multiplication. Similarly, a double-length accumulator is used in division to permit, for example, division of a 20-digit dividend by a 10-digit divisor to obtain a 10-digit quotient and a 10-digit remainder. The two halves of this double-length accumulator are designated in several ways: (1) as upper (UA) and lower (LA) accumulators,[3] (2) as A register and R register,[4] or (3) as accumulator (AC) and M-Q (multiplier-quotient) register.[12] Other combinations are possible. In multiplication and division, these double-length registers hold the dividend before division or the product after multiplication. However, the location of the multiplier before multiplication or the positions of the quotient and remainder after division vary from computer to computer. The designations R and M-Q are obvious, since the remainder is held in one system and the multiplier or quotient is held in another.

In many computers yet a third register for coding is also available. This is usually a separate one-word register called a distributor. The contents of the address referred to in the instruction are stored in it. This operand in the distributor combines with the contents of the accumulator to produce the result which is stored in the accumulator. The distributor is also called a D, or memory register. Its primary function is to hold temporarily information being transferred between the computer storage and the accumulator of the arithmetic unit. All words going to or from the arithmetic unit pass through the distributor.

Although a distributor is present in most computers, its availability and usefulness vary. In some it is present and its contents visible to the operator, but there is nothing in the instruction code which refers to it or indicates its presence. In other computers the distributor (or its equivalent) is separately available through the instructions. One method of doing this[3] is to make it addressable in the same manner as any other storage location, simply by assigning a number to it. By also making the two halves of the accumulator individually addressable, three interconnected zero-access-time registers are available in the arithmetic unit, whereby a number of basic operations (such as doubling a number) can be performed without reference to the relatively long access time of the main storage. This system has disadvantages, however, for although the distributor and the two halves of the accumulator are separately addressable, any information to or from them will disturb the contents of the distributor.

TYPES OF INSTRUCTIONS

The instructions used in a computer are variously categorized. The breakdown followed here is (1) arithmetic, (2) information transfer, (3) logical, (4) input-output, and (5) miscellaneous.

ARITHMETIC OPERATIONS

Addition, subtraction, multiplication, and division are the basic computer arithmetic operations. There are a few computers which do divide not directly but by a coded routine.[17] In these cases the equivalent of division is achieved by multiplying by the reciprocal of a number, which is obtained by an iterative process. On the other hand, some computers have a basic built-in square-root instruction in addition to the other basic arithmetic operations.

Absolute Value. The basic arithmetic operations are usually algebraic; that is, plus and minus signs are associated with the numbers being operated on. However, it is sometimes desirable to deal with the *absolute* value of numbers. In this case the numbers are considered to have no sign. In practice, they are all taken as positive. Absolute-value instructions are generally restricted to ADD and SUBTRACT instructions. "ADD absolute value" is one example; "RESET AND SUBTRACT absolute" is another.

Multiplication is generally available either with or without *round-off* or *half-adjust*. In a decimal machine, multiplication of one 10-digit number by another results in a 20-digit product if there is no round-off. However, if only the 10 most significant digits of the answer are required, the round-off operation will cause the tenth digit to increase by 1 if the eleventh digit is 5 or more. After this the 10 least significant digits will be erased. Similarly, in many machines round-off is available independently of the multiplication operation.

Division operations may have more than one form depending on how the remainder is handled. In many computers, as a result of division the quotient is in one register and the remainder in another. In single-register computers, the quotient is rounded off and the remainder lost.

SHIFT. SHIFT instructions are considered arithmetic since they are equivalent to multiplying by powers of the radix. For example, shifting a decimal register to the left three places is the same as multiplying by 1000. Similarly, a right shift of four places is the same as if the number had been multiplied by .0001. Most computers have SHIFT instructions for shifting right or left. The instructions differ as to the disposition of overflow and as to whether or not registers other than the basic accumulator register are involved in shifting. This may include the sign digit or overflow toggle. In our academic set of instructions only one register was involved and digits shifted off either end were lost—a fact often used to advantage. However, where two registers are used together as one double-length register, it can be arranged, if desired, that digits shifted off to the right are lost and not recoverable but that digits shifted off to the left reenter at the right of the double register. Another shifting system involves a single register in which digits shifted off the left reenter at the right. Generally, shifting significant digits off the left (most significant position) does not cause an overflow indication.

Shifting instructions are examples of *nonaddress* or *zero-address* instructions, in that the location of the data to be shifted does not have to be specified, since the SHIFT instruction involves only what is already in the accumulator. The address portion of the instruction normally contains digits indicating the number of places to be shifted.

INFORMATION TRANSFER

The ability to transfer numbers (words) between the arithmetic unit and storage is extremely important. All one-address computers have instructions which will bring the contents of a specified storage address and place it in the arithmetic unit. In cases where there is more than one register in the arithmetic unit, these instructions may refer to the registers by their individual addresses. Bringing a word from storage never alters the word in storage, which can be changed only by reading a new word in. It is a duplicate of the word in storage that is left in the arithmetic unit as the result of an instruction to transfer from storage.

Transferring a number from storage to the arithmetic unit generally results in adding the number to the number in the accumulator. Hence a TRANSFER instruction is actually an arithmetic operation. This accumulating is the basic ADD (or SUBTRACT) operation of the computer. Frequently the accumulator is cleared immediately before adding the contents of the storage location specified. Then the result is simply a trans-fer from storage to the arithmetic unit.

Transfer of information from the arithmetic unit to storage does not destroy the contents of the register in the arithmetic unit. Thus most computers also have a second instruction which causes the arithmetic unit register to be reset at 0 after transfer (duplication) of the information at the storage location specified. Such operations are sometimes called "to memory and hold" and "to memory and clear," respectively.

Clear and Erase. There is a distinction between *clear* and *erase*. Clearing means that all digits or characters of a word are filled with numerical 0s; erasing means that all bits for any digit or character have a zero value. In many computers these two conditions are the same; however, in an excess-three computer they are not, for numerical 0 is binary 3.

Return Address. An important facility of information transfer involves branching to some other storage location, executing the subroutine program there (see Chapter 12), and then returning automatically to the correct place in the main program. At the time of exit from the subroutine it is necessary to place a jump instruction whose address will be correct for return to the main program.

The information needed is present in the control unit of the computer. The control counter or equivalent device normally contains the address of the next instruction. It is necessary to transfer this information from the control unit to the arithmetic unit. Once there, the coding of link instructions for exiting to the subroutine and reentering from it is straightforward.

In a computer where the instructions are normally executed in sequence, one method of doing this is to have an instruction which will *record* the number of the control counter plus 1 as the address of an UNCONDITIONAL-TRANSFER instruction in a specified storage location *m*. Thus, with storage location *m* as the last instruction in the subroutine, the linking procedure would be to execute such a record instruction and then unconditionally transfer to the beginning of the subroutine.

Similarly, this *record* or *return-address* instruction could place the contents of the control counter—after it has advanced 1—into an arithmetic register of the computer. Other instructions can be used to form from it a return-address instruction which can be transferred to the end of the subroutine. Exit to the subroutine again would be by an unconditional transfer to the start of the subroutine.

There are also instructions where only the address digits of a word in the accumulator or similar arithmetic register will replace the corresponding digits of a word in a specified storage location. This *store-address* instruction facilitates address modification.

LOGICAL OPERATIONS

One important set of logical instructions are branching or transfer control instructions. These instructions, under specified conditions, cause the computer to branch to one or the other of two storage cells for the next instruction. In the academic set, the computer examined the contents of the accumulator; if zero or positive, it went on to the next instruction in order, but if negative, it cleared the accumulator and took its next instruction from the alternate address specified in the instruction. Most computers have several branch instructions, as there are a number of circumstances which the computer can examine in order to determine when and where to branch.

For example, the instruction may be, with regard to accumulator contents, "branch on zero," "branch on nonzero," "branch if positive," or "branch if negative." Moreover, the contents of the accumulator or corresponding register may be compared to the contents of some other storage register or cell. Thus, "transfer on equal," "transfer if less," or "transfer if more" are operations included in some computers.

The computer can sense other conditions to determine when to transfer control. For example, the computer may have switches which, depending on whether they are on or off when sensed, would result in transfer of control. This permits the operator to exercise some control of the problem and can also be used to monitor other processes. For example, if some input or output device were not ready to operate, the computer could sense this and go to some alternate program until it was ready. Similarly, a computer used for process control in an industrial plant would have to know the status of the process it is controlling.

Overflow as Conditional Transfer. Heretofore, causing a register to overflow by adding together two numbers whose sum is greater than the capacity of the register has been described as a situation to be avoided. In many computers, however, overflow serves a very useful purpose as a CONDITIONAL-TRANSFER control. After an operation has been performed which could cause an overflow, the computer can branch to a specified alternate address or go to the next address in order, depending on whether an overflow had occurred. The overflow itself is sometimes stored in an *overflow toggle,* which is then sensed to determine if an overflow has occurred.

Overflow can be used for tallying. The number used for tallying would contain a tens complement of the desired tally; for example, a three tally is 999 999 9997 in a 10-digit machine. When 1 is added the first or second time, no overflow occurs. However, adding 1 a third time will cause an overflow, indicating that the count of 3 has been attained.

Another use is in floating-decimal operations (Chapter 11). When two numbers are added and an overflow occurs, the most significant digit of the sum is lost. However, it is always a 1; thus the overflow can cause this digit to be added in, and the corresponding realignment of numbers and altering of exponents can be accomplished.

EXTRACT. Another logical instruction is the EXTRACT or logical-multiplier type. In general, the EXTRACT operation results in a digit-by-digit modification of a word as the result of a comparison with another (*extractor*) word. It is frequently used to separate different items of information stored in a single word. Assume that an employee's payroll number (0278), his salary scale code (142), and the number of hours he has worked (080), are packed into one 10-digit word thus: 0278 142 080. This would define the gross pay due that individual during the pay period. However, the computer would need the three items of information separately to make the computation. One type of EXTRACT instruction would use 0000000111 as the extractor, where a 1 in the extractor would cause the corresponding decimal digit in the word being extracted to remain unaltered and a 0 would cause that digit to be set to 0. Thus the result of the EXTRACT would be 080 as the number of hours worked. Similarly, 0000111000 as an extractor would result in 0000 142 000, which separates the salary code from the original packed word. Lastly, 1111000000 is used to recover the payroll number 0278 000 000.

This general type of operation is frequently called logical multiplication. Each digit in the output is the result of the multiplication of the corresponding digit in the input by either 1 or 0.

Other logical operations are available in some binary computers. A logical AND instruction would cause each digit of the extractor to be compared logically with the corresponding digit in the original word. If there is a 1 in both, the extracted word will have a 1 in that position; if not, there will be a 0. Thus 0110 and 1010 in a logical AND operation both result in 0010. Notice that this corresponds basically to logical multiplication. Similarly a logical OR instruction will have a 1 in each position of the output if either the original word or the extractor contains a 1. For example, 0110 and 1010 would result in 1110 in a logical OR operation.

The essential characteristic of such logical operations is that they are digit-by-digit operations in which the result in one position does not depend on or influence the result in any other position.

INPUT-OUTPUT INSTRUCTIONS

There are many kinds of input-output instructions. An important computer factor is ability to communicate with input-output devices. The more sophisticated the computer, the larger the repertory of input-output instructions.

It is difficult to generalize in this area. Specific techniques for input-output differ considerably from one computer to another. They are a function, certainly, of the number and kind of input-output devices. For example, a punched-paper-tape computer has quite a different communication problem from that of a punched-card computer.

Input-output instructions are generally READ, WRITE, and CONTROL. The WRITE instructions, of course, are punch instructions for paper tape or card output. The control operations would include REWIND, SEARCH for a specific block address, and BACKSPACE ONE BLOCK for magnetic tapes. They could also include control functions for a typewriter or tabulating-machine output.

Addressing Input-Output Devices. One important consideration is how a coder specifies an input-output device. One method is to have certain nonaddress, nonoperation digits in the instruction word designate the device. Obviously, unique digits or characters in the operation portion of the instruction word can also be used to address input-output. Still another generally used method is to designate input-output units through the address portion of the instruction. Thus, in addition to the addresses used for the storage associated with the computer, other addresses are used for various input-output devices.

Buffering. Another consideration involves whether the input-output device is buffered from the computer. Since many input-output devices are comparatively slow in comparison with the computer itself, it is generally inefficient to have the computer stop while, for example, waiting for a card to be read or punched. A preferable arrangement is to store the information going to or from the input-output device in a buffer register. This can be done at the relatively rapid internal speed of the computer. Having loaded or unloaded the buffer, the computer can continue its operation while independently and in parallel the buffer unloads or loads to or from the input-output device. In such a buffered system, the computer would not directly cause, for example, a punched card to be punched. The computer would write its information into the buffer register and continue computing. The card punch would activate and punch the information from the buffer into the card and await the next new set of information. Other buffered devices would operate in a similar manner. The use of buffers means that the instruction refers to the buffer, not to the input-output device directly.

MISCELLANEOUS INSTRUCTIONS

Some instructions in most computers fall outside the limits of the previous categories.

Table Look-up. In many problems the desired output is somewhat arbitrarily related to the input. For example, the amount of withholding tax per pay period depends on the gross pay and number of dependents and is generally given in a table. It is not practical to use a mathematical formula to compute withholding tax as a function of the *argument* (income and dependents). Another example is a salary table in terms of different job classifications, in-grade promotions, and longevity. In using a computer in these or similar cases, a table-look-up operation must be performed.

One way of doing this in the withholding-tax example is to store the amounts to be withheld in consecutive storage locations and have the addresses of these locations depend on the gross income and number of dependents. For example, if there are 25 ranges of gross salary and eight different dependent categories, 200 storage locations would be required. The routine for such a table look-up can be coded using the instructions already considered.

However, in many table-look-up operations the argument designations are so arbitrary or irregular that it is difficult to use them to determine the storage location containing the desired answer. To facilitate this operation, a table-look-up instruction is available in one computer.[3] In it, the argument for which a search is to be made is stored in an arithmetic register. The arguments are stored in order, in consecutive storage locations. The computer instruction specifies the location of the first argument in the table, and the computer goes to that location and searches through the succeeding storage locations until it finds an argument which is equal to or, if no equal exists, higher than the first. The address of this argument is recorded in another arithmetic register.

This greatly facilitates certain types of table-look-up operations, although many such operations are better done with instructions normally available in a computer.

No Operation. Most computers have instructions whereby the computer performs no operation but merely steps to the next instruction.

Also known as IGNORE instructions, they generally serve no useful purpose in themselves but are used temporarily to take the place of other instructions when checking out a problem or to fill gaps when something is removed.

STOP. STOP or HALT instructions in some computers are conditional. For example, with an external switch in one position, the computer will stop; if the switch is in another position, the STOP would be ignored. Some STOP instructions specify a jump to be performed on restarting; some simply cause the computer to stop.

BIBLIOGRAPHY

The specific, detailed instructions which will be executed by any digital computer are given in the operation or programming manuals of the manufacturer. The student is encouraged to obtain such manuals for any computer(s) of special interest to him. In addition each of the references below includes the definition of a set of instructions which is much more practical and useful than the minimum set given in Chapter 3. A comparative study of them will indicate the general nature of instructions which are useful in more than an academic sense.

Booth, A. D., and K. H. V. Booth: "Automatic Digital Calculators," pp. 144–157, Academic Press, Inc., New York, 1953.

Canning, R. G.: "Electronic Data Processing for Business and Industry," pp. 103–133, John Wiley & Sons, Inc., New York, 1957.

Chapin, N.: "An Introduction to Automatic Digital Computers," pp. 386–398, D. Van Nostrand Company, Inc., Princeton, N.J., 1955.

Eckert, W. J., and R. Jones: "Faster, Faster," pp. 145–148, McGraw-Hill Book Company, Inc., New York, 1956.

Engineering Research Associates: "High-speed Computing Devices," pp. 56–73, McGraw-Hill Book Company, Inc., New York, 1950.

Goode, H. H., and R. E. Machol: "System Engineering," pp. 244–257, D. Van Nostrand Company, Inc., Princeton, N.J., 1957.

Gotlieb, C. C., and J. N. P. Hume: "High-speed Data Processing," pp. 78–94 and 187–188, McGraw-Hill Book Company, Inc., New York, 1958.

McCracken, D. D.: "Digital Computer Programming," pp. 98–110 and 219–226, John Wiley & Sons, Inc., New York, 1957.

Richards, R. K.: "Arithmetic Operations in Digital Computers," pp. 377–378, D. Van Nostrand Company, Inc., Princeton, N.J., 1955.

Wegstein, J. H., and S. N. Alexander: Programming Scientific Calculators. *Control Eng.*, vol. 3, no. 5, pp. 87–92, May, 1956.

CHAPTER 11

Accuracy, Precision, Checking

A review of digital computers and their applications must include consideration of the validity of the answers obtained. Assuring that the results are valid is of importance to the designer, builder, and user. A reasonable portion of initial and operating costs is devoted to assuring valid answers.

In this chapter validity will be treated in terms of equipment that is, or can be, built into the computer itself. In the next chapter means other than equipment will be considered.

ERROR, MISTAKE, MALFUNCTION

Deviation from the correct answer can be caused by (1) imprecise mathematical procedure, that is, some *error* in the method used, (2) a *mistake* of the human programmer, coder, or operator, or (3) computer *malfunction*. These distinctions among *error*, *mistake*, and *malfunction* are generally accepted and will be used here. It does seem a shame, though, that to err is no longer exclusively human.

Certain aspects of the validity of answers, such as the study of error analysis, are beyond the scope of this text. The errors due to the approximations necessary to permit "simple-minded" digital computers to solve involved and abstruse mathematical problems need to be known. Error studies, however, can be quite involved and hence will not be considered in detail here, although certain limited aspects will be mentioned.

The error in any computation depends on the precision and range of the numbers involved. Even mathematically simple problems are subject to errors. Computers are, or can be, built to reduce these errors by means of *floating-point* and *multiple-precision* techniques. Human mis-takes are considered elsewhere in this text. As yet little has been done to compensate for human frailty by means of equipment.

152

Computer malfunction, on the other hand, has been thoroughly investigated, and all modern computers have some means for checking malfunctions. Checking is very important both to the computer operation itself and to the various applications. Here we have to depart from the definition of "error" given above, since devices for checking computer malfunctions are generally referred to as "error-checking" devices. The term *validity checking* is sometimes used [3] to avoid this conflict.

FLOATING-POINT OPERATIONS

The size of the word (its number of digits) in many digital computers is fixed, insofar as arithmetic operations are concerned. Commonly used word sizes are 10–12 decimal digits and 30–40 binary bits. This has proved to be a reasonable compromise and one that considers the requirements both of the user and the designer. Many operations can be fitted into this range. Of course, the scaling of a problem in a fixed-decimal-point operation—on the one hand, to prevent overflowing the register and, on the other, to prevent losing significance—is frequently difficult and time-consuming. There are occasions, also, when ordinary fixed-point operation will not give the desired accuracy over the desired range. When this occurs, there are two other general techniques available, floating-point or multiple-precision computation.

As previously mentioned, fixed-point operation means that the numbers in the computation have decimal points which, for a given parameter, do not change throughout the problem. The coder knows where the decimal point is and scales appropriately, and he, not the computer, keeps track of it. However, since the computer is adept at keeping account of other figures, obviously it might also keep track of the decimal point and, further, always place it in an optimum place for each computation. Since the location of the decimal point may change from one operation to another, this method is generally called *floating point*. In business applications of the same sort it is called *floating dollar sign*.

Notation. All numbers can be expressed as a fraction less than 1 but more than one-tenth, times some integral power of 10. This notation (examples are given in Table 11.1A) is similar to that frequently used in practical engineering representation of data for the ease of computation. The engineering system uses a number between 1 and 10 with the appropriate exponent base 10. Although floating-decimal-point computers have been built using this system, general practice is to express the number as a fraction less than 1, since most computer designers and users are familiar with fractional operation.

Table 11.1. Floating-decimal Notation and Examples

(A)	$236 =$	$.236 \times 10^3$
	$-1107 =$	$-.1107 \times 10^4$
	$-.0127 =$	$-.127 \times 10^{-1}$
(B)	$236 =$	2360000053
	$-1107 =$	-1107000054
	$-.0127 =$	-1270000049
(C)	$236 =$	0236000054
	$-1107 =$	-1107000054
		-0871000054
	$-871 =$	-8710000053
(D)	$236 =$	2360000053
	$-.0127 =$	-1270000049
		-0309720052
	$-3.0972 =$	-3097200051
(E)	$83.7 =$	8370000052
	$20.7 =$	$\vdots 2070000052$
		$* \vdots 0440000052$
	$104.4 =$	1044000053

* Overflow.

The two important phases of floating-point notation have various names. Because of their analogy with logarithms, the two parts are sometimes called *mantissa* and *characteristic,* respectively, but since this analogy is rather forced, the practice is not universal. Various mixed systems, such as *mantissa* and *exponent,* are sometimes used. The terms *digits* and *exponents* are also useful, particularly when pertaining to an integral arithmetic unit. We will use the terms *fractional* and *exponent* parts.

To permit a computer to handle such numbers we need not show the decimal point nor the 10 itself. Thus the number 236 is defined adequately by the fractional part 236 and the exponent 3. Further, it is generally desired to include the fractional part as well as the exponent in one word. However, a word contains only one sign; hence it is not possible to carry an exponent negative sign if there is a negative sign associated with the quantity itself. It is common practice, therefore, to assume a value of 50 added to the actual power of 10 associated with a decimal number, that is, to *bias the characteristic.* The result, as shown in Table 11.1*B*, is that a 10-digit word contains eight digits for the fractional part and two for the exponent, which denotes the location of the decimal point. This permits the numbers to range from about 10^{+50} to

10^{-50} and yet be contained in a 10-digit word. This is an adequate range for most purposes. It is certainly far less restrictive than fixed-point operation.

Although the range in floating point is quite large, it is possible to obtain numbers which exceed this range. A number which is too small (yet is not 0) will cause an "underflow." This generally occurs because of a mistake in the program and must be anticipated in order to take appropriate corrective action.

Manipulations. Floating point can either be programmed or built into the computer. The latter is more desirable, for then floating point can be done operationally as easily as fixed point. Further, it generally takes no more time (frequently less) to perform the arithmetic operations. The obvious disadvantage is the additional equipment required.

If not built in, floating point can be programmed as a subroutine (see Chapter 12), but since each floating-point operation consists of many fixed-point operations, floating-point operation is thereby much slower. Many fixed-point computers have special instructions to facilitate floating-point programming.

The nature of these instructions will be indicated by examples. First, Table 11.1C shows how the computer adds 236 and 1107 in floating form. Since the exponents are not equal, before the addition is performed the smaller number is shifted right until the exponents match. The addition is done only on the fractional part; the exponents are not altered. As shown, the 236 000 0053 becomes 023 600 0054 to permit adding it to −110 700 0054. The immediate result, −087 100 0054, is not in final form. The *normal (standard)* form of a floating-decimal number has a non-0 in the most significant position. Thus −087 100 0054 must be normalized (standardized) to −871 000 0053.

To facilitate normalization, many computers have a special instruction—sometimes called a *cyclic, logical,* or *nonarithmetic shift*—that counts the positions the number must be shifted left to be normalized. This count is then used to modify the exponent. Where floating-decimal operation is built into the equipment, no special programming is needed.

Normalization is also required in multiplication. The example of Table 11.1D illustrates floating-decimal multiplication of 236 and −.0127. Assuming a fractional computer, the product of 236 000 00 and 127 000 00 is 030 972 00. This fractional part must be normalized to obtain the correct answer. Note also that in multiplication the exponents are summed and 50 is *subtracted* to obtain the exponent of the product. In division the exponent associated with the divisor is subtracted from that of the dividend and 50 is *added* to this difference.

Floating-point operations require special representation for 0. Obviously, this is one number which cannot be normalized. A mid-range exponent value is sometimes assigned to it.

Floating-decimal operations must provide for other ramifications. For example, in addition or subtraction (Table 11.1E) overflow may occur. If it does, the sum must be shifted right and the value of the exponent increased by 1. Further, overflow indicates that the most significant digit in the sum (always a 1) has been lost. It must be replaced when the sum is shifted right and the exponent changed. Again, in some computers without built-in floating decimal, a special instruction facilitates addition of this 1. The usefulness of the floating-decimal system is so great that it is widely employed for many classes of problems, even though designing or programming for it is far from trivial.

Although the examples given have been for a 10-decimal-digit machine, similar schemes can be used in binary computers or decimal computers of other word lengths. Further, the exponent (of 2 or of 10) could be at the left in the word instead of the right, since the computer must separate and act on each individually.

Significance. In our example of a 10-decimal-digit register maximum possible significance is eight digits, and it can be much less. The loss of significance is marked, for example, when the difference between two numbers of about the same value is taken. The unnormalized form may have several 0s at the left which, when normalized, would result in 0s at the right. Subsequent operations may result in non-0 digits at the right, although the answer is no more significant. This loss of significance in floating-point operations is frequently considered disadvantageous. Certainly one needs to know more about the significance of numbers to code for fixed-point operation. Of course, it is possible to have the computer keep account of the decimal point and determine how significant the answers may be as well.

Floating point permits handling of numbers over a wide range of values—but to a limited precision.

MULTIPLE PRECISION

The precision of the numbers handled often must be in excess of that implied by the basic word size of a computer. In a 10-decimal-digit machine these 10 digits are the maximum number of significant figures in ordinary (single-precision) operations. Thus addition or subtraction results in 10-decimal-digit sums and differences; multiplication will have a 20-decimal-digit product, and division of a 20-digit dividend by a 10-digit divisor produces a 10-decimal-digit quotient and a 10-digit remainder. Multiple-precision operations occur where twice as many digits (double precision), three times as many (triple precision), etc., are possible for each basic arithmetic operation. This is achieved by a sequence of single-precision operations. However, one computer at least [16] has some built-in multiple precision.

Table 11.2. Multiple-precision Addition

	a	b	
	xxxxx	xxxxx	
	c	d	
	xxxxx	xxxxx	
	carry ⤵		
		xxxxx	← $b + d$
$a + c$ →	xxxxx		
e →	xxxxx	xxxxx	← f

Addition. For example, as shown in Table 11.2, consider *double-precision (double-length)* addition. Let the letters a through f represent single-length words. First let a represent the 10 most significant digits of a 20-digit number in which b represents the least significant digits. Similarly, c and d represent another 20-digit word. Addition is achieved by the following single-precision operations. First b is added to d and the sum stored in f as the 10 least significant digits of the sum, and the overflow (if any) is noted. Next a is added to c and the overflow from $b + d$ is added to this to obtain the most significant digits denoted as e. This technique can obviously be extended to higher orders of precision. Note that the sign associated with a multiple-precision word must be determined separately.

Multiplication. Double-precision multiplication is illustrated similarly in Table 11.3. In this case, the 20-digit word represented by 10-digit

Table 11.3. Multiple Multiplication

	a	b		
	xxxxx	xxxxx		
	c	d		
	xxxxx	xxxxx		
carry →	xxxxx	xxxxx	← $b \cdot d$	
carry → xxxxx	xxxxx	← $a \cdot d$		
	xxxxx	xxxxx	← $b \cdot c$	
xxxxx	xxxxx	← $a \cdot c$		
g	h	i	j	
xxxxx	xxxxx	xxxxx	xxxxx	

words a and b is multiplied by 20-digit c and d. The 40-digit product will be stored in four single-precision 10-digit words g, h, i, and j. First b is multiplied by d and the 10 least significant digits of this product are j. Next c is multiplied by b and a by d. The 10 least significant digits of these products are added to the 10 most significant from $b \times d$. The sum (disregarding overflow) is the i portion of the double-precision product. Now a is multiplied by c and the 10 least significant digits of this product are added to the 10 most significant from $c \times b$ and $a \times d$. Also, the overflow which may have occurred in forming i must also be added. This results in the value for h. The 10 most significant digits from $a \times c$ along with the overflow from the formation of h will determine g. This, too, can be extended for multiple-precision operations, but it gets difficult as the order increases.

Multiple-precision division is also possible. It is, comparatively speaking, very difficult to do. The procedure for double precision (40-digit dividend and 20-digit divisor yielding 20-digit quotient and 20-digit remainder) is left as an exercise for those interested. Extension to general multiple-precision operations is also left open.

Multiple-precision operations are not often used and hence are generally programmed rather than built into the computer. The proper use of single-precision operations is sufficient for most purposes. There are problems, however, such as inverting large matrices, for which the solution requires many arithmetic operations in which significance can be lost through the propagation of round-off errors. Assurance of reasonable significance in the answer may require double precision in intermediate operations. Multiple precision to a high order is required in some rather academic investigations, such as determining the value of π to thousands of decimal places.

CHECKING

The validity of a computation must often be checked. In this chapter means and techniques for checking machine malfunctions is the primary concern. However, we will also consider some aspects of mathematical checks and of errors in certain mathematical methods. The third general area affecting validity, that is, human mistakes, will be taken up in the next chapter.

Reliability. Malfunctions of digital computers must be checked not because they occur frequently but because of the great damage a single malfunction can cause. Actually, digital computers malfunction less than most devices which are considered so reliable that no checking is required, such as hand-operated calculators. A digital computer is so fast that in a few hours it can do more operations than such a calculator can do in a lifetime of operation.

A human may make a mistake once in 10^3 (1000) operations. A computer malfunction rate must be less than one in 10^{12} (1,000,000,000,000). Even though malfunctions thus occur extremely rarely on a per-operation basis, the tremendous speed of computers means that they can occur often enough to require checking.

The basis for all checking is redundance. More than the basic job is done. This excess provides the check. Redundancy can be of two general forms (1) additional operations in the calculation or (2) additional equipment in the computer. Although all computers have some built-in checks, some have more than others. "Business" type computers usually have more than "scientific" computers. However, it is difficult to generalize, since the differences between the two computers are becoming less and less. The progressively improved reliability of computer components has made built-in checking less important.

Programmed checks are used to supplement built-in checks when there is a need. This permits great flexibility in checking, particularly when the programmed check does not operate until the built-in check indicates a fault.

Checking of Scientific Problems. Despite high reliability and hence an extremely small possibility of malfunction, some malfunctions are bound to occur. How serious this may be depends on several factors. In many scientific computations this is less serious than it would be in business applications. For example, if in the solution of a scientific problem where the result of one computation is independent of a similar computation on other data, a wrong answer can easily be tolerated. Many scientists realize the possibility of experimental error in input data; hence they are more likely to recognize and allow for the result of a computer malfunction in the output. They check only to see that the answers are reasonable and consistent or that they show continuity or smoothness. Frequently, since the data refer to a physical system, checks may merely consist of noting whether the indicated result is physically possible.

There are types of scientific problems in which an error in one step will not prevent obtaining the correct answer. This is true of certain iterative procedures which are strongly convergent (self-correcting). For example, taking the square root of a number is a rapidly convergent iterative procedure. If the square root of .01 is computed with a 10-decimal-digit computer and the first approximation is .999 999 9998, subsequent approximations will be .505 000 0000, .262 400 9900, .150 255 3012, .108 404 3468, .100 325 7852, .100 000 5290, and finally, .100 000 0000. However, assume that there is a computer malfunction and that the third computed approximation is .550 255 3012 instead of .150 255 3012. Subsequent approximations would then be .084 214 3418, .101 479 4808, .100 000 0006, and finally, .100 000 0000. Notice that convergence led to the correct answer despite the perturbation, taking the same number of steps as if the intermediate error had not occurred. Mathematical procedures which will arrive at the correct answer despite such errors are said to *settle*.

Other types of scientific problems are nonsettling, and an error in an intermediate result will be propagated as an *inherited error* into later results at the same or even larger magnitude. The solution of differential equations is such an example. Since such equations involve not only the basic parameters themselves but their rates of change as well, the solution for a specific value of a parameter usually depends on previously computed values involved in the rates of change. Thus an error for one value will induce an error in subsequent answers as well. Actually, an error causes the computer to solve a different differential equation than the original one. These mathematical errors may be due to the round-off of the numbers used and the *truncation error* (the error due to the approximation used for the integration process).

Business Problem Checking. In business applications the consequences of an error are considered more serious. A check for $1,000,032.17, if the correct amount were $32.17, would be looked on dimly by most bankers. In accounting, the general rule is that figures must "balance to the cent." Thus a bank's assets may be listed as $347,986,531.21 (implying 11 significant digits) when actually the values are not known that precisely.

In business applications, one wrong number among many thousands could cause the books not to balance, and this is considered intolerable. However, there is a growing tendency to rely more on mathematical significance than on the "its-got-to-balance-to-the-cent" attitude which is, and has been, the basis for business record keeping. Nevertheless, no rapid changes can be expected, as there is so much precedent for existing procedures. Legal concepts and auditing principles would be affected if it was admitted that the actual assets of a bank were not known to 11 significant figures. Even the scientist who is tolerant of an error in the data he gets from a computer has an entirely different attitude if his pay check differs from what it should be, especially if the mistake causes it to be "short."

Mathematical Checks. An example of a mathematical check on data is the general technique of *differencing*. This is a form of the smoothness test. An elementary example is given in Table 11.4, where the squares of the digits 1 through 9 are given. The first difference between the squares (D_1) results in 3, 5, 7, and so on. Doing this again results in a second difference (D_2) of 2 in all cases. However, as also shown in Table 11.4 if an error occurs (the square of 5 is indicated as 26 instead

Table 11.4. Use of Difference to Detect Errors in Data

	Correct			Incorrect		
n	n^2	D_1	D_2	n^2	D_1	D_2
1	1			1		
		3			3	
2	4		2	4		2
		5			5	
3	9		2	9		2
		7			7	
4	16		2	16		3
		9			10	
5	25		2	26		0
		11			10	
6	36		2	36		3
		13			13	
7	49		2	49		2
		15			15	
8	64		2	64		2
		17			17	
9	81			81		

of 25), then the second difference is not constant. This kind of check is used in many forms.

Another mathematical checking technique involves *complementary* operations. For example, if a program requires addition, multiplication, and square-root operations, then the answer could also be checked by squaring, dividing, and subtracting and then comparing with the original data. Again, agreement within the accuracy of the computations would be required. This method has the obvious advantage of requiring a different set of operations to be performed in checking than in the original solution, thus minimizing the possibility of the same malfunction occurring twice.

These and other checking systems which essentially require the problem to be done twice have an obvious disadvantage: The indicated error may be in the checking procedure, or in the equipment itself. Thus, more malfunctions are indicated than occur in the basic computer.

Another mathematical check which does not require complete duplication and is useful for checking decimal calculations involves *casting out nines*. It uses the residual modulus nine (*rmn*), which is the remainder after each of the numbers is divided by 9. Consider this addition problem:

535	remainder 4
129	remainder 3
664	remainder 7

Note that the *rmn* of each of the two numbers checks with that of the sum. Similarly, if they had been multiplied

535	remainder 4
129	remainder 3
69,015	remainder 3

This checks also, since the product of 4 × 3 is 12, which is 3 *rmn*. Comparable rules could be used for subtraction or division.

Actual division of the entire number by 9 is not required. The digits of the number, when added, have the same remainder as if the entire number had been divided by 9. Thus, using the examples again, the sum of the digits in 535 is 13 (giving an *rmn* of 4) and in 129 is 12 (*rmn* 3).

Duplication. A simple example of complete redundance would be where each operation is done twice and the two results compared. If they disagree, a malfunction is indicated. This, of course, fails if the same malfunction occurs in both computations. This method requires nothing redundant in the computer itself but rather in the computer program. Moreover, it takes longer to solve the problem. Similarly, two separate computers could be used to solve the same problem, with step-by-step comparison. Again, disagreement would indicate a malfunction. Such complete duplication is generally considered impractical because of the obvious expense. However, *companion* (*twin*) *arithmetic units* which, for checking purposes, duplicate the operations of the regular unit are sometimes used.[6]

Parity Checks. Fortunately, there are many useful and widely employed checks which do not require complete duplication or 100 per cent redundancy. One popular check employs the principle of *parity;* that is, it causes all numbers or characters to be equal in some manner. An example already considered is the character systems of Chapter 9. Although only six bits are required for the basic information, seven are used. The last, *check bit,* is added by the machine to assure that all characters contain an odd number of 1s. An even number of 1s may be

used for checking. For this reason, it is sometimes known as an *odd-even check*. Circuitry for testing to see if there is an odd or even number of 1s provides a good check. Of course, two simultaneous errors could occur, and they would be unde-
tectable. Odd-even checking is used where such a possibility is negligible. An odd number of 1s is sometimes used in preference to an even number, since complete failure would result in all 0s, which is an even (zero) number of 1s. This can be avoided in an even check by having the checking system also assure that there is at least one 1 in the character or number.

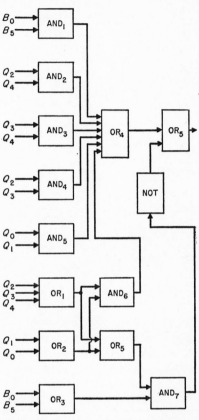

Various parity checks have been considered in other parts of this text. The ability to provide a check was one of the important considerations of the binary-coded-decimal systems considered in Chapter 4. As a matter of fact, this is the sole reason that five- or seven-bit codes are used when four is more than sufficient to represent 10 numbers. The checks used were parity—all numbers have two 1s and only two 1s. The logical circuit for making this check in the biquinary system [3] is shown in Fig. 11.1. It checks that one and only one of the two *bi* bits (B_0 and B_5)

FIG. 11.1. Logical circuit to check for one *bi* bit and one *quinary* bit of the bi-quinary code.

and one and only one of the five *quinary* bits (Q_0, Q_1, Q_2, Q_3, and Q_4) are 1. It is suggested that various wrong combinations be tried to demonstrate how this checking is accomplished. This is called a *validity* check.

Parity checks are also frequently used with magnetic tapes. Generally the tape will have several parallel tracks including one to provide *lateral parity*. This would be analogous to the seven-bit system just discussed. In addition, however, *longitudinal parity* checking could also be used. In this case, each row would be checked for parity after a certain number of digits in a field or block has been read in. An example [5] is given in

Fig. 11.2. Each of the six characters in the field has a lateral parity check indicated in the top row. This permits a check on each character as it is stored or read from the record. In addition, at the end of the field an extra column provides a longitudinal check on the entire field. Thus although double errors would be undetected in either system, the possibility is very small that they would be undetected in a system that checks both ways.

Obviously, this double-checking system would be used only in a storage system where the error rate is high enough to make simultaneous failures significant. Relatively speaking, magnetic tapes are more likely to malfunction than other storage devices.

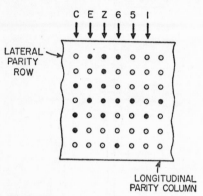

Summation Check. Another checking procedure is *summation checking*. For example, after a group of numbers is placed on magnetic tape, a programmed check is

Fig. 11.2. Basic example of both longitudinal and lateral parity checking for magnetic tape.

often made to determine that the numbers are correctly recorded. The numbers in storage would be summed (ignoring overflow) and the sum recorded along with the numbers. Subsequently, the numbers could be read back from magnetic tape and again summed. The two sums, of course, must agree. Sometimes examination of the difference between them is useful in determining the error. This kind of check is sometimes called a *hash total*.

Forbidden-combination Checks. In a decimal computer there is some redundancy in representing the 10 states with four bits, since four bits will accommodate 16 different states. Hence, in a 1-2-4-8 code, the six combinations 1010 through 1111 are generally not used; they may be considered *forbidden*.[4] If such a combination occurs it can be detected as an "error."

The forbidden-combination check is, however, limited. In the 1-2-4-8 example, if the correct number is 5 with the 1 and 4 toggles on, then an error would be indicated if the 8 toggle was on instead of the 1 (forbidden combination of 12) but would not if the 2 were on instead of the 1 (a combination of 6, which is not forbidden). Similarly, other binary-coded-decimal systems allow forbidden-combination checks. An excess-three computer could simply check for 0000 and 1111, as they are the most likely failures.

Even in non-*bcd* computers it is possible, by mistake or malfunction, to obtain invalid digits or characters which the computer tries to interpret as instructions. These *unallowable order (instruction) digits, improper commands, improper operation codes,* or *unused orders (instructions)*, as they are variously called, are detected by the computer and cause it to stop. Various other terms are used to describe these combinations, including *false code, nonexistent code,* or *unused code.*

Error-detecting and -correcting.* Generally if an "error" is detected it causes the computer to stop and await further instructions. Sometimes the malfunction is so serious that this is the only practical recourse. However, many times the malfunction is temporary. It may be caused by a transient condition in the computer or it may be a random error. If the operation which failed were repeated, it would quite likely be correct. Thus it is obviously desirable not only to have the computer detect malfunctions but also to correct them. It can do this in various ways.

For example, if, in reading a block of information from a magnetic tape, the sum check fails, the computer can cause the information to be reread and checked again. It is likely that it will pass the check the second time. However, the checking programming must take into account the fact that it may continue indefinitely to fail. In case of such a "hang-up," human intervention is required.

In some computers, failure on a validity check will cause the computer to go to a specific location for a further instruction. This instruction could be to restart the program or to use some other method of correcting the difficulty and then to continue with the problem. Of course, the fact that such a malfunction had been detected—even though subsequently corrected—is recorded, for it may well be an indication of marginal operation rather than a random error.

Even more elaborate check indicator systems are used, in which any of several different types of errors can cause corresponding check indicators to be turned on. Further, each *error indicator* can be individually addressed in the program. If no error of a given type has occurred, the computer continues normally. However, if there has been an error, the computer will transfer control to an alternate address for instructions on how to clear or circumvent the error, and the error indication is also turned off. Of course, it is possible to have the computer stop on any of the various types of "errors." It is simply not practical to program around certain errors.

This reflects the design trend of having computers refer first to them-

---

* The definitions of error, mistake, and malfunction preclude using error-detecting to pertain to detection of the *malfunctions*. However, since it is widely used, it is given here.

selves for corrective measures. In an addressable magnetic-tape system, where, for example, because of mistake or malfunction, the address being searched for is not present, the tape unit could hang up and indefinitely search around the correct address but never find it. Some tape units, however, have built-in equipment which would thereupon cause the computer to transfer control to a specific location for further instructions. Again, the computer could be instructed as to how to handle the situation. Likewise, other malfunctions or mistakes in tape operation would cause the computer to refer to still other locations, each of which would contain instructions on alternate courses of action.[15]

The ideal computer would solve problems without human intervention, even after malfunctions or mistakes. Of course, only a few of the possible malfunctions or mistakes actually can be covered, but even those result in more efficient computer utilization.

Part of this general technique involves *error-detecting and -correcting codes* in which enough redundant information is sent along with the word to check for the existence of an error and to arrange for its correction. Various systems for this have been proposed, but none is used in commercially available computers. Briefly, the redundant information required is less than that in the word itself, when detecting and correcting a single error.

An example of an error-detecting and -correcting code is given in Table 11.5. It uses seven bits to represent decimal 0 through 15. The three extra bits permit checking for an error and correcting it. The usual four-bit representations for these numbers are in columns 3, 5, 6, and 7. In addition, column 1 contains a parity bit so that there will be an even number of 1s in columns 1, 3, 5, and 7. Similarly, the bits in columns 2 and 4 are such that there will be an even number of 1s in columns 2, 3, 6, and 7 and in 4, 5, 6, and 7, respectively. With 5 as the number, the representation would be 0100101. If there were an "error" in the third digit and it was a 1 instead of 0, then the column-4 check (even number of 1s in 4, 5, 6, and 7) would pass, but the column-2 and column-1 checks would fail, since each involves column 3. Thus recording, left to right, a 0 for passing a check and a 1 for failure, we have 011, which is the binary representation of the erroneous position. It can therefore be corrected. The "error" can be in any position including, of course, the three *partial-bit* positions.

Still more redundance and error detecting and correcting are required if two simultaneous errors are to be detected. Again, however, the possibility of two random errors is so much smaller than that of a single error as to be generally negligible. If two or more errors do occur

Table 11.5. Example of an Error-detecting and -correcting Binary Code

Decimal number	Seven-bit code						
	1	2	3	4	5	6	7
0	0	0	0	0	0	0	0
1	1	1	0	1	0	0	1
2	0	1	0	1	0	1	0
3	1	0	0	0	0	1	1
4	1	0	0	1	1	0	0
5	0	1	0	0	1	0	1
6	1	1	0	0	1	1	0
7	0	0	0	1	1	1	1
8	1	1	1	0	0	0	0
9	0	0	1	1	0	0	1
10	1	0	1	1	0	1	0
11	0	1	1	0	0	1	1
12	0	1	1	1	1	0	0
13	1	0	1	0	1	0	1
14	0	0	1	0	1	1	0
15	1	1	1	1	1	1	1

simultaneously, they are quite likely to be indicative of a general failure, which would probably be detected by other means.

PROBLEMS

1. Try various examples of floating-decimal addition, subtraction, multiplication, and division. Use the notation of Table 11.1. Include in your examples cases which require normalization and where overflow occurs.

2. Repeat the above problem assuming a 35-bit binary word where the exponent is the eight most significant digits, and it is biased by 2^{128}. As an example, 236 is: 100010001110110000000000000000000000.

3. Practice multiple-precision operations by taking specific examples. Assume a computer where normal (single-precision) operation in multiplication is one-decimal digit by one-decimal digit for a two-decimal-digit product. Similarly, assume addition to be limited to a single-decimal-digit sum. For example, multiply 89 by 37 as a double-precision operation. Note how it differs from the customary (single-precision) arithmetic learned in grade school.

4. Do triple precision in a manner similar to that suggested in the problem above. Multiply a three-decimal-digit number by another three-digit number.

5. Assume that the second approximation in the square root example of page 21 is erroneously .0624009900 instead of .2624009900. Calculate the

successive approximations and number of iterations to arrive at the correct answer.

6. Students with a statistical background can consider the error in round-off. What is the probability of a cumulative $10 error if 100 items are each rounded to the nearest dollar and then added. Repeat for 1,000 items.

7. A single error for the value of N^2 in Table 11.4 was indicated by the fact that three of the second differences were not the correct value. If the basic computation is cubing, which difference can be used for checking? Further, a single error affects how many of these differences?

8. Test by the casting-out-nines method whether 22,043,005,544,886,271,869 could be the product of 3,469,271,943 and 6,353,784,283.

9. Try various combinations of correct and incorrect inputs in the error-detecting circuit of Fig. 11.1. As examples, (a) assume 8 is correctly represented by B_5 and Q_3 being 1 and the other five bits being 0. Note which (including OR_5) of the logical elements have 0 outputs and which have 1 outputs. (b) Assume that only the Q_2 input was 1. Note how a 1 output is obtained from OR_5. (c) Assume that Q_1 and Q_2 are the only 1 inputs. (d) Assume B_0, Q_3, and Q_4 are 1.

10. Table 11.5 gives the 16 valid combinations in the seven-bit error-detecting and error-correcting code. Try some of the 112 other combinations and determine which of the seven bits are indicated as being in error and the corrected decimal number intended.

BIBLIOGRAPHY

Eckert, W. J., and R. Jones: "Faster, Faster," pp. 98–104, McGraw-Hill Book Company, Inc., New York, 1956.

Gotlieb, C. C., and J. N. P. Hume: "High-speed Data Processing," pp. 146–163, McGraw-Hill Book Company, Inc., New York, 1958.

Hamming, R. W.: Checking Techniques for Digital Computers, *Control Eng.*, vol. 4, no. 5, pp. 111–114, May, 1957.

Hamming, R. W.: Error Detecting and Error Detecting Codes, *Bell System Tech. J.*, vol. 29, pp. 147–160, April, 1950.

McCracken, D. D.: "Digital Computer Programming," pp. 121–131 and 191–197, John Wiley & Sons, Inc., New York, 1957.

Phister, M.: "Logical Design of Digital Computers," pp. 326–339, John Wiley & Sons, Inc., New York, 1958.

Stibitz, G. R., and J. A. Larrivee: "Mathematics and Computers," pp. 192–199, McGraw-Hill Book Company, Inc., New York, 1956.

CHAPTER 12

Programming and Coding

Only very basic aspects of programming and coding have been examined up to now. To go into these important topics exhaustively is beyond the scope of this presentation. However, it is appropriate that certain terminology and applications of programming and coding techniques be considered in some detail. In this chapter subroutines, interpretive routines, translating routines, compilers, automatic coding, and universal code will be examined.

The programming examples previously considered have been quite simple, and deliberately so, to permit basic principles to be presented without encumbrance. Hence the examples are almost trivial in themselves. Simple as they are, however, they reveal that there is much red tape involved in preparing a problem in a form a computer can use.

THE CODING PROBLEM

Getting the basic state of a problem into machine language is important. Generally, much more time and money are spent in preparing a problem for solution than in solving it. In previous examples the few instructions available made coding more complicated than it is when there are many instructions. For practical problems using a practical instruction system, the number of instructions required to solve a problem is large. Sometimes hundreds, often thousands of detailed machine-language instructions are required. Just to set down these instructions is quite time-consuming; in addition, however, a significant amount of time is also necessary to *debug* the program once it has been set down. Most programs will have errors at first, which cost time and money to find and correct.

This situation is caused by the need to communicate with the computer in what have been called *microsyllables*. Although it is good that general-purpose automatic computers are extremely versatile and flexible, this fact makes great demands on those who code problems, for hundreds or thousands of instructions must be gotten correct, word for word and digit by digit. *The machine does what it's told to do, not what you want it to do.*

This is counter to normal human operations where everything does not have to be spelled out precisely. In speech, for example, proper information is conveyed when sounds and even words are missing. The redundancy of the language permits one to follow the thought anyway. It has been estimated that English, for example, is 60 per cent redundant. Gap filling is practically second nature to humans. Getting everything down precisely correct the first time is not.

Further, it will be noted that the detailed coding for a problem involves many routine (*bookkeeping*) operations. These unchallenging operations are even more likely to result in mistakes than are the more challenging parts of programming. To aid in the mechanics of preparing, checking, and correcting the coding of a problem several aids have been devised.

ROUTINE

Even in the most elaborate computers, all basic operations are not built in. Although a computer may execute a hundred different instructions, some cannot be done directly. For example, in scientific problems calculating the square root, determining a trigonometric value, raising a number to a power, or taking a logarithm are not generally built in. In business applications FILE, MERGE, COLLATE, or SORT operations might be left out. In all cases, however, it is possible to accomplish the desired operation by a sequence of machine-language instructions, that is, a routine.

Subroutine. In general each of these operations will need to be done many times in a given problem. There may be a number of sines or cosines to be computed, or sorting or merging to be done. It is obviously useful to have, say, a sorting routine applicable to all sorting, so that the step-by-step details of the sorting procedure need not be recoded for each time the operation is required. Further, such a routine would be devised so that, no matter where it entered the program, it would, after execution, cause the main program to be reentered at the proper place. Thus if sorting is required at five different places, one general sort routine would be entered from each of these five places and the main program afterward would be reentered at the correct place.

When used in this manner, a routine becomes a *subroutine*. The obvious first step in simplifying coding is to accumulate a number of subroutines to do repetitive jobs or portions of jobs. Subroutines for square-root, sine, cosine, logarithm, complex-arithmetic, sort, merge, and collate operations are only a few examples. A library of subroutines is often developed in the hope that problems may be solved by "patching together" subroutines already available.

Assembly Routine. It is possible to use the computer itself to put together (*assemble*) a program. For example, a number of subroutines may be used. If each subroutine occupies a separate, distinct portion of storage and there is a large amount of storage available, then patching the subroutines together is not necessarily difficult. However, a subroutine assigned to a specific set of storage locations in one problem is quite likely to be located in another set of storage locations for another problem. When the location is changed, it is necessary to alter the references to the subroutine as well as certain addresses in the routine itself. This is a tedious job and one which can be done by the computer itself as a part of an assembly routine.

Actually, the general problem of assigning specific locations for instructions and data is handled by an assembly routine. Many computers have limitations which the programmer must remember when specifying the exact storage location for each word. Mistakes occur if he forgets. For example, in some computers an optimum address for the next instruction or data word must be determined to minimize computer idle time between the execution of instructions. In others, instructions can be located only in certain portions of storage, read-in or read-out storage is restricted, the number of words in a quick-access loop is limited, and so on. To avoid these difficulties, the coder codes in a *relative* or *pseudo-address* system, and the computer itself (through an assembly routine) will allocate *absolute* addresses, taking into account the pertinent rules and restrictions and thereby relieving the coder of this chore and making mistakes less likely. The coder, for example, can assign relative or pseudo-addresses as if the storage were much larger than it actually is. Yet, as long as the actual storage capacity is not exceeded, the assembled program will be efficient in its allocation of absolute addresses for the program, including, when pertinent, those for relocated subroutines.

An assembly routine may also accommodate *mnemonic instruction* systems. In computers the operation to be performed is indicated by the digits in a certain portion of the instruction word. These digits are generally arbitrary so far as the coder is concerned. If, for example, he were using the instruction set of Chapter 3, he would need to remember that ADD is 1, SUBTRACT 2, MULTIPLY 3, and DIVIDE 4. For a few instructions such association is not difficult or demanding. However, when the instruction set consists of a hundred or more operations with a somewhat arbitrary set of digits for each, the possibility of mistakes increases. For this reason, many computer groups have a set of *mnemonic* alphabetic abbreviations for specifying operations. This is translated into the digits actually used by the computer by an assembly routine. For example, the above operations would be specified as ADD, SUB, MUL, or DIV, and the routine would provide the 1, 2, 3, or 4, respectively.

Interpretive Routine. Another aid to preventing mistakes in coding is to use an instruction code which is not directly in machine language. The intelligent use of, for example, a set of 70 single-address fixed-decimal-point instructions pertaining to a computer without index registers requires a high level of experience and training. On the other hand, to use a set of 10 three-address floating-decimal instructions involving 10 index registers would surely require less. The latter system could be used more readily by persons unfamiliar with the computer who have problems to solve, if it is desirable to have them program and code their own problems.

Although the second set of instructions (sometimes called a *macrocode*) may not pertain to an actual computer, an interpretive routine could cause almost any computer to execute programs written in it. This would require that each instruction of the macrocode be interpretable by a specific sequence of actual machine-language instructions. The set of instructions defined and used in Chapter 3 are for a nonexistent computer. However, an interpretive routine was used to take programs written in this instruction set and cause them to be executed on a computer with a different set of instructions.

An interpretive routine is generally inefficient and slow. Instructions in the macrocode will generally require the execution of a large number of machine-language instructions. Further, each individual instruction is interpreted one at a time. Routines which would more efficiently translate from a pseudo-language to an actual language are called *compilers* and will be considered in a moment. Interpretive routines are easily written and used in situations where machine inefficiency is outweighed by the advantages to coding which accrue from the use of a special instruction set.

Interpretive routines can, of course, be used to interpret from one actual machine instruction set to another. This is not generally done, however, since computers of various types differ enough to make this inefficient. An operation which in one machine language may consist of a few instructions would require a large number of interpreted instructions. The ratio of instructions is so high and the interpreting so inefficient that interpretation is impractical.

DEBUGGING

Mistakes will necessarily occur, and means to facilitate their location are in order. Finding the mistakes in a program is called *debugging*. Known answers for a given set of input parameters can be used to check the computation. Generally, however, it is necessary to break the problem into sections and to check each section. The contents of the registers can be observed at various check points and compared with the correct value for a sample problem whose answers are known.

Break Points. To permit the computer to stop at selected parts of the problem a system of break points is frequently used. The instruction at which a stop is desired is identified in some distinctive manner. One method is to put digits in a portion of the instruction reserved for this purpose.[4] With a switch set for break-point operation, the computer will operate in the normal manner until it encounters a break-point instruction. It will then stop and the register contents can be examined. Operation can be resumed by a control on the computer and will continue until the next break-point instruction is encountered. This sequence can be continued as required.

Generally more than one level of break-point operation is provided. This permits flexibility in that the lower levels can permit checks on minor individual portions of the program, and as they are corrected, the upper levels of break point will permit checking of major portions skipping over the lower-level break points between. In general, the break-point system makes it possible, after checking has been completed, for the program to be executed without break-point stops, simply by operating the appropriate control on the computer. It is not necessary to alter the instructions.

Monitoring and Tracing. The debugging technique of looking at the contents of the registers is not practical if a large number of instructions must be monitored. It is just not economically feasible to allow an expensive computer to be held up while a coder looks at the registers as he goes through the program step by step. Not only is this a slow process, but it does not provide a detailed record of the operations. For this reason, *automonitor* and *tracing* routines are available for most computers. Basically, they cause a record to be made of the computer's operations as it executes the program.

One level of monitor or tracing routine would print out (on a typewriter or line printer) the contents of all registers for every step of the problem. Thus would be shown the instruction being executed, the address(es) referred to, the contents of the address(es), the contents of the accumula-

tor and other registers, and other pertinent information, such as the condition of the overflow toggle. The program listing in Chapter 3 is an
example of this kind of tracing. Such detailed tracings are not always
practical. Making a record of all this information on each step requires
considerable output. If a typewriter-type output is used this would
mean that the tracing would be quite slow; line printers, being faster,
are better suited to complete monitor tracing.

Generally detailed tracing of all steps is not needed or desired. To
speed up the process and to eliminate marginal information, monitor routines which record only selected portions of the program are frequently
used. For example, the monitor may record only those instructions which
have altered the contents of a storage location or have caused a decision
to be made. Monitoring at these levels will permit checking on most of
the mistakes in programming and/or coding.

Post-Mortems. A logical extension of the above technique is called a
post-mortem. An unchecked program, when first put on a computer, will
frequently not go all the way to the end. It may stop because the computer tries to execute as an instruction a word that was never intended as
an instruction; it may stop because of an unanticipated overflow; or it
may stop because of some other mistake. When this happens, the program "dies." A post-mortem of what happened is in order. A post-
mortem routine anticipates many common mistakes and checks to see
if they have occurred. To use such a routine it may be necessary to
restrict the operations which are legitimate. For example, in a general-
purpose digital computer it is possible arithmetically to modify the operation portion of an instruction. In a post-mortem monitored system, this
operation may be defined as forbidden, although modification of the
address portion would still be allowed. If this forbidden operation were
attempted, the post-mortem routine would note it and so indicate to the
operator. Other forbidden operations, such as unanticipated overflow,
would also cause the computer to print out or otherwise indicate the
mistake. Further, a post-mortem generally remembers a number of previous storage alterations or branching operations, so that they too may
be printed out when the program dies.

AUTOMATIC CODING

It is possible to go beyond this in using computers to prepare their own
programs, that is, to code problems automatically. Suppose that the
identical problem is to be coded for two different computers, having different characteristics and instruction systems. Further, assume that,
when coded, the problems would take about the same amount of time to

solve on either computer. Thus we could say that their solutions would be equivalent. However, the detailed machine-language instructions would differ considerably, just as the steps in execution of the problem would also differ.

Within reasonable limits, each of the computers, by means of an interpretive routine, could solve the problem as stated in the language of the other. However, as noted, this process is quite slow and inefficient.

Translators and Compilers. An interpretive routine resembles a word-for-word literal translation from one language to another. Word-for-word translations are, of course, inefficient. Efficient translation from one language to another requires interpretation of phrases, sentences, ideas, and concepts. The basic concepts of one are frequently expressed quite differently in the vocabulary, syntax, idioms, etc., of the other. A good translation extracts the concept from the words in one language and expresses it in the words of another. Similarly, a program which will take the machine language of one computer and produce a reasonably efficient program in another machine language is called a *translator*. Translators are very difficult to derive. Further, they are generally limited to translating from the machine language of one specific computer to that of a second specific computer. The problem of translating is solved only for some cases. The general case, in which the characteristics and language of any two different computers would specify or generate a suitable translating routine, has not been solved.

It is very advantageous to have an easy means for adapting solutions of problems from one type of computer to another. Many computer groups, either as they expand and/or as the state of the art advances, will procure different types of computers. In general, the advance is to bigger, faster, or otherwise more useful computers. Yet the programs for one installation represent many man-years of effort which must be redone when another type computer is procured and no translation system is available. This is obviously quite wasteful.

For two species of computers, only two translators (one each way) would be required; for three computers, six; for four, twelve; for five, twenty; and so on. As the number of computer types further increases, the number of translators required soon becomes unreasonable.

Universal Language. The obvious method to avoid a multiplicity of translators is to use one universal language. This *universal language* (*code*) would be independent of the machine language of any specific computer and aimed rather at expressing the basic concepts involved in solving a problem. Thus a problem stated in a universal code could be solved by any computer, with only one translator per computer required. These one-way translators are easy to devise, for they need only translate from concept to machine language rather than from language to concept to language.

Actually there are several different universal languages. Some are mathematical; they take the basic operations and associated symbols of mathematics and compile a detailed machine-language routine for solving a mathematically expressed problem. In a mathematical compiler, not only the variables and parameters but the operations indicated (for example, the parentheses, the exponents, radicals, vinculums, and arithmetic symbols) are all expressed in a systematic manner. The compiler then produces a program which will perform the operations represented in these symbols. IBM's FORTRAN is one example.

Compiling means that a set of instructions are formed for solving the problem, not that the problem itself is solved; that is, the steps involved in the solution are not executed. After compilation, the solution can be achieved as any other machine-language program would be. Further, a compiler generally must examine all of the universal-language instructions before it can produce an efficient set of corresponding machine-language output instructions. This is in contrast to an interpretive routine, which operates instruction for instruction.

Another universal language is used for solving business-type problems. Input instructions are English-language words such as FILE, MERGE, SORT, and so on. The compiler would take this representation of basic concepts and operations and translate into an orderly set of machine-language instructions. Again, the usefulness of such compilers is that they do not merely assemble a piecemeal set of instructions but rather consider the over-all problem as expressed in the universal language and develop a system of machine instructions for the solution.

The fact that there is more than one universal language is not so unfortunate as it may at first appear. Such languages, since they exist at the concept, rather than at the detailed machine-language, level, are relatively easy to translate. The basic ideas expressed by mathematical symbols are almost universally defined and used. Also, although translating English words into computer operations is subject to greater leeway, nevertheless, such words are susceptible of definition and hence are useful for automatic coding.

PROSPECTS

Techniques for producing computers are ahead of techniques for using them. The technique of step-by-step coding of machine-language programs is wasteful of time, money, and personnel. This "hand production" of programs seems fortunately destined to be overshadowed by the "mass production" possible with automatic coding, in which the computer itself does much of the work. This is fortunate because soon there will not be enough programmers and coders to produce the programs required by the ever-increasing number of computers. Another advantage is that the designer can design primarily for other features, such as reliability and cost. If the computer user no longer codes in machine language, then the basic machine operations no longer need be those which he finds convenient to use. Instead the set of machine operations may well be one which is impractical for direct coding but more practical for automatic coding than traditional instructions. Actually these unconventional instructions and operations may be even more efficient than the traditional. There are computer designs which already indicate this trend.[18]

BIBLIOGRAPHY

Goode, H. H., and R. E. Machol: "System Engineering," pp. 254–257, McGraw-Hill Book Company, Inc., New York, 1957.

Gotlieb, C. C., and J. N. P. Hume: "High-speed Data Processing," pp. 290–303, McGraw-Hill Book Company, Inc., New York, 1958.

Livesley, R. K.: "Digital Computers," pp. 37–38, Cambridge University Press, New York, 1957.

McCracken, D. D.: "Digital Computer Programming," pp. 159–190 and 211–216, John Wiley & Sons, Inc., New York, 1957.

Richards, R. K.: "Arithmetic Operations in Digital Computers," pp. 363–384, D. Van Nostrand Company, Inc., Princeton, N.J., 1958.

Mathematics of Logic

The subject of this appendix is mathematical symbols. However, the mathematics is not complex. In fact, it is too simple. Many of the complications of the algebra of continuous functions (the usual type) disappear when considering the algebra of two-state logic.

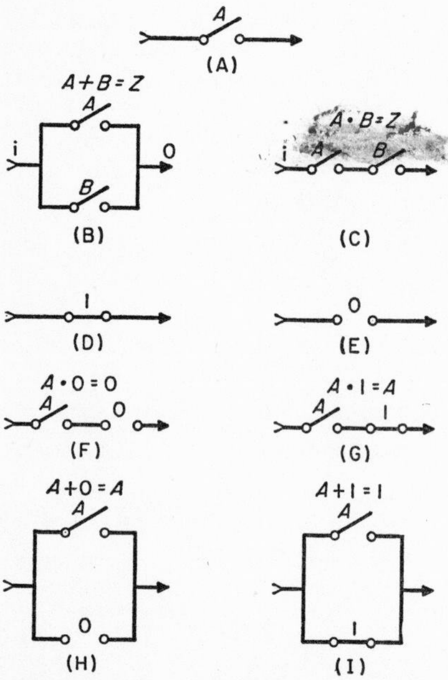

Those who appreciate a physical point of view may consider useful the representation of logical elements by on-off electrical switches. Many of the examples will be of this type. The usefulness of representing basic logical operations by what is called Boolean Algebra (after the English logician George Boole), the basic manipulations possible, and the limitations of the method will be considered.

FIG. A.1. Basic switching configurations and their Boolean algebraic representation.

BASIC SWITCH CONCEPTS

Let us consider the basic operations in two-state logic in terms of switches. Being a two-state device, a switch is either *off* or *on*. There is continuity between the two terminals or there is not. Symbolically, a switch is shown in Fig. A.1(A); the symbol A represents the switch. Further, 0 represents an open circuit (*off* condition or no continuity) and 1 represents a closed circuit (the *on* condition or continuity). Thus

$$A = 1$$

means "switch A is on" and

$$B = 0$$

means "switch B is off."

Two switches connected in parallel are shown in Fig. A.1(B). We will consider Z to be the combined effect between the input and output, that is, between i and o. In this case the result is obvious. If either A or B (or both) are on, then there is continuity between i and o. In terms of a truth table where Z is the over-all effect, this is

A	B	Z	
0	0	0	(1)
0	1	1	(3)
1	0	1	
1	1	1	(5)

Or. Except for the last condition, this is equivalent to the binary addition table. Hence, arbitrarily, let us symbolize INCLUSIVE OR by the symbol $+$. Fig. A.1(B) can then be written

$$A + B = Z$$

However, remember that this means only "if either A or B (or both) are closed, Z is a closed circuit." It is not to be interpreted in terms of addition in the usual sense.

And. Let us consider the effect if, as shown in Fig. A.1(C), two switches A and B are connected in series. Again it is obvious that Z is on if A and B are both on. Using a truth table, the four possible combinations are

A	B	Z	
0	0	0	(6)
0	1	0	(4)
1	0	0	
1	1	1	(2)

This is equivalent to the binary multiplication table. We will use the symbol $\times$ for the AND logical connective. Thus

$$A \times B = Z$$

represents the series circuit of Fig. A.1(C). Incidentally, as in arithmetic representation, the $\times$ is sometimes omitted but is implied, as in

$$AB = Z$$

It is further apparent, from Fig. A.1(B), that

$$A + A = A \tag{11}$$

and, from Fig. A.1(C), that

$$A \times A = A \tag{12}$$

These are sometimes referred to as the *idempotent* laws.

If a switch is on (closed) under all circumstances it is considered to have a value of 1 (Fig. A.1(D)) and if off (open) a value of 0, as in Fig. A.1(E). In Fig. A.1(F) is an always-open switch in series with a switch A which may be open or closed. The combined result is an always-open circuit, that is,

$$A \times 0 = 0 \tag{10}$$

Similarly, in Fig. A.1g, an always-closed switch in series with switch A is nothing more than A itself, that is,

$$A \times 1 = A \tag{8}$$

In Fig. A.1(H), we see that an open circuit across a switch does not affect it, that is,

$$A + 0 = A \tag{7}$$

And that, in Fig. A.1(I), a direct closed circuit remains a direct circuit no matter what is connected in parallel with it; hence

$$A + 1 = 1 \tag{9}$$

MATHEMATICAL LAWS

This mathematics of logic has the three basic mathematical properties of being *commutative, associative,* and *distributive.* The commutative law is illustrated by

$$A + B = B + A \tag{13}$$

$$AB = BA \tag{14}$$

and the associative by

$$(A + B) + C = A + (B + C) \tag{15}$$

$$(AB)C = A(BC) \tag{16}$$

We will consider these as obvious.

The distributive law may not be so obvious. In Fig. A.2(A), we see the switch equivalent of

$$AB + AC = A(B + C) \tag{17}$$

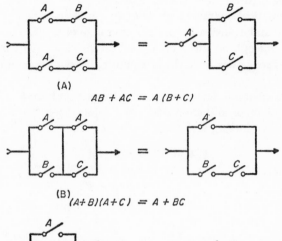

(A)

$AB + AC = A(B+C)$

(B)

$(A+B)(A+C) = A + BC$

(C) $A(A+B) = A$

Fig. A.2. Examples of network simplification where the circuits on the right involve fewer elements than the circuits on the left.

which itself is not difficult. However, consider Fig. A.2(B), which is

$$(A + B)(A + C) = A + BC \tag{18}$$

If there is some doubt of this, remember

$$(A + B)(A + C) = AA + AB + AC + BC$$

but from (12) above,

$$= A + AB + AC + BC$$

and from (17) above,

$$= A(1 + B + C) + BC$$

but since from (9),

$$1 + B + C = 1$$

then

$$(A + B)(A + C) = A \times 1 + BC$$

and from (8),

$$(A + B)(A + C) = A + BC$$

Notice that the manipulations and concepts involved are quite simple; perhaps their greatest fault is that they are too simple. In comparison to the mathematical operations of ordinary arithmetic, there are only two coefficients, 0 and 1, instead of an infinite range of coefficients. There is no negative concept, no subtraction, and no division. All variables exist either to the zero power or to the first power. There are no other powers, no roots.

As another example, let us prove that the network on the left of Fig. A.2(C) is equivalent to that on the right. Again, by inspection it may be obvious, but formalizing it,

$$
\begin{aligned}
A(A + B) &= AA + AB \\
&= A + AB \\
&= A(1 + B) \\
&= A \times 1 \\
&= A
\end{aligned}
$$

Using a truth table and taking the over-all characteristic as Z, then the left-hand network is

$$A(A + B) = Z$$

Now, considering the four and only four possible states for the two switches A and B and tabulating the corresponding value of Z, we get

A	B	Z
0	0	0
0	1	0
1	0	1
1	1	1

Inspection of the respective four values for Z shows that for all cases Z is the same as A and is not at all dependent on B. Where all possible

:ases can be set down and examined, the truth-table technique is quite ıseful.

NEGATION

In addition to AND and OR, which have been considered above, NOT s also a basic logical connective used in computers. NOT (*negation*) neans the opposite state or condition. It is symbolized in different ways. We will use a line over the symbol. Thus

$$\bar{0} = 1 \tag{19}$$

$$\bar{1} = 0 \tag{20}$$

imply states that a not-open switch is closed and a not-closed switch is ipen. Simple enough.

Similarly, a switch which is always in the opposite state or condition as A is $\bar{A}$. Thus if A is in the 1 condition, then $\bar{A}$ is 0; if 0, then $\bar{A}$ is 1.

The two negation relationships,

$$A + \bar{A} = 1 \tag{21}$$

$$A\bar{A} = 0 \tag{22}$$

ıre called the *complementarity* laws. Figure A.3 illustrates these principles in terms of switches. The first [Eq. (21)] merely states that if a switch A and its opposite $\bar{A}$ are connected in parallel, the combination is always on, continuity being obtained through one switch or the other. The second [Eq. (22)] states that the over-all effect of a switch and its opposite being connected in series will always be an open circuit.

Another example involving negation which may not be obvious is

$$A + \bar{A}B = A + B$$

From Eqs. (17) and (12) we know the left side can be expressed as

$$(A + \bar{A})(A + B) = A + B$$

and from Eqs. (21) and (8) that

$$A + B = A + B$$

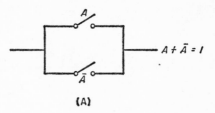

(A)

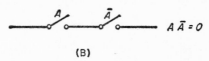

(B)

Fig. A.3. Complementarity laws of Boolean algebra.

This relationship and the corresponding one

$$\bar{A} + AB = \bar{A} + B$$

are called *reduction formulas*.

The *dualization laws* (De Morgan's theorem or *inversion formulas*) are not so obvious. They state, for the two-switch case, that

$$\overline{AB} = \bar{A} + \bar{B} \tag{23}$$

$$\overline{A + B} = \bar{A} \times \bar{B} \tag{24}$$

Table A.1 shows the truth-table proof of Eq. (23). In columns 1 and 2, all four possible combinations of A and B are shown. Column 4 shows

Table A.1. Truth-table Proof of the Dualization Law

1	2	3	4	5	6	7
A	B	AB	$\overline{AB}$	$\bar{A}$	$\bar{B}$	$\bar{A} + \bar{B}$
0	0	0	1	1	1	1
0	1	0	1	1	0	1
1	0	0	1	0	1	1
1	1	1	0	0	0	0

the resultant values of $\overline{AB}$, while by columns 5 and 6 the values for $\bar{A} + \bar{B}$ are also derived. In column 7, they are the same in all cases as column 4. Equation (24) could be proved in a similar manner.

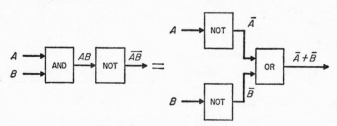

Fɪɢ. A.4. Duality or inversion principle.

Figure A.4 shows the corresponding logical circuits for each side of Eq. (23). Notice that only general AND, OR, and NOT blocks are given instead of a specific switch circuit. It is often not desirable to try to xtend the simple switch concept to a logical problem such as this, although it can be done. Indeed the control panel wiring of EAM equipment does this extensively.

The specific means for implementing the logical connectives AND, OR, nd NOT is not important and need not be limited to switch arrangements. Specific implementation changes with the state of the art. Vhether an actual switch, a flip-flop, a magnetic decision element, or ny of many other possible devices is used doesn't matter. The basic logic s the same.

The last law of the set involves negation and is called *involution*. It is

$$\bar{\bar{A}} = A \tag{25}$$

vhich simply states that a double negative is the same as an affirmative.

All of the above basic identities are summarized in Table A.2. This epresents all possible basic two-element mathematical manipulations of Boolean algebra. They can be extended to three or more variables.

DUALITY

A critical analysis will reveal two arbitrary choices of symbols. The use of the multiplication symbol for AND and of the addition symbol for OR vas arbitrary. Actually, it could be done quite the other way around, nd indeed some groups do just this. However, if this is done, the second arbitrary premise—that 1 represents the desired output state—must also be reversed. Note that as we used it, a 1 represents a closed circuit, and ill our consideration was given to the circumstances which resulted in obtaining a 1 or whatever it represented. Thus a 1, besides being a closed circuit (continuity), also implies "yes." Yet obviously there are many circumstances where "no" is the correct answer. The negative approach s a widely used technique.

When both changes are made the results are still valid, that is, if he AND and OR are interchanged and if 0 and 1 are also interchanged. This is a form of the duality principle. By applying this to the identities n the left column of Table A.2, one can derive the corresponding identities in the right column and vice versa. Hence Eq. (1) becomes Eq. 2), Eq. (2) becomes Eq. (1), etc. There is no dual for Eq. (25), ince it involves neither AND nor OR.

USE OF BOOLEAN ALGEBRA

Boolean algebra is used in the analysis of logical circuits because it permits consideration of a variety of ways of implementing any given logical problem. Thus one would set down the problem in terms o AND, OR and NOT as represented above. Then, by using the identitie summarized in Table A.2, it is possible to rearrange this mathematics int other equivalent forms, but ones which would take different numbers o types of logical connectives.

Table A.2. Summary of the Basic Boolean Algebraic Identities

(1)	$0 + 0 = 0$	(2)	$1 \cdot 1 = 1$
(3)	$0 + 1 = 1$	(4)	$1 \cdot 0 = 0$
(5)	$1 + 1 = 1$	(6)	$0 \cdot 0 = 0$
(7)	$A + 0 = A$	(8)	$A \cdot 1 = A$
(9)	$A + 1 = 1$	(10)	$A \cdot 0 = 0$
(11)	$A + A = A$	(12)	$A \cdot A = A$
(13)	$A + B = B + A$	(14)	$A \cdot B = B \cdot A$
(15)	$(A + B) + C = A + (B + C)$	(16)	$(AB)C = A(BC)$
(17)	$AB + AC = A(B + C)$	(18)	$(A + B)(A + C) = A + B($
(19)	$\bar{0} = 1$	(20)	$\bar{1} = 0$
(21)	$A + \bar{A} = 1$	(22)	$A\bar{A} = 0$
(23)	$\overline{AB} = \bar{A} + \bar{B}$	(24)	$\overline{A + B} = \bar{A} \cdot \bar{B}$
(25)	$\bar{\bar{A}} = A$		

Network Simplification. At this point some of the usefulness of thi mathematical representation and manipulation of two-state logic begin to appear. The network on the left of Fig. A.2(B), which involved fou switch elements, has been found to be exactly replaceable by the simple three-element network on the right in Fig. A.2(B). The process of chang ing one to another involved simple mathematical manipulations. Al though this example may not be striking, there are many examples i which a complicated logical network can be reduced by such technique to a much simpler equivalent network.

Another example was given in Fig. A.4. The left side used one o and one AND device to obtain an output the same as that obtained wit two NOT and one OR devices at the right. Which of these two possibilitie would be used in a given design of a logical device depends on many othe factors. Perhaps in some, considerations in implementing an AND devic would make it practical to use a NOT and an OR device in its place Hence one would use the circuit on the right rather than the one wit fewer elements on the left.

The principle of duality mentioned above is of more than academi interest. There are circuits which, when being analyzed by either system will not appear subject to a useful modification, but when cast into th dual form will result in a simpler form. However, this technique is not widely used because of the obvious confusion from reversed concepts.

Analysis of logical circuits also may indicate that some parts are logically redundant and hence need not be used. This has already been illustrated in the logical circuits of Fig. A.2. In each of the three

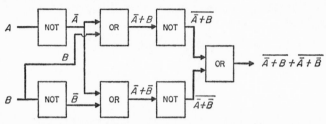

Fig. A.5. Logical circuit which is equivalent to A.

examples, the circuit on the right required fewer switches than that on the left. Although the simplification may be obvious and not require mathematical manipulation in these cases, there are many logical problems for which useless elements exist but cannot be easily detected.

As an example, consider the circuit of Fig. A.5, to prove that it is equivalent to A. The logical equations for this two-input, four NOT, and three OR circuit is the left side of

$$\overline{\overline{A} + B} + \overline{\overline{A} + \overline{B}} = A \qquad (26)$$

From Eq. (24) we derive

$$\overline{\overline{A} + B} + \overline{\overline{A} + \overline{B}} = \overline{\overline{A}}\overline{B} + \overline{\overline{A}}\overline{\overline{B}}$$

and from Eq. (25)

$$= A\overline{B} + AB$$

Further, from Eq. (17)

$$= A(\overline{B} + B)$$

while finally, Eq. (21) results in

$$= A$$

Equation (26) is an example of a logical combination which is useful for analyzing logical circuits. When so applied, it is a part of a *not-not* technique. In many devices (especially those involving relays, as in industrial controls) it is easy to obtain the negative or inverse of a logical function and sometimes, through Eq. (26), this results in circuit simplification.

Although only of academic interest in this particular example, the principle is the same in actual problems; the recasting of the logical equations results in determination of a simpler form. The proof of Eq (26) can be obtained by the truth table in Table A.3. All combinations of A and B are shown in columns 1 and 2. The intermediate steps are given in columns 3–8, with the value of the entire expression given in column 9. Examination shows that it is the same as A for all cases of A and B.

A similar exercise would involve the proof that

$$AB + AC + B\bar{C} = AC + B\bar{C}$$

This is a third *reduction formula*.

Limitations. The algebra of two-state logic is of particular value to the designer of a computer. Its usefulness is limited, however. It is a good tool for analysis, that is, for determining the characteristics of a circuit. But a designer needs a synthesis tool, too, that answers the question, What circuit has given characteristics? Such a tool is difficult to find, although substantial advances are being made.

Table A.3. Truth-table Proof of Logical Network of Fig. A.5

1	2	3	4	5	6	7	8	9
A	B	$\bar{A}$	$\bar{B}$	$\bar{A}+B$	$\overline{\bar{A}+B}$	$\bar{A}+\bar{B}$	$\overline{\bar{A}+\bar{B}}$	$\overline{\bar{A}+B}+\overline{\bar{A}+\bar{B}}$
0	0	1	1	1	0	1	0	0
0	1	1	0	1	0	1	0	0
1	0	0	1	0	1	1	0	1
1	1	0	0	1	0	0	1	1

Further, the designer needs to derive an optimum design. The engineering, logical, economic, and other factors which affect the choice of a system or of components are generally too complex to be fully evaluated. Certainly, such nonlinear parameters as politics, patent-infringement possibilities, and so on, limit the area of usefulness of his results even if he were master of the subtleties of Boolean algebra.

PROBLEMS

1. Prove the following:

    (a) $A + \bar{A}B = A + B$

    (b) $A + C(A + B) + B(\bar{A} + \bar{C}) = A + B$

    (c) $AC + (\bar{A} + D)(B + C) + C(B + \bar{A}D) = C + B(\bar{A} + \bar{D})$

    (d) $A + AC + B + \bar{A}B = A + B$

2. Write the dual of the above examples and re-prove the identities.

3. One of the following three terms is superfluous; that is, it can be dropped without affecting the logical operation indicated. A truth-table approach is probably best.

    (a) $AB + \bar{B}\bar{C} + A\bar{C}$

    (b) $AB + AC + B\bar{C}$

4. Prove the validity of the following equation by writing the Boolean algebraic expression and reducing to an identity.

5. The network on the right is equivalent to the one on the left. Indicate the proper designation $(A, \bar{A}, B, \bar{B}, C, \bar{C})$ for the three unmarked switches on the right.

6. Reduce the network on the left to the equivalent form on the right.

7. Write the Boolean algebraic expression for:

BIBLIOGRAPHY

Boole, G.: "An Investigation of the Laws of Thought," Dover Publications, New York, 1951 (reprint of the 1854 original).

Caldwell, S. H.: "Switching Circuits and Logical Design," John Wiley & Sons, Inc., New York, 1958.

190   *Digital Computer Primer*

Courant, R., and H. Robbins: "What Is Mathematics?", pp. 108–116, Oxford University Press, New York, 1941.

Culbertson, J. T.: "Mathematics and Logic for Digital Devices," pp. 115–212, D. Van Nostrand Company, Inc., Princeton, N.J., 1958.

Humphrey, W. S.: "Switching Circuits," pp. 13–64, McGraw-Hill Book Company, Inc., New York, 1958.

Phister, M.: "Logical Design of Digital Computers," pp. 30–111 and 393–398, John Wiley & Sons, Inc., New York, 1958.

Richards, R. K.: "Arithmetic Operations in Digital Operations," pp. 26–80, D. Van Nostrand Company, Inc., Princeton, N.J., 1958.

Richardson, M.: "Fundamentals of Mathematics," pp. 176–196, The Macmillan Company, New York, 1958.

Shannon, C. E.: A Symbolic Analysis of Relay and Switching Circuits, *Trans. AIEE*, vol. 57, pp. 713–723, 1938.

APPENDIX B

Word Distribution

A study of the distribution of words in this book was made using a digital computer and electronic accounting machinery. It was facilitated by having the entire text punched into IBM cards, and indeed the original manuscript submitted to the publisher was a listing of these cards on a line printer normally used for accounting purposes.

The version studied differs somewhat from the final version in the text. However, the differences are not great and the general conclusions hold. The term "word" as used here defines simply a group of alphabetic characters (excluding punctuation, special symbols, and numbers) which is or would be separated from other "words" by a space. Included in the definition are one-letter words such as *A* and *B*, as used in the discussions on logic, as well as lengthy hyphenated terms. A different sequence of letters was considered another word, although only the plural, obtained by adding an *s*, was involved.

FREQUENCY DISTRIBUTION

A total of 57,936 words was used. However, there were only 3,653 different words, so that each was used an average of 15.8 times. The range of use was wide. The word *the* was used 4,515 times, and yet there were 1,420 words which appeared just one time. Table B.1 lists the 15 most frequently used words and the number of times used. Similarly, Table B.2 shows the other end of the scale, giving the number of words used from 1 to 15 times in the text.

In Table B.1 many of the words are articles, prepositions, conjunctions, and verbs that do not indicate the substantive nature of the text. By eliminating all but nouns or noun equivalents (Table B.3), a better indication is obtained. Here, plurals and equivalent forms are combined so that the figures do not necessarily agree with those of Table B.1. Notice that AND, OR, and NOT are included as substantives since they are used

191

Table B.1. List of 15 Most Frequently Used Words in This Book

Word	Number of Times Used
the	4,515
of	2,016
a	1,712
in	1,680
is	1,611
to	1,493
and	1,177
be	851
this	711
for	659
are	600
or	547
it	545
as	544
computer	486

in that sense in the text. Unfortunately, these counts include their use in a nonsubstantive sense. Hence, there is not as much emphasis on these words as the figures indicate. Nevertheless, Table B.3 gives a clear idea of the emphasis and intent of the text. Incidentally, certain terms are deliberately deemphasized. For example, *memory* occurs only 14 times, in comparison to 330 for *storage; calculator* occurs 30 times, as compared to *computer* with 800; and *command* 8 in contrast to *instruction* with 414.

WORD LENGTH

Statistics are given in Table B.4 on the length of the words used in the text. Note that these are cumulative figures. For example, under a word length of 5 letters, the numbers indicate that there are 953 different words of 5 letters or less, which make up 37,624 words of the total of 57,986, well over half the total count.

ZIPF LAW

It has been empirically determined that if the words used in the English language are ranked, the product of the rank R of a particular word and S, its size, is a constant. Considering the ranking of which Table B.1 is a part, where *the* is 1, *is* is 5, *for* is 10, etc., the value of M is indicated for various values of R in Table B.5. Note that a value of 9,000 for M is indicated for ranks between 100 and 300, although the agreement is good over a much wider range.

Table B.2. List of the Number of Words Appearing from 1 to 15 Times

Times Used	Number of Words
1	1,420
2	502
3	282
4	191
5	142
6	110
7	93
8	55
9	64
10	55
11	55
12	28
13	32
14	38
15	32

SENTENCE LENGTH

The text was also examined for the length of all the sentences in number of words. There were 2,896 sentences for a total of 56,305 words. (The discrepancy in word count as compared to that given above is due to fact that titles were included in total word count but were not sentences. Further, sentences containing mathematical expressions were not counted. Finally there were some errors in each count.) The range was from two sentences of two words each to one with 75 words. The average length was 19.4 words. The distribution is skew with a median of 17.5 words and a mode of 16 words for 149 of the sentences. One-quarter of the words counted were in sentences of 16 words or less, one-half 21 words or less, and three-quarters 29 words or less.

Table B.3.   List of the First 30 Substantives with Number of Times Used.
(This includes plurals and substantially equivalent forms.)

Word	Number Used	Word	Number Used
and	1,177	example	208
computer	800	time	196
or	575	bit	193
number	417	two	191
instruction	414	logic	188
operation	412	word	182
one	412	code	168
digit(al)	404	pulse	166
not	352	binary	159
storage	330	register	156
device	243	address	153
input	219	location	140
information	218	arithmetic	137
output	215	control	123
decimal	209	accumulator	119

Table B.4.   Summary of Word Length

Length of Words in Letters	Inclusive Words in Text	Inclusive Number of Different Words
1	2,343	21
2	13,933	83
3	24,186	229
4	32,083	560
5	37,624	953
6	41,681	1,390
7	46,595	1,883
8	50,679	2,382
9	53,455	2,777
10	55,167	3,103
11	56,667	3,343
12	57,413	3,492
13	57,634	3,563
All	57,936	3,653

Table B.5. Rank and Size of Word Frequency Distribution as It Obeys Zipf's Law

Rank	Size	M
1	4,515	4,515
5	1,611	8,055
10	659	6,590
20	344	6,880
50	154	7,700
100	90	9,000
200	45	9,000
300	30	9,000
500	16	8,000
1,000	6	6,000
2,000	2	4,000
3,000	1	3,000

BIBLIOGRAPHY

The analysis was similar to that described by Busa for studying an author's vocabulary in the following:

Casey, R. J., et al.: "Punched Cards," 2d ed., pp. 357–373, Reinhold Publishing Corporation, New York, 1958.

Frequency distribution of words in written material is considered in the following:

Zipf, G. K.: "Human Behavior and the Principle of Least Effort," Addison-Wesley Publishing Company, Reading, Mass., 1949.
Goode, H. H., and R. E. Machol: "System Engineering," p. 135, McGraw-Hill Book Company, Inc., New York, 1957.

General Bibliography

Since the field of digital computers is expanding so rapidly, it is difficult to keep abreast of the developments. One of the best sources of the latest information is directly from the manufacturers. They issue operation, coding, and other manuals which are of value for detailed study of any specific computer or for comparative studies of various computers.

COMPARISONS

Published summaries and comparisons of digital computers run the risk of becoming quickly obsolete. However, the following references do a good job of summarizing as of the time they were written.

Carr, J. W., III, and A. J. Perlis: Comparing Large-scale Calculators, *Control Eng.*, vol. 3, no. 2, pp. 83–92, February, 1956.

Carr, J. W., III, and A. J. Perlis: Small Scale Computers as Scientific Calculators, *Control Eng.*, vol. 3, no. 3, pp. 99–104, March, 1956.

Chapin, N.: "An Introduction to Automatic Digital Computers," pp. 423–497, D. Van Nostrand Company, Inc., Princeton, N.J., 1957.

Gotlieb, C. C., and J. N. P. Hume: "High-speed Data Processing," pp. 305–309, McGraw-Hill Book Company, Inc., New York, 1958.

Weik, M. H.: A Second Survey of Domestic Electronic Digital Computing Systems, *Ballistic Research Laboratories Report* 1010, Aberdeen Proving Grounds, Md., 1957.

GLOSSARIES

The terminology pertinent to digital computers is given in the following works.

"First Glossary of Programming Terminology," Association for Computing Machinery, New York, 1954.

Glossary of Terms in the Field of Computers and Automation, *Computers and Automation*, vol. 5, no. 10, pp. 17–36, October, 1956.

IRE Standards on Electronic Computers: Definition of Terms, 1956, *Proc. IRE*, vol. 44, pp. 1166–1173, 1956.

Berkeley, E. C., and L. Wainwright: "Computers, Their Operation and Applications," pp. 333–358, Reinhold Publishing Corporation, New York, 1956.

Chapin, N.: "An Introduction to Automatic Computers," pp. 500–516, D. Van Nostrand Company, Inc., Princeton, N.J., 1957.

BOOKS

The following listing includes books which have already been used as references in the main text. In addition there are several others where there has been no attempt to select sections corresponding to the chapters of this text.

Aronson, M. H.: "Computing Handbook," Instruments Publishing Company, Pittsburgh, Pa., 1955.

Berkeley, E. C.: "Giant Brains," John Wiley & Sons, Inc., New York, 1949.

Berkeley, E. C., and L. Wainwright: "Computers, Their Operation and Applications," Reinhold Publishing Corporation, New York, 1956.

Boole, G.: "An Investigation of the Laws of Thought," Dover Publications, New York, 1951 (reprint of the 1854 original).

Booth, A. D., and K. H. V. Booth: "Automatic Digital Calculators," Academic Press, Inc., New York, 1953.

Bowden, B. V., ed.: "Faster than Thought," Pitman Publishing Corporation, New York, 1953.

Caldwell, S. H.: "Switching Circuits and Logical Design," John Wiley & Sons, Inc., New York, 1958.

Canning, R. G.: "Electronic Data Processing for Business and Industry," John Wiley & Sons, Inc., New York, 1957.

Carnap, R.: "Introduction to Symbolic Logic and Its Applications," Dover Publications, New York, 1958.

Chapin, N.: "An Introduction to Automatic Digital Computers," D. Van Nostrand Company, Inc., Princeton, N.J., 1957.

Courant, R., and H. Robbins: "What Is Mathematics?", Oxford University Press, New York, 1941.

Culbertson, J. T.: "Mathematics and Logic for Digital Devices," D. Van Nostrand Company, Inc., Princeton, N.J., 1958.

Eckert, W. J., and R. Jones: "Faster, Faster," McGraw-Hill Book Company, Inc., New York, 1956.

Engineering Research Associates: "High-speed Computing Devices," McGraw-Hill Book Company, Inc., New York, 1950.

Gardner, M.: "Logic Machines and Diagrams," McGraw-Hill Book Company, Inc., New York, 1958.

Goode, H. H., and R. E. Machol: "System Engineering," McGraw-Hill Book Company, Inc., New York, 1957.

Gotlieb, C. C., and J. N. P. Hume: "High-speed Data Processing," McGraw-Hill Book Company, Inc., New York, 1958.

Grabbe, E. M., ed.: "Automation in Business and Industry," John Wiley & Sons, Inc., New York, 1957.

Grabbe, E. M., S. Ramo, and D. E. Wooldridge, eds.: "Handbook of Automation, Computation, and Control," vol. II, "Computers and Data Processing," John Wiley & Sons, Inc., New York, 1959.

Gruenberger, F.: "Computing Manual," University of Wisconsin Press, Madison, Wis., 1952.

Hartree, D. R.: "Calculating Instruments and Machines," University of Illinois Press, Urbana, Ill., 1949.

Higonnet, R. A., and R. A. Grea: "Logical Design of Electrical Circuits," Mc-Graw-Hill Book Company, Inc., New York, 1958.

Humphrey, W. S.: "Switching Circuits," McGraw-Hill Book Company, Inc., New York, 1958.

Ivall, T. E., ed.: "Electronic Computers," Philosophical Library, Inc., New York, 1956.

Jeenel, J.: "Programming for Digital Computers," McGraw-Hill Book Company, Inc., New York, 1959.

Livesley, R. K.: "Digital Computers," Cambridge University Press, New York, 1957.

McCracken, D. D.: "Digital Computer Programming," John Wiley & Sons, Inc., New York, 1957.

Phister, M.: "Logical Design of Digital Computers," John Wiley & Sons, Inc., New York, 1958.

Richards, R. K.: "Arithmetic Operations in Digital Computers," D. Van Nostrand Company, Inc., Princeton, N.J., 1955.

Richards, R. K.: "Digital Computer Components and Circuits," D. Van Nostrand Company, Inc., Princeton, N.J., 1957.

Richardson, M.: "Fundamentals of Mathematics," The Macmillan Company, New York, 1958.

Smith, C. V. L.: "Electronic Digital Computers," McGraw-Hill Book Company, Inc., New York, 1959.

Stibitz, G. R., and J. A. Larrivee: "Mathematics and Computers," McGraw-Hill Book Company, Inc., New York, 1956.

Wilkes, M. V.: "Automatic Digital Computers," John Wiley & Sons, Inc., New York, 1956.

Wilkes, M. V., D. J. Wheeler, and S. Gill: "Preparation of Programs for an Electronic Digital Computer," Second Edition, Addison-Wesley Publishing Company, Reading, Mass., 1957.

PERIODICALS

The following is a list of periodicals on the field of digital computers. In addition, various subject-matter fields such as business, science, technology, etc., have specialized periodicals which have material pertinent to their uses of computers.

Communications of the Association for Computing Machinery, Association for Computing Machinery, New York.

Computers and Automation, Edmund C. Berkeley and Associates, New York.

Computing News, J. W. Granholm, Seattle.

IBM Journal of Research and Development, International Business Machines, New York.

Journal of the Association for Computing Machinery, Association for Computing Machinery, New York.

Mathematical Tables and Aids to Computation, National Academy of Sciences, National Research Council, Washington.

Transactions of the IRE Professional Group on Electronic Computers, Institute of Radio Engineers, Inc., New York.

List of Computers

The computers and parts of computer systems which are referred to are as follows:

Number	Type	Manufacturer
1	IBM 7070	International Business Machines
2	LGP 30	Royal Precision Corporation
3	IBM 650	International Business Machines
4	DATATRON	Electrodata Division, Burroughs
5	IBM 705	International Business Machines
6	UNIVAC II	Sperry-Rand
7	UNIVAC SCIENTIFIC	Sperry-Rand
8	IBM RAMAC	International Business Machines
9	READIX	J. B. Rea
10	Data Transceiver	International Business Machines
11	IBM 709	International Business Machines
12	IBM 704	International Business Machines
13	SC 3000	Stromberg Carlson-Haloid
14	RW 300	Thompson-Ramo-Wooldridge
15	NCR 304	National Cash Register
16	G-15	Bendix
17	BIZMAC	Radio Corporation of America
18	STRETCH	International Business Machines

Index

203

F